LANGUAGE LEARNING

Insights for Learners, Teachers, and Researchers

Andrew D. Cohen

School of Education
Hebrew University of Jerusalem

NEWBURY HOUSE PUBLISHERS
A division of HarperCollins*Publishers*

Director: Laurie E. Likoff
Production Coordinator: Cynthia Funkhouser
Cover Design: Edward Smith Design, Inc.
Compositor: Crane Typesetting Service, Inc.
Printer and Binder: McNaughton & Gunn

NEWBURY HOUSE PUBLISHERS
A division of HarperCollins*Publishers*

Language Science
Language Teaching
Language Learning

Language Learning: Insights for Learners, Teachers, and Researchers

Library of Congress Cataloging-in-Publication Data

Cohen, Andrew D.
   Language learning : insights for learners, teachers, and
researchers / Andrew D. Cohen.
      p.   cm.
   Includes bibliographical references and index.
   ISBN 0-06-632097-6
   1. Language and languages—Study and teaching. I. Title.
P51.C58   1990
418'.007—dc20
                                        90-6267
                                        CIP

63-20972   93 92 91 90 9 8 7 6 5 4 3 2 1

Contents

Foreword

Acknowledgments

Chapter 1   Introduction   1

Chapter 2   Learning Vocabulary Words   21

Chapter 3   Attending to Ensure Learning   41

Chapter 4   Speaking to Communicate   53

Chapter 5   Reading for Comprehension   73

Chapter 6   Writing As Process and Product   103

Chapter 7   Research on Vocabulary Learning, Attending,
            and Speaking   133

Chapter 8   Research on Reading and Writing   159

Chapter 9   Conclusions   189

References   197
Index   211

Foreword

Andrew Cohen has been involved in researching and teaching second language learning strategies for years—long before it was in vogue to do so. This book brings together his considerable insights into ways that learners can actively participate in their own learning. It outlines ways that can enhance learners' abilities to understand, speak, read, and write in a second language.

One major audience for this book are language learners themselves. Five chapters speak directly to them, providing them with detailed ideas and exercises that will augment their learning whether in a formal classroom setting or learning on their own. These very same chapters will provide teachers of second (or foreign) languages with a multitude of suggestions to help learners participate more actively in their own learning. They will give teachers ideas about how to teach their lessons with more sensitivity to the way learners go about learning and to the possibilities open to them for improving their choice of strategies.

Particular strategies are emphasized. The choice of emphasis derives from Andrew Cohen's own program of research. It is a significant strength and a unique feature of this book that the strategies outlined in its initial chapters are based on the author's extensive research related to language learning strategies. This research is described in two chapters, giving the inquisitive and motivated learner and teacher an understanding of the knowledge base underlying the strategies. These chapters also offer the researcher a sampling of different research methods as well as productive avenues of research to pursue.

Thus, this book is highly relevant to learners, teachers, and researchers for the insights it gives into how to enhance second language learning. The practical suggestions are founded in empirical research and are taught through exercises so that learners can appreciate the benefits of the strategies immediately. Improbable as it may seem, the book is written in a way that is accessible to all three audiences—learners, teachers, and researchers.

Merrill Swain
The Ontario Institute for Studies in Education
August, 1989

Acknowledgments

I would like first like to acknowledge those colleagues who inspired me to begin my research effort and who encouraged me during my many years of research, namely, Joan Rubin, David Stern, Anita Wenden, and Carol Hosenfeld. Next I would like to acknowledge those who gave me feedback on this manuscript. My heartfelt thanks go to Rebecca Oxford and Gissi Sarig who read through the manuscript carefully and provided many useful comments.

In addition, I would like to thank a number of other colleagues for their insightful comments on the manuscript: Alister Cumming, Elaine Tarone, Paul Nation, Earl Stevick, Henri Holec, Mike Scott, Andrea Gevurtz-Arai, Sandra Harper, and Polly Ulichny. There is no doubt in my mind that the manuscript is much improved due to their most helpful input. I would also like to extend my gratitude to the many learners whose insights about their target language learning provided the basis for this book.

Finally, I wish to acknowledge my wife, Sabina, and my children, Judy and Daniel, for all they have taught me about language learning, and for their steadfast and loving support, without which this book would never have come to fruition.

Chapter 1

Introduction

We would not think of undertaking many of our lifelong pursuits without coaching or formal training. For example, when we learn how to drive, we have a driving instructor. When we learn how to play tennis, we usually have a teacher there to make sure our backhand and our serve are reasonable. Yet when it comes to learning a target language, we usually do not have a coach to help us *learn* more effectively. It is somehow taken for granted that we will know how to do it. It may also be felt that the target language course will implicitly or explicitly transmit to us guidelines for how to learn the particular language under the given circumstances. The truth is that this may not be the case.

In instance after instance, the course ends and the learner has managed to write down a considerable amount of information about a given language in a course notebook, but much of it never gets learned by the learner. It stays in the notebook. The concern of this book is on getting more of the language into the learners' heads.

The dissemination of notions about learner strategies in language learning means the supplying of potentially beneficial means for improving target language learning. It does *not* mean the imposition of dubious and largely irrelevant categories on learners from cultural groups for which such categories may be inappropriate. As will be discussed below, research is demonstrating that learners from a multiplicity of backgrounds can find benefit in one or another set of learning strategies. Once learned, some of these strategies become automatic among learners, while others need to be consciously called into play by the learner or by the teacher in order to be accessible. It has also been demonstrated that learners are increasingly interested in receiving training in how to learn a target language (see Oxford 1990)—hence, the justification for this book.

MULTIPLE AUDIENCES: A JUGGLING ACT

This book is intended for three audiences at the same time because it is the contention of the author that the material can be of benefit to all three groups simultaneously. Granted, it calls for flexibility on the part of readers to pay special attention to those sections of greatest interest to them. In a way, this could be considered part of learner training in reading since an important strategy in reading in native and target language alike is identifying those points of keen interest and being selective in reading.

The first audience that the book is written for is that of *learners* who are in the process of learning a target language,[1] either individually or in group. It may also be fair to say that the insights for learners contained in these pages may have their greatest payoff for adult learners at an intermediate or advanced level, though some of the discussion clearly has the beginner in mind (e.g., in Chapter 2 on vocabulary). For the sake of the learner group, large sections of the book are addressed to the reader in the second person, "you," and include practical exercises intended for the learner.

The second audience is that of *teachers* and *teacher trainers* of a target language who are interested in training language learners to become more aware of how to make better use of their time as learners. This group of readers actually constitutes the *primary* focus of the book. As will become evident, much of the book is written with this group in mind. Although every effort is made to present concepts at a level that well-motivated learners will be able to grasp on their own, there is material in the book that classroom teachers may best be able to convey effectively to learners —either directly through learner training exercises or indirectly through language exercises making use of the strategies or techniques discussed at length in the book. The book includes sample exercises that teachers can conduct in class as one means of including learner training in the instructional process.

Every time teachers come upon a reference to "you" meaning "the learner," they are requested to make the necessary translation. Actually, the best language teachers are often those who from time to time put themselves in the role of language learner—in part, so as not to forget what the experience of language learning entails. Some prominent teacher-training programs actually require of their students that they take a semester or more of a target language—ideally one that is completely unlike any that they have already studied. Hence, some teachers reading this book may, in fact, be part of different audiences at the same time—learners, as well as teachers or teachers-in-training.

The third audience is that of *researchers* who are interested in areas of

[1]In this book, the language to be learned will be referred to by the inclusive term, *target language*. The intention is to include both *second language learning*, the learning of a language that is spoken in the community in which it is being learned, and *foreign language learning*, the learning of a language that is not spoken in the local community. Even though the two situations are subsumed under the same rubric, *target language*, we must bear in mind that there are important differences between the two learning situations—with the former, second language learning, implying more direct exposure to the language being learned.

investigation regarding the learning of a target language. The book has as its main research focus the role of the learner in a target language learning situation, and specifically, the cognitive processes that the learner uses in learning and using the target language. This overriding interest motivated the author's research that is reported on in this volume.

The researcher audience may well include teachers who are interested in classroom research. In fact, much of the research reported on in the book reflects naturalistic classroom research on learner strategies, research in which teachers can play a substantial role, as they have in some of the studies which will be described (e.g., Cohen, Glasman, Rosenbaum-Cohen, Ferrara, & Fine 1979). For this reason, the reader will note the emphasis on case studies and quasi-experimental designs.[2] In effect, the research reported on in this book reflects applied linguistic research in its true sense—research in applied areas, with an emphasis on tapping learning strategies while they are being employed or just subsequent to their use.

The researcher will find references to research studies throughout the book, as well as ideas for studies worth conducting. Furthermore, the two chapters at the end of the volume are reserved for more detailed description primarily of some of the author's research, with a "Further Readings" section at the end of each of these chapters for those interested in reading about the work of others in related areas.

The reader will note that many of the studies reported on in this book have not produced definitive answers. In some cases, the descriptions of research are simply meant to be illustrative or suggestive of research that could be conducted. The number of learners in most of the studies is small and there are also biases regarding how these subjects were chosen—a problem quite common to applied linguistic research in the real world. Moreover, the report of research is intended to demonstrate that studies need not be experimental to be informative.

WHERE CURRENT TEACHING METHODS SEEM TO BE FALLING SHORT

However learner-proof today's language teaching methods may be, they are still only as successful as the learners would have them be. Even innovative teaching methods may well fall short in that the learners do not do what is appropriate for them in order to succeed at the method. In fact, it has become clear both to learners who have spent many long and some-times frustrating hours in language classrooms, and to their teachers, that

[2]*Quasi-experimental* designs reflect studies conducted in educational and training situations in which the researcher lacks control over certain variables such as which students are exposed to a given program. So, for example, in such situations the researcher cannot randomly assign students to the experimental and control groups.

the mastery of—or even the rudimentary control of—a new language can be painfully elusive.

Innovative approaches to language teaching have made claims to producing dramatic results among language learners regardless of the level of awareness that the learners have about their learning strategies. Teaching methods such as Total Physical Response, Community Language Learning, Silent Way, and Suggestopedia are among some of the most cited (see Larsen-Freeman 1986, Richards & Rodgers 1986). Even if such methods are capable of eliciting dramatic levels of learning even from language learners who as a rule pay little attention to their learning strategies, the bulk of language instruction in the world takes place in more traditional language classroom settings, without access to the latest innovations.

It is, in fact, possible that the so-called traditional language classrooms put an emphasis on approaches that are currently held in esteem by leading foreign language educators—such as development of listening comprehension and reading skills before speaking, vocabulary input in meaningful contexts, limited grammatical sequencing and downplaying of grammatical analysis, exposure to authentic language, language practice in social contexts, and the continual review of previously introduced language material in cyclical fashion (see Schulz 1986). It is *still* possible, and even probable, that individual learners under such circumstances are benefiting only partially from their language learning experiences. And one explanation for reduced benefit is that the learners do not have strategies for enhancing their listening, do not have ways for holding onto newly encountered vocabulary words, and/or do not have a grasp of strategies for improving their communication skills.

Whatever the language teaching environment may be, learners' attention to strategies can, in fact, make a real difference. Under such conditions, the difference between "getting by" and producing noteworthy results may depend on the degree of responsibility that the learners take for their own learning experience. Thus, it would appear that learners can benefit substantially from a heightened awareness of ways for improving daily learning, for bridging gaps, and even for achieving dramatic breakthroughs in areas in which they have felt stuck on a plateau.

Perhaps 15 years ago, the message began to appear in the professional literature that there is value in focusing on language learning strategies and learner strategy training (e.g., Rubin 1975, Stern 1975). Although it has now become fashionable to speak about language learner training in the use of strategies, the actual training of learners to be better language learners is still being conducted in relatively few places in the world (see Oxford 1990; Oxford, Cohen, Crookall, Lavine, & Sutter, in press). Perhaps now there will be a shift to greater application of learner training as the available books on the topic have become noticeably more abundant. There is no doubt that numerous teachers have now become aware that there may well be a need to train their learners to learn—instead of just focusing on teaching them the language.

For the purposes of this book, *learning strategies* are viewed as learning processes which are consciously selected by the learner. The element of *choice* is important here because this is what gives a strategy its special character. These are also moves which the learner is at least partially aware of, even if full attention is not being given to them. For example, a learner may use the strategy of skimming a portion of text in order to avoid a lengthy illustration. If a learner's move is totally unconscious, then it would simply be referred to as a "process," and not a "strategy."[3]

Before the specific purposes of this book are presented, an effort will be made to describe other related literature in the field so that the reader will have more of a sense of how the various publications interrelate and relate to the current volume.

THE LEGACY OF PUBLICATIONS ON THE TRAINING OF LANGUAGE LEARNERS

Over the last 15 years, books and monographs dealing with learner strategies and learner training in target language learning have begun to appear and will be described in some detail below as a way of providing a context for this book. These publications have tended to represent a dramatic departure from those volumes aimed at the training of language *teachers*—for example, works by Allen and Valette (1977), Rivers (1981b), and Omaggio (1986). In these "how-to-teach" volumes, reference to learner strategies and to what learners can do to improve their language learning are treated briefly and primarily as a complement to the many suggestions regarding the teaching act.

For instance, within the context of what teachers can do to teach a language skill, there may appear tips for better learning, such as when Allen and Valette provide tips for vocabulary acquisition (1977:155ff.). At times, the steps for teaching strategies for improving a skill may even be listed (e.g., Omaggio 1986:170–171, who lists reading strategies from Hosenfeld, Arnold, Kirchofer, Laciura, & Wilson 1981). In addition, the issue of learner strategies may be raised in discussion questions (e.g., Rivers 1981b:80ff.) or in suggested activities (e.g., Rivers 1981b:218–219). Hence, there is some mention of learner strategies, particularly in the revised editions, but the emphasis is secondary.

In the *learner* training publications, the focus is more directly and especially on the learner and improving learner strategies. On occasion,

---

[3]This view is not held by some of my colleagues who feel that strategies need not be consciously employed. I maintain that there must be some level of awareness of strategies, regardless of whether they are being attended to.

the influential studies have been reports of research—for example, that of Naiman, Frolich, Stern, and Todesco (1975). Although this monograph did not deal directly with learner training, the focus was on finding out more about the successful language learning experience by extensive learner interviews and case studies, classroom observation, and teacher question-naires. This study was a pioneering effort in that many of the techniques used were innovative at the time, and the findings gave much food for thought to researchers. There then followed other smaller-scale studies, usually case studies, such as Wilga River's study of her learning of Spanish (Rivers 1979) and Schmidt's (1984) study of a learner. Studies such as these also contributed to our understanding of learning strategies. In recent years, many such case studies of language learning strategies have appeared—in itself a validation of the importance of this type of work.

The published materials relating specifically to learner training range mostly from those aimed primarily at language learners to those intended for teachers, who in turn are expected to pass on insights to the learners. Likewise, the publications range from those with an emphasis on the study of a language in a formal classroom environment to those focusing on the learning of a language in the field. To have a better sense of where the present work fits into the picture of learner strategies and learner training, let us take a brief look at some volumes that have appeared previously.

The Learner As Intended Audience

The early books mentioning the learning of a target language tended to have as their emphasis the general area of good study habits, rather than a specific focus on that which makes the learning of language skills different from the learning of other kinds of skills. Two of these books were Yorkey's (1970) *Study skills for students of English as a second language* and Martin, McChesney, Whalley, and Devlin's (1977) *Guide to language and study skills for college students of English as a second language.*[4] While both of these books have sections on developing vocabulary skills—the latter being somewhat more complete (e.g., mentioning how to prepare vocab-ulary cards), their major thrust is on study skills for college (e.g., note-taking, test taking, library skills, and the writing of term papers).

1. *A Guidebook for Self-Instruction in Isolated Areas.* One of the early books

---

[4]There are, of course, those books directed at general study habits, such as those by Deese and Deese 1979, Casey 1985, and Chibnall 1987, just to mention a few. Such volumes characteristically have a brief section on how to read more effectively (especially with respect to the reading of textbooks), how to take lecture and reading notes, and how to write term papers. Actually, the book by Deese and Deese also has a brief section on studying a foreign language (84–92), in which the authors make passing mention of some important areas of concern, such as dictionary use, word analysis, the learning of cognates, the use of flash cards, and the mastery of grammar.

to focus specifically on the learning of another language was *Language acquisition made practical* (Brewster & Brewster 1976), written primarily for missionaries and others working in locations in the world where they would essentially be on their own, learning the local language and culture with the assistance of local interpreters.[5]

The Brewster and Brewster book provides a detailed day-by-day program for learning a language, including directions as to how to chart daily progress. Despite its many fine features, the book espouses a rather lock-step approach which is not consistent with some current thought and practice in the field. There is, for example, a premium put on extensive mimicry and other mechanical language drills. Also, learners are told to learn new words *only* in meaningful sentences whereas learning of words in word lists may be a practical and efficient way of learning certain basic vocabulary (see discussion in next chapter). No mention is made of the use of flash cards or mnemonic devices (see Chapter 2). Learners are also discouraged from seeking translations for words because of the lack of accurate equivalents across languages, whereas at the early stages of learning a succinct translation may be quite helpful.

The claim the authors make is that by means of the book, users will learn not only a new language but also how to learn languages. Their claim is probably justified, with the qualifier that users will essentially be learning one system for learning a language. Current learner training materials are less prescriptive, catering more to differences in learning styles.

2. *A Brief Manual for Prospective Language Learners.* A second book, *How to be a more successful language learner* (Rubin & Thompson 1982), appeared at a time when interest was beginning to grow in the differences among language learners—why some succeed at target language learning while others fail. Rubin actually began her own observational research into the topic over a decade before the book appeared. She would sit in on language classes in French, German, and other languages, and pay attention almost exclusively to learners and what they were doing—at a time when the field was paying almost exclusive attention to the teachers. In 1975, her influential article, "What the 'good language learner' can teach us" appeared, followed in the same year by a similar article written by Stern. Perhaps that year marked a decided shift in focus away from the teacher in favor of greater concern for the learner and learning strategies.

The book by Rubin and Thompson devotes its first section to the role of learner characteristics in language learning, objectives for language learning, the instructional setting, and the nature of language. The second section is devoted to strategies for being a better language learner such as

---

[5] I can relate personally to this kind of an experience as I was a Peace Corps volunteer for two years on the High Plains of Bolivia and learned the local language, Aymara, largely through the assistance of local informants.

organizing, being creative, making intelligent guesses, and learning for-malized routines. The last section is concerned with aids for language learning—such as textbooks, dictionaries, and tapes. While the book pro-vides only brief mention of each of these topics—brevity which may have limited the book's usefulness to the learner somewhat—Rubin has most recently produced a videodisc program for training language learning strat-egies, known as the "Language Learning Disc" (see Rubin 1987).

The program, designed for adults (high school and above), is presented on a two-sided (one-hour) interactive videodisc with five accompanying diskettes providing an average of eight hours of instruction. The videodisc program provides training in language learning—for example, learning how to select appropriate strategies for use in the particular learning con-text, making better use of memory, dealing more effectively with errors, and using resources wisely. The disc provides an opportunity for the stu-dents to choose the language, topic, and level of difficulty from a wide variety of languages for their interactive exercises which are embedded in a number of dramatic scenarios.

3. *A Monograph Directed at a Specific Population.* By the mid-1980s, Re-becca Oxford had become quite active in the field of learner strategies and learner strategy research. One of her main concerns was that of classifying types of strategies in the form of a taxonomy (Oxford 1985). Shortly there-after, she and her colleagues produced a brief monograph for Peace Corps volunteers who need to learn a foreign language for use in their country of assignment. The monograph, entitled *Improving your language learning: Strategies for Peace Corps volunteers* (Grala, Oxford, & Schleppegrell 1987), dealt with common questions about language learning (e.g., age, best way, mistakes, lack of understanding, time to master, and success), general management strategies, organizing to learn, building memory, and learn-ing in different contexts.

4. *A Course in Learner Training.* This course entitled *Learning to learn English: A course in learner training* (student's book, cassette tape, and teach-er's book; Ellis & Sinclair 1989) is intended for lower-intermediate to in-termediate level learners of English, and is meant to be flexible, so that it can either be integrated into a course of language instruction or used sep-arately in learner training sessions. In this course, learners determine which areas they will focus on and then record their needs, priorities, aims, and progress. The course starts with preparation for learning: expectations, learning styles, needs, organization, and motivation. Then it treats the skill areas: vocabulary, grammar, listening, speaking, reading, and writing. A variety of strategies are presented, along with frequent quotes from learners who use these strategies. While the teacher's book has an introduction to the theory of learner training, there is no overt research basis to the specific techniques that are presented to the students.

The Teacher As Intended Audience

There have also appeared a series of books and monographs directed primarily at the teacher, with the intention that the teacher will provide the training for the learner—whether this training takes the form of (1) a separate workshop or minicourse, (2) a prelude to a language course, (3) material presented during the course and integrated into it, or (4) material presented during the course but separate from actual language instruction.

1. *A Guidebook of Learner Strategies for ESL.* One of the early learner strategy guidebooks written for teachers of ESL was prepared by Stewner-Manzanares, Chamot, O'Malley, Kupper, and Russo (1983). It emphasized strategies for learning how to understand and speak the language, with the strategies intended for application both to activities occurring "in ESL classrooms, and to language activities occurring outside formal language learning environments." The guide was divided into two parts: (1) definitions of various types of cognitive and metacognitive strategies[6] and examples of how they are used by students, and (2) specific examples of how the learning strategies can be taught in the context of the teacher's ongoing instructional program, with the intent that learners become active, independent users of the strategies wherever they see opportunities to do so. The authors warn that certain strategies may be most useful only with certain types of learning activities or for certain types of students.

An example of a metacognitive strategy would be that of self-management—students identifying learning preferences such as listening to and speaking on favorite topics and directing conversations to their own areas of interest. Here is an example from a student.

> (To facilitate social communication,) I try to choose the topic of conversation. For instance, I know a lot about football, so I choose this as a topic for conversation with friends. I can have a friendly conversation when I initiate the theme of it. (Stewner-Manzanares et al. 1983, Part II, 5)

An example of a cognitive strategy would be that of the use of imagery— relating new information to visual concepts in memory via familiar, easily retrievable images. Here is an example from a student.

> We make a log of drawings in class to illustrate what we are studying, writing in the dates of each event. We have made a whole series of pictures to illustrate an idea, and this helps communicate the meaning.

---

[6]The authors define *cognitive strategies* as those involving the direct application of a strategy to the information to be learned. *Metacognitive strategies* are defined as those involving thought about the learning process or the regulation of learning, entailing the use of planning, monitoring, or evaluation of a learning activity.

Looking at the pictures helps us recall the meaning. . . . (Stewner-Manzanares et al. 1983, Part II, 22)

2. *A Guidebook with a Focus on Learning Styles.* Another guide for teachers, that written by Willing (1989), also appeared recently. While the primary focus is on learner training, the teachers' guide includes a few activities intended for in-service teacher training, teacher self-study, or as a lead-in to the material. The author stresses that learners differ in their learning styles and that teachers need to accommodate to these different styles. A research study conducted by the author (Willing 1985) found that there were essentially four learning-strategy types: communicative (e.g., learning by listening to natives, talking to friends, or using the language in shops), concrete (e.g., learning by games, pictures, or using cassettes at home), authority-oriented (e.g., learning through teaching explanations, writing everything in a notebook, reading, or studying grammar), and analytical (e.g., learning by studying grammar, studying alone, finding own mistakes, or doing homework).

The first part of the handbook deals with managing the learning process, and includes activities designed to help learners become aware of the nature of language and language learning, and of their own preferences, habits, strengths, and weaknesses as learners. The topics covered include learning plans, managing communicative situations, practicing, and monitoring. The second part of the handbook deals with managing information, and is aimed at encouraging learners to take more responsibility for planning and evaluating their own learning. The focus is on information-processing strategies (selective attending, associating, categorizing, pattern learning, and inferencing).

3. *Reports of Programs Emphasizing Autonomous and Self-Directed Instruction.* Three volumes have recently appeared which emphasize programs in self-directed learning, where the teachers give less frontal instruction and instead assume other kinds of roles—such as counselor, materials preparer, program developer, researcher, and evaluator.

a. *Self-Directed Learning in Australia.* One such monograph for teachers was written by Helen Helmore (1987). The monograph defines and describes self-directed learning as "the opposite of teacher-directed learning"—an approach whereby "learners make decisions, alone or with the help of others, about what they need or want to know, how they will set objectives for learning, what resources and strategies they will use, and how they will assess their progress" (Helmore 1987:6). Then, the planning of the course, the nature of counseling sessions, the drawing up of learning contracts, monitoring of learning, and self-assessment are conducted through interaction between the learner and the staff. Two reports have also been issued regarding the self-directed learning course, one an evaluation (Helmore 1985a) and the other a set of three case studies of representative learners within the program (Helmore 1985b).

b. *Self-Instruction in Europe and Scandinavia.* A second volume on autonomous learning, written by Leslie Dickinson (1987), is primarily based on programs of self-instruction developed by the Centre de Recherches et d'Applications Pédagogiques en Langues (CRAPEL) in the University of Nancy II, France; the Open Access Sound and Video Library at Cambridge University; and the Scottish Centre for Education Overseas in Moray House College of Education, Edinburgh. The book describes what self-instruction is ("situations in which a learner, with others or alone, is working without the direct control of a teacher") and why it is useful.

The Dickinson volume then looks at facilitation of learning through self-instructional systems, materials for self-instruction, learner support through analysis of learner needs and learner contracts, self-access resources, preparation of teachers and learners for self-instruction, and self-assessment (i.e., the selection of formative assessment measures for self-monitoring, but also for placement and diagnostic purposes as well). While this book pays only passing mention to actual learner strategies detailed in other volumes (Dickinson, 1987:130–131), it sets the stage for them by describing types of self-instruction programs where such learner training is in many ways essential.

c. *Autonomous Learning in Europe and Scandinavia.* The third volume on autonomous learning, edited by Henri Holec (1988), constitutes a collection of 12 reports, each describing some effort at autonomous and self-directed learning in secondary schools and universities in the United Kingdom, in Scandinavia, and elsewhere in Europe. The following are brief descriptions of four reports selected from the volume.

A report by Dam and Gabrielsen (1988) describes a six-year project in which Danish school children from the fifth to the tenth form at the Danmarks Laerererhojskole, Copenhagen, planned, organized, and evaluated their classroom learning of English as a foreign language. The learners had as class objectives to develop: (1) strategies for use in learning in class and outside, (2) a realistic concept of their own capacity to learn and how to learn, (3) awareness of their own role and that of others in the learning-teaching process (e.g., cooperative strategies, peer tutoring), and (4) a sense of responsibility for social aspects of classroom interaction. The learners were involved in developing materials which encouraged self-expression and which were open to elaboration. With regard to evaluation, the learners answered the questions, "What are we/am I doing? Why? How? What is it used for?"

While the learners' achievement on exams was reported to be similar to that of learners in traditional classrooms, the learners in the program felt more secure about their learning and were more motivated to learn.

The program showed that learners could be more involved in nontrivial decision making and take more responsibility for their learning in school.

Huttunen (1988) reports a similar program of autonomous language learning at the senior secondary school of Lassinkallion Lukio in Oulu, northern Finland, from 1982 to 1985, where students took increased initiative and responsibility for the learning of three foreign languages at the same time—English, Swedish, and German. The learners monitored the choice of materials, the performance of work, participation in activities, homework, and presentation of the results. At the top level (level 3), the learners gave themselves their grade for the course, along with a justification. Whereas the overall performance of the pupils on the matriculation exam was no different from that of pupils in the standard language courses, the experimental group was better at communicative ability as measured by written composition, as well as being better on grammar tests. While still maintaining the role as final arbiter, *the seven participating teachers shifted from being leaders of activities to "help and resource person."* The teachers also became more aware of their attitudes and of areas where they lacked skills or experience.

Muller, Schneider, and Wertenschlag (1988) reported on a different kind of autonomous program, namely, that of tandem learning—the learning of language by exchange. At the University of Fribourg in Fribourg, Switzerland, pairs of learners were reported to be meeting for two-to-three-hour sessions each week in order to teach the partner their language (i.e., German, French, or English, and occasionally, Italian or Spanish) for an equal amount of the time. The report indicated that such meetings often included spontaneous, relaxed conversation over drinks and joint reading of articles. The sessions were either integrated into the language courses, accompanied by them, or detached from any particular course, with the partners fixing their own objectives and methods.

Muller et al. reported that most of such tandem arrangements (70 percent) have proven successful. On the plus side, *students have found that tandem learning allows them to have extended, relaxed learning sessions where they can feel responsible for their own learning.* On the minus side, students have mentioned the lack of materials to give the sessions structure. In addition, students sometimes disagreed on certain issues such as how to handle correction for style and grammar. In general, the system has been found to make participants more sensitive to the problems not only of learning, but of teaching as well.

Gremmo (1988) reports on an evaluation of a program for self-directed learning of EFL in effect for 12 years at the University of Nancy II, the Système d'Apprentissage Auto-dirigé avec Soutien (SAAS). A questionnaire was distributed to a small sampling of learners who had gone through the program (N = 19) in an effort to get honest answers to questions regarding difficulties in learning (e.g., scheduling, methods, programs, studying individually) and areas of success and failure (e.g., progress in English, ability to work alone) and to get suggestions for improving the program. While most of the respondents were positive in their responses, some felt that they lacked motivation and were even somewhat traumatized by having to learn at home on their own. While all learners received group counseling on how to learn, several felt that what they had learned about "learning how to learn" was not adequate for their needs.

4. *Textbooks on Learner Strategies and Learner Training.* Perhaps the first textbook to appear on the topic of learner strategies was that of Wenden and Rubin (1987), *Learner strategies in language learning,* which grew out of a series of TESOL colloquia on the topic and which was perhaps intended as much for researchers as for teachers. This volume has an important feature which distinguishes it from other volumes. It provides both a theoretical overview in chapters by Wenden ("Conceptual background and utility") and Rubin ("Learner strategies: Theoretical assumptions, research history and typology"), as well as six empirical in-depth studies on different approaches to language learning (written by Thompson, Cohen, Chamot, Abraham & Vann, Wenden, and Horowitz, respectively) and three chapters on experiments in learner training (written by O'Malley, Holec, and Wenden, respectively). This compendium of research articles has helped not only to provide information regarding learner strategies and how to train learners to use them, but also to further legitimize that area of target language research dealing with what learners say about their language learning and what they do about it.

The second textbook for teachers on learner strategies and learner training was that of Rebecca Oxford, *Language learner strategies: What every teacher should know* (1990). The Oxford book integrates the theoretical underpinnings of the learner strategy literature with practical suggestions for teachers concerning how to train their students to be more successful language learners. The book presents the taxonomy of learner strategies mentioned above, offers means for assessing students' learning strategies, and provides a model for strategy training accompanied by numerous strategy training exercises. The concept of learner training is exemplified by a chapter describing a number of actual learner training projects.

A field testing of the book also helped to shed some light on the issue of whether it pays to integrate learner training with classroom instruction or to detach such training from the regular classroom activities. The field assessment revealed that incorporating strategy training exercises into regular classroom activities and treating learning strategies as a means of enhancing progress students were already making was more beneficial than having the exercises constitute a separate entity, disconnected from ongoing classroom work.

A third textbook which has recently appeared is that by O'Malley and Chamot, *Learning strategies in second language acquisition* (1990). The book considers the contribution of cognitive theory to an understanding of the research on learning strategies, and looks at the role of strategies in second language instruction. The book is intended to respond to the need among second language teachers for guidance on how to present instruction that capitalizes on the knowledge and skills that learners already possess, while encouraging the learners to develop new and more effective strategies for learning. The authors review the literature on learning strategies and present an instructional model for learning-strategy training, the Cognitive Academic Language Learning Approach (CALLA), which teachers can apply to their own classes. Their model for learner training was developed and field tested with numerous groups of learners.

Now that we have considered the books and monographs that provide a backdrop for this book, let us consider the contributions of the present volume—a book that focuses on a limited number of specific learner strategies, viewing them from the vantage point of the learner, but reviewing their underpinnings from the vantage point of the teacher and researcher.

THE BACKGROUND FOR THE BOOK

This book is based on accumulated insights from research on processes in target language learning. Much of the research that provides the empirical basis for the book has been conducted by the author during the last 20 years. Insights from the work of students that I have supervised and from the work of colleagues are also drawn upon. The book represents applied linguistics in its truest sense—the application of research findings to language learning. Most of my ideas have been tried out on learners on a monthly basis over the last eight years at Ulpan Akiva, a Hebrew and Arabic language learning center for tourists, immigrants, and residents in Netanya, Israel. Learners there have been participating in semiformal lectures and in informal group and individual discussions on the learning of vocabulary, attending, speaking, reading, and writing a target language.

The book is written in the same spirit as the Wenden and Rubin book and the Oxford book, with a blending of theory and practice. Unlike the other two volumes, it focuses in detail on just a few selected areas of language learning strategies—essentially those that have interested the author as a researcher over the years. Hence, the book does not represent a survey of possibilities in learner training, as the Oxford book does, but rather is reflective of my particular research interests. The reader will, for example, note that certain language learning strategies are emphasized more in the discussion of one language skill than in the discussion of another. Hence, vocabulary learning is discussed with an emphasis on *recall* strategies, conversational discourse in terms of *attending* strategies on the aural side and *synthesizing*[7] strategies on the oral side, reading largely from the point of view of *self-awareness* and *monitoring*, and writing from the perspective of *modeling* and *feedback* (see Table 1.1).

It is important to point out, however, that these learning strategies often play a role in the other language skill areas as well. The lack of mention of these strategies in conjunction with other language skills simply reflects my personal choices as a researcher. In effect, this book presents a given skill area simply to highlight certain selected learning strategies and not others. The reader is requested to keep that caveat in mind while reading through this book—that is, rather than being comprehensive, this book is selective both with respect to learning strategies and with respect to the facets of language skills that are discussed.

Whereas it would be attractive to present the most effective strategies for language learning, it is fair to say that there is no such thing. Rather, learners differ notably both in the strategies that they can use effectively in language learning and in the ways that they make effective use of a given strategy in a given instance. The view that strategies are inherently good for all learners or that their use would produce successful results for the same learners each time has been found to be simplistic. Rather, it is important to lay out a series of options and to let the particular learner choose according to taste and results from using a given strategy.

Table 1.1   LEARNER STRATEGY AREAS DEALT WITH IN THIS BOOK BY SKILL AREA

| Learning strategies | Language skills | | | |
	Vocabulary learning	Conversational discourse	Reading	Writing
		Aural Oral		
Recall strategies	X			
Attending strategies		X		
Synthesizing strategies		X		
Self-awareness and monitoring strategies			X	
Modeling and feedback				X

[7]A cover term for the strategies used in bringing together and utilizing language material for the purpose of oral language communication.

A MIX OF THEORY, RESEARCH RESULTS, AND
PRACTICE

It is not an easy task to write both to learners and to the trainers and researchers of learners at the same time. There is a need to be practical, and yet not simplistic or unempirical. Hence, the reader will note that theory and practice are intertwined in different ways from chapter to chapter, with the highest level of integration in the more practical chapters, Chapters 2 through 6. At times theory precedes practice, and sometimes vice versa. The book also has two chapters at the end which provide the theoretical underpinnings for practical suggestions made; for example, an exercise in the use of the technique of reformulation in writing is presented in Chapter 6, and then, in Chapter 8, a description of the research conducted to validate the technique is described. Thus, this book provides a "how-to" approach, while at the same time indicating when and how certain techniques were tried out systematically and the theoretical implications of the research.

Learners and teachers are encouraged to focus on the more practical aspects of the book for the purposes of learner training. In certain sections of the book, learners are encouraged to take a more active role in what goes on in the classroom so as to maximize the payoff they get from the time spent. For example, students are encouraged to discuss with their teachers alternate means for the correction of oral and written language if current practices do not seem to be working. Clearly, such suggestions run directly counter to the approach that says learners should leave the teaching to the teacher. Although there is a lot to be said for this approach of *learner as consumer*, it is also true that teachers usually leave the learning to the learner. Hence, it becomes the learners' responsibility to let the teacher know what is working and what is not working in their efforts to learn the target language and, possibly, to suggest alternate approaches in areas where they are not satisfied with the results of their learning.

As suggested above, the references to the research may be of interest to those teachers interested in doing *classroom research*, whether they refer to it by that name or not. For instance, if teachers divide readers up into pairs so that there is an "investigator" and a "reporter," with the former eliciting verbal report data on the reading strategies used in reading a passage and the latter providing the data (see Chapter 5), the teacher would have a rich source of data as well as a useful class exercise for the students.

The reader will note that some of the research reported on in the book leads to relatively clear conclusions about potentially beneficial language learning strategies (e.g., the reading strategies listed in Chapter 5), while other research has produced only speculative or tentative results, given the limited number of studies or limitations in the research methods. In the latter case, too little may still be known about certain areas to permit unequivocal recommendation of given strategies as beneficial (e.g., preferred vocabulary learning strategies in Chapter 2, or the effects of feedback on written work in Chapter 6).

The book is susceptible to such a weakness because an effort is made to bring research results to bear on most of the strategies and techniques presented in Chapters 2 through 6. It is easier to include pronouncements from experience without empirical evidence, since such empirical evidence is difficult to obtain given the current level of development of applied linguistic research on target language learning. For example, valuable research on mnemonic techniques for learning vocabulary would entail assessing a learner's success at using a mnemonic each time the need arises in speaking. It would appear that no such research has yet been undertaken, due primarily to the difficulty of staging such vocabulary retrieval events and the unwillingness or inability of learners to write down their "take" of each such retrieval situation when it occurs.

WHAT THE BOOK COVERS

The book begins with a section of practical suggestions on how to learn vocabulary (Chapter 2). This is the leadoff chapter because vocabulary is so central to language learning. The approach is largely that of dealing with lower-level strategies rather than providing a global framework for vocabulary learning in the way that a global framework is presented in the chapter on reading (Chapter 5). The vocabulary chapter considers the use of notebooks, flash cards, and dictionaries, and pays particular attention to the use of mnemonics in remembering words. The chapter presents language vocabulary to learn (from an Andean Indian language), a list of approaches to mnemonics, a task, a quiz, and a discussion. This chapter is intended for learners at all levels of language learning.

Chapter 3 discusses techniques for paying attention to language input more effectively, in classroom settings primarily, though the principles could apply out of class as well. Successful language intake for the purposes of language learning starts with attending to language input systematically. This chapter is also intended primarily for beginning and intermediate learners who have yet to attain a comfortable level of listening ability in the target language.

Chapter 4 looks at demands put on speakers in producing utterances. It views speaking as a matter of negotiating for meaning and considers the role of communication strategies in the pursuit of meaningful interchange. Next, the chapter considers the correction of oral errors and its role in the learning process. Finally, the chapter explores what is entailed in producing a situationally appropriate utterance, such as an apology, and what learners may wish to do in order to produce speech acts in a target language with greater success. The chapter is intended primarily for advanced intermediate and advanced learners of a target language.

Chapter 5 considers effective reading strategies in target language learning. This chapter is perhaps most consistent with the view that learners need a global sense of the task in context, in this case reading, before they can relate profitably to the lower-level activities (Collins, Brown, & Newman, in press). The chapter gives this global perspective initially before dealing with specific reading tasks. It gives readers an opportunity to perform an inventory as to the reading strategies they tend to use and to become more aware as to the full array of options open to them. The chapter is primarily for intermediate and advanced readers—readers who have reached a level where reading comprehension is now a major concern.

Chapter 6 looks at writing strategies against the backdrop of a process and product approach to writing. It pays particular attention to means for obtaining useful feedback, such as through the technique of reformulation. It considers a possible repertoire of strategies learners might use to make most profitable use of feedback from others. This chapter is intended for intermediate and advanced writers, although some matters of feedback would pertain to beginning writers as well.

Chapters 7 and 8 provide the research basis for many of the techniques presented in the preceding pages, as well as providing suggestions for further readings. Chapter 7 focuses on research on vocabulary learning, attending, and speaking. The main concern of the research on vocabulary learning is the benefit derived from using mnemonic devices such as keywords as an aid to memory. The research on attending looks at the issue of students' patterns of attention during typical teacher-fronted classroom sessions. The research on speaking deals with a particularly complex form of speech, namely, the execution of speech acts such as apologizing. Apologies are of interest in that they demand both a certain mastery of the forms of a target language and also some understanding of the conditions under which it is appropriate to utilize one or another of those forms. Hence, apologies provide a window onto the processes involved in learning how to speak another language.

Chapter 8 looks at research concerned with the processes involved in reading texts of a more academic nature and in writing essays. The reading research is based primarily on mentalistic data obtained in a series of studies from readers who provided verbal report data (introspection, retrospection, and think-aloud data) while reading. The writing research focuses on the issue of feedback, considering the process involved in the teacher making comments on a learner's essay and then returning it to the learner to deal with. The research points up some of the shortcomings of this process as it is usually carried out. Then, research regarding the innovative technique of reformulation is presented and discussed, with consideration of the pros and cons of this technique.

The final chapter, Chapter 9, highlights some of the key points that have emerged from each of the skills chapters (Chapters 2 through 6) by way of conclusion.

TOPICS BEYOND THE SCOPE OF THE BOOK

Since the book deals with those areas that have been the subject of my research over a number of years, there are numerous areas that are not treated in the volume. Nonetheless, these are still important topics for consideration in learning training. For example, the book does not deal with possible differences in choice of language learning strategies according to cultural group—such as the learning style preferences of target language learners (visual, auditory, kinesthetic, tactile; Reid 1987) or the use of memorization techniques by the Chinese (see Huang & van Naerssen 1987), nor does the book deal with aptitude and how it relates to learning strategies (see Skehan 1989, for new insights on this topic).

A sampling of other areas that are not addressed include child-adult differences in the use of learning strategies, the role of diagnostic testing in determining the areas for which learning strategies would be needed, the setting of goals and planning the learning program (see Cumming 1986, Wenden 1987), and the relationship between language learning strategies and other kinds of learning strategies (e.g., why learning strategies conventionally used for subject matter study may be inappropriate for target language learning).

Chapter *2*

Learning Vocabulary Words

The purpose of this chapter is to assist you, the learner, in becoming more aware of your own personal approaches to learning vocabulary in a target language and in broadening your repertoire of approaches. Certain chapters in this book, like the one on reading (Chapter 5), lead with a theoretical introduction and have exercises at the end. In this chapter, the exercise will come first in order to get you thinking about what vocabulary learning actually entails. Some theoretical material is inserted within the exercises, both to provide information and to shift the focus away from the learning task briefly so that you have an opportunity to see how your mind works.

This chapter provides suggestions for learning vocabulary through mnemonics, word analysis, and cognates. The role of the dictionary, flash cards, and grouping of words is also discussed. In addition, some effort to relate these suggestions to theories of second language acquisition is made. There is a problem that emerges when consulting the research literature, because experts do not have many definitive theories for the learning of target language vocabulary. In fact, second language acquisition researchers have noted that the study of vocabulary acquisition has until recently been one of the most neglected areas of research (Levenston 1979, Meara 1980). Hence, some of the recommendations are in need of greater empirical validation. The chapter also makes a connection between research in second language acquisition and metacognitive strategies in psychology (in the section on mnemonics).

In the exercise that leads off this chapter, you will be asked to learn words out of context—in lists, a practice which some specialists hold in disfavor. As Stevick puts it, "The memorization of vocabulary lists is out of favor these days among many thoughtful and creative teachers" (1982:76). Stevick goes on to point out that all the same, many learners do, in fact, learn words in lists (including himself from time to time), either because their teachers tell them to, out of "a sense of moral obligation toward any word once it has come up," or out of a desire to improve their "word-image" for that word (e.g., problems in individual sounds or syllables or in the meaning) (1982:77). Stevick sees the learning of isolated vocabulary items as "very useful in increasing the range of vocabulary that you have

available to you in designing experiences [that lead toward acquisition]"
(1982:79).

Nation (1990, Chapter 8) also notes that, whereas learning words in
lists (i.e., of target language words with native language equivalents) has
been "unfashionable among many language teachers for quite a long time,"
research has shown that it is an effective means for learning a large number
of words in a short time—over 30 per hour, with retention several weeks
later. Nation feels the strongest argument for learning words out of context
is that it can be regarded as the *beginning* of learning of any word and that
such learning will be enriched by later encounters with the word in context.
These later meetings then provide an opportunity for enrichment of the
word meaning, rather than a frustrating struggle to find the meaning (Nation, personal communication).

When considering the role of *context* in vocabulary learning, it is important to note that there are many types of contexts—some that provide
clues to the meaning of words and some that do not. Moreover, after
surveying the field of research on the learning of vocabulary in context,
Carter concludes: "It has not been convincingly demonstrated that the
information learners obtain from meeting words in a variety of contexts is
more beneficial, either in terms of knowledge of forms or meanings of
lexical items, than either translation or simply looking up the word in a
dictionary" (1987:168–169).

Actually, Carter ends by concluding that a mixture of approaches should
be adopted—such as learning words both *in* and *out* of context (e.g., through
using mnemonics). Cognitive psychologists concur with this view when
they take the position that if you really want to learn words, it pays to
analyze and enrich them by associations or images—the "depth of processing" principle (Craik & Lockhart 1972, Craik 1977). This chapter considers multiple approaches to vocabulary learning, and in particular, discusses
(1) strategies for remembering words, (2) word attack strategies (i.e., discovering word meaning through word analysis and through dictionaries),
(3) strategies for practicing words, (4) the knowledge natives have about
their vocabulary, and (5) considerations in selecting vocabulary to learn.

STRATEGIES FOR REMEMBERING WORDS

An Exercise in Vocabulary Learning

Let us suppose that you already know some words of a language called
Aymara. You are now going to be given a list of Aymara words. We will
assume that you have already gotten a sense of their meaning in context
in that these words appeared in a short passage. The passage was about
a young man who was sick due to an infection in his leg and about his

new girlfriend. This new girlfriend brought flowers to his hospital bed, but found him sleeping, and so she wrote him a note and left quickly.

Take whatever time you need to learn the following 10-word list taken from that passage. Learn them so that you can produce the Aymara form when given the English equivalent. Also pay attention as best you can to the process you use to learn each word. Below, you will be asked to label this process.

AYMARA[1]	ENGLISH
wayna	young man
usuta	sick
cayu	leg
machaka	new
aca	this
pankara	flower
ucampisa	but
iquiña	to sleep
kellkaña[1]	to write
laka	quickly

After you feel you have learned these words, continue reading on in this section. For the purpose of the exercise, do not refer back to this list until told to do so.

The words selected come from Bolivian Aymara and conform more or less to the sound system of Spanish. They reflect common vocabulary in everyday Aymara. Aymara belongs to the same language family as Quechua and is spoken by about 600,000 people in Bolivia and Peru, most of whom reside on the High Plains in and around Lake Titicaca.

The purpose of this first exercise is to give you the opportunity to observe how you learn vocabulary. Much of our language study—as in other fields as well—is conducted unconsciously or at a low level of consciousness. It is the premise of this chapter that if you become aware of the actual processes which you use as a vocabulary learner, you may gain insights about those learning strategies that work for you and those that do not. Then it is possible to modify or eliminate the less effective strategies.

For example, you may be a person who feels that repeating a word over to yourself a number of times will fix the word in your memory, and yet in reality this approach may not work well for you—if you were to

---

[1] In Aymara, c and qu are pronounced like the initial consonant in "kiss" and k is pronounced like the initial consonant in "cool."

keep a tally of its effectiveness over a number of words. On the other hand, you may not be aware of just how greatly you benefit from seeing a visual image of words or concepts that are picturable. Sometimes we use a certain approach to vocabulary learning not because it works, but because we think that we *should* be able to learn that way. Perhaps we use it because we know that it works for someone else, because a teacher once told us to do it that way, or because we did it that way once and it worked then. For instance, you may once have kept an alphabetical listing of target language words and their native language equivalents, not because this listing genuinely contributed to your vocabulary learning, but rather because it seemed like the appropriate thing to do—since other students were doing it.

You will notice that you will be asked to perform what is considered to be the more difficult vocabulary learning task, namely, producing a target language word when given the native language equivalent. The easier task would be to ask you simply to supply the native language equivalent when given the target language word. The intention is to provide you an opportunity to see how you learn vocabulary when it is not easy to do so.

Now take the following list of English words and supply the appropriate Aymara forms.

this	_____
flower	_____
leg	_____
but	_____
young man	_____
to write	_____
new	_____
sick	_____
quickly	_____
to sleep	_____

Now check back to the original list to see how many of the words you got right. See if you can retrace the process whereby you learned each word. Below is the list of Aymara words with a list of categories of possible ways that each word was learned. The category "Used an associational link" refers to any association you might have made between the word to be learned and something else. For example, if you learned *usuta* 'sick' by linking the word to "used up" ("someone who is sick is used up"), you would enter this association into the box provided. Note that at first recall you may think you used rote memory to learn a word, but if you give it more thought, you will remember that you used some memory aid. Fill in the relevant box(es) for each word.

	GOT RIGHT	USED ROTE MEMORY	USED AN ASSOCIATIONAL LINK
wayna	_____	_____	_____
usuta	_____	_____	_____
cayu	_____	_____	_____
machaka	_____	_____	_____
aca	_____	_____	_____
pankara	_____	_____	_____
ucampisa	_____	_____	_____
iquiña	_____	_____	_____
kellkaña	_____	_____	_____
laka	_____	_____	_____

The purpose of this exercise is for you to see how you actually go about learning new words. It is true that many words come into your target language vocabulary without your actually going about learning them consciously. Rather you just seem to learn them automatically or "acquire" them, as Krashen and others have referred to as more automatic learning (Krashen 1982). In this chapter the focus is specifically on those words that you *do* go about learning consciously.

Now take a look at the Aymara words that you produced correctly and incorrectly when given the English equivalents. Here you have an opportunity to see how well rote memory of vocabulary worked for you on a short-term basis. Here we are referring to those words you just repeated to yourself a few times, let us say, without attempting to link them to something else. If you used some associational links to remember the words, you can see how well these associations worked as well.

Using Mnemonic Associations

One of the ways of improving your performance in learning new words is by using *mnemonic*[2] links. The following is a list of eight types of links. It was originally compiled on the basis of questionnaire responses from college-level target language learners. They reported both the types of mnemonic associations that they tended to use (if any) and those that they actually used in tasks assigned to them (Cohen & Aphek 1979). This is not

---

[2]*Mnemonic* means "aiding the memory" (Higbee 1979) and mnemonic techniques "involve physically transferring to-be-learned materials into a form that makes them easier to learn and remember" (Bellezza 1981:61).

a definitive list of all possible types of associations. Rather it is intended to be suggestive of some of the more popular approaches to generating associations.

List of Associations   You can create associations between a target language word to be learned and something else.

1. By linking the word to the sound of a word in the native language, to the sound of a word in the language being learned, or to the sound of a word in another language.
2. By attending to the meaning of a part or several parts of the word.
3. By noting the structure of part or all of the word.
4. By placing the word in the topic group to which it belongs.
5. By visualizing the word in isolation or in a written context.
6. By linking the word to the situation in which it appeared.
7. By creating a mental image of the word.
8. By associating some physical sensation to the word.
9. By associating the word to a keyword.

Let us go through these categories one by one and give examples, with the assumption that the native language is English.

1. *By linking the word to the sound of a word in the native language, to the sound of a word in the language being learned, or to the sound of a word in another language.* Suppose you want to learn the Aymara word *pankara* 'flower,' for example. You could think of a pancake shaped like a flower—an example of linking *pankara* by sound to a word in your first language. Or if you want to learn the Hebrew word *cosher* 'aptitude,' you could associate it to *kasheh* 'difficult': "Something that is difficult takes aptitude." This is an instance of associating the target word to another word in the target language through sound. Finally, if you want to learn the Hebrew word *me'arbolet* 'whirlpool,' you could associate part of the word to the Spanish word *árbol* 'tree': "An *árbol* is whirling around in the water." This last example actually combines sound with another form of associating, creating a mental image—to be discussed below (item 7).

2. *By attending to the meaning of a part or several parts of the word.* If you wish to learn the German word *Frühstuck* 'breakfast,' you could take the first part of the word *früh-*, 'early,' and think of "an early bird at breakfast."

3. *By noting the structure of part or all of the word.* Assuming that you want to learn the French word *brouille* 'misunderstanding,' you could make a link to *se débrouiller* 'to get out of trouble,' an expression that you already know. Or, you want to learn the Hebrew word *mas'ait* 'truck,' and you remember it by structural association to *laset* 'to carry.' Both words are formed from the same Hebrew base.

4. *By placing the word in a topic group to which it belongs.* For instance,

you could learn a word by its association to other words dealing with the same type of object (e.g., clothing, food) or concept (e.g., states of annoyance, things that are beautiful, expressions of apology). For example, you could learn the three key words for expressing apologies in Hebrew— *mitsta'er* 'am sorry,' *mevakesh slixa* 'ask to be excused,' and *mitnatsel* 'apologize'—by grouping them together and then contrasting their respective meanings and functional limitations.

5. *By visualizing the word in isolation or in a written context.* By visualizing a word in isolation, a learner may remember the word by its configuration of letters, by the number of letters, or by one or more letters. For example, you could learn the Hebrew word *be'emtsa* 'in the middle,' by remembering that there is an 'm' in the middle of the word. You could likewise link the word to the list that you learned it in, to a particular sentence or passage in the text in which it appeared, or to the sign on which you saw it.

6. *By linking the word to the situation in which it appeared.* You could link a word to a poem or song you heard it in, to a group discussion in which the word came up, or to some encounter in which the word played an important part. If you are in a rap group and people are talking in Hebrew about *tina* 'resentment,' you could link the word to the rap session itself.

7. *By creating a mental image of the word.* You could envision a gesture or action that encompasses the word. For example, you could learn the Spanish word *chueco* 'bowlegged' by seeing an image of someone walking bowlegged.

8. *By associating some physical sensation to the word.* It might be that a way to remember a word is by a sensation that comes up in association to the word. For example, you hear the Hebrew word *umlala* 'miserable' (fem. sing.) and you begin to feel bad because of the tone of voice with which the word was said. Or you remember the French word *marron* 'chestnut' by association with the distinctive taste of ground chestnut paste spread on toast.

9. *By associating the word to a keyword.* For example, in order to learn the Spanish word *pato* 'duck,' you could create an image of a duck wearing a *pot* (the keyword) on its head. When you are called upon to retrieve the meaning of *pato*, this evokes the keyword *pot*, which in turn reevokes the image of the duck wearing the pot on its head (Atkinson 1975). This method combines the approaches in item 1 and item 7 above to a certain extent. The target language word is "recoded" into a more familiar word, the keyword. This keyword—a native language word or phrase—is similar in sound to part or all of the target language word. Next, an interacting image is created between the keyword and the native language word or phrase. The intended result is that an encounter with the foreign word will evoke the keyword, which in turn reevokes the imagery link, and finally the native language equivalent can be retrieved from this interaction or imagery link (Atkinson 1975, Levin 1981).

Now that you have read through this list of possible types of association, go back to the table of words above, to see if you used one of these types to learn any of the words. If you did use a type of association, indicate which one you used. Note that two of the categories may both apply for a given word—for example, you associated it with a street sign (item 5) and with a song that you heard (item 6). Some of you may have used few or no associations. Others may have used associations extensively.

At this point review the list of suggested types of associations. Familiarize yourself with them. Think of examples you could give from languages you have learned.

Another Exercise in Vocabulary Learning

Now here is another list of 10 Aymara words to learn. Assume that these were new words from a passage about a young woman and her girlfriend. The young woman opens her door just as the sun is rising, sees her girlfriend standing there, looks her in the eye, and at once starts to laugh because of what she learned about her from a neighbor the previous day while she was spending time talking to her neighbor in the fields.

This time make a decided effort to learn the words with the assistance of mnemonic links. Select some association for each word, if at all possible. Sometimes it takes longer to come up with an acceptable association than other times. It depends on your language background and on the nature of the word that you are learning. Here are the Aymara words to learn:

AYMARA	ENGLISH
tawako	young woman
puncu	door
inti	sun
nayra	eye
ucspacha	at once
larusiña	to laugh
cunalaycuti	because
yatekaña	to learn
pacha	time
parlaña	to talk

After you have learned these words, again do not look back at this list until told to do so—for the sake of the exercise.

Research with learning of vocabulary in a variety of languages has generally demonstrated that the use of some associative technique, particularly using mental images, is a more effective means of vocabulary learning than simple rote memory (see Cohen & Aphek 1980 for references). It has been claimed that people can correctly identify hundreds of slides seen once and can learn, say, 300 words in native language/target language pairs in a single sitting with some *visual* association but just 10 pairs when relying simply on a *verbal* association—that is, putting the word in a sentence (Jahn, n.d.).[3]

As with any technique, the use of mnemonics has been the subject of criticism. One criticism is that mnemonics encourage the learner to learn just one meaning of the target language word—to match only that meaning with its translation equivalent in the native language (Meara 1980). For this reason some educators suggest learning target language words by association to a picture and not to a native language word, when the word can be pictured (Jahn, n.d.). Of course, linking a word to a picture may cause the same result—that is, the learner may only remember that meaning of the word which is depicted.

In fact, the learning of the various meanings of words with multiple meanings is always a problem. Often, a given course of study will only introduce one meaning at a time, usually starting with the most frequent meaning. However, sometimes a less frequent meaning of a word is introduced because it is important in a given context. For example, in Hebrew the word *levaker* means both 'to visit' and 'to criticize.' The first meaning is more frequent, but in the context of, say, work supervision the latter meaning, 'to criticize,' may be just as important or more so.

Also, there is a concern that linking the target language word to a similar sounding, but not identically pronounced native language word might interfere with the learning of the precise pronunciation of the target language word. So, for example, if the Aymara word *pankara* 'flower' is learned by association to "pancakes," the learner may erroneously pronounce the first vowel just like the *a* in "pan" rather than like the *a* in "swan." For this reason, users of mnemonics need to be careful to hear how the target word actually sounds and to treat mnemonic links simply as aids which trigger the retrieval of the target word.

There is also substantial evidence that learners differ in how they best learn new words, both in a target language and in the native language. Some learners like to visualize the word or imagine it in a specific concrete context—if it is abstract. Others like to spell it out. There are others who like to learn the word by its sound (rhythm, tone). Still others respond to a word in terms of some activity—some physical or emotional feeling (Reinert 1976). Also certain words lend themselves more easily to the generation of associations than do others (Cohen & Aphek 1980). In a study

[3]A pre-publication version of Jahn's book was slated for publication with Marcel Didier (Montreal) in the early 1970's, and apparently was never published.

with English-speaking learners of Hebrew, for example, the students generally had little trouble finding an association for *pekiah* 'cracking.' Most used the sound of the word to suggest cracking. On the other hand, students had difficulty finding an association for the word *sharui* 'in the state of' (masc. sing.). Not only was the root difficult to identify, but also there is no equivalent word in English. It also appears to be the case that target language nouns—especially concrete nouns—may be easier to learn than verbs, and verbs easier than adjectives (Raugh & Atkinson 1975).

Now, at this time, continue the second exercise by supplying the appropriate Aymara forms for the English words which appear in the following list.

at once	_____
to talk	_____
eye	_____
sun	_____
because	_____
to laugh	_____
door	_____
time	_____
to learn	_____
young woman	_____

At this point check the original list and see how many of the words you got right.

	GOT IT RIGHT	USED ROTE MEMORY	USED ASSOCIATIONAL LINK (Specify which type)
tawako	_____	_____	_____
puncu	_____	_____	_____
inti	_____	_____	_____
nayra	_____	_____	_____
ucspacha	_____	_____	_____
larusiña	_____	_____	_____
cunalaycuti	_____	_____	_____
yatekaña	_____	_____	_____
pacha	_____	_____	_____
parlaña	_____	_____	_____

Put a check next to all the Aymara words that you produced correctly. Also indicate how you went about learning each word. See if there is any pattern to how you used associations in the instances where you used them. For example, did you look mostly for native language words that sounded like all or part of the Aymara word? Did you use a combination of sound and meaning—for example, linking *ucspacha* to the English word "to dispatch," producing the link "to dispatch at once." Note the words that you did not come up with mnemonic associations for, if any. Is there any pattern to these words? Have you learned anything about how you learn vocabulary? Did you get any insights about how you *can* learn vocabulary—about the options that are given to you to make associational links? Did you use more associations in learning this set of 10 words than with the last set? Did your performance on the memory task improve?

How might you have created associations for the Aymara words? Let's take some examples. First, let us assume that you are just a beginning student of Aymara. Not having a rich source of vocabulary in Aymara to draw on for structural associations, you may well have relied largely on sound and meaning links. For example, you remembered *larusiña* 'to laugh' through association to the word "ruse" in English—"They all laughed at the silly ruse." As for *tawako* 'young woman,' you may have envisioned a young girl smoking tobacco. In this case, "tobacco" would serve as the keyword mnemonic. As for *puncu* 'door,' you could have pictured a young punk standing by a door—and hence, "punk" would be the keyword. For the word *nayra* 'eye,' you may have remembered it because it has the sound of the word "eye" in it. You may have learned *ucspacha* 'at once' by noting that it was actually formed from the words *pacha* 'time' and the adverb for 'immediately,' *ucsa*. This then would be a good example of linking two target language words by their structure.

Now let us assume you have some background in Aymara, and perhaps you are currently taking a course in Aymara. Assuming you already knew that *achaku* means 'mouse,' you could associate *machaka* 'new' to it by sound, by the meaning of a part of the word, and by a mental image through picturing a new mouse coming into your house. If you knew some French, perhaps you remembered *parlaña* 'to talk' by associating it by sound and meaning to the French *parler* 'to speak, talk.' If you knew that *pacha* means 'time,' then you could have provided a link for remembering *ucspacha* 'at once.' If you knew that *yatichaña* meant 'to teach' and *yatiña* 'to know,' then you could have used the base form *yati*/*yate* 'knowledge' to remember *yatekaña* 'to learn.' Both these examples combine the use of associations by meaning and by structure.

If you knew that *usu* meant 'sickness,' then you could do a structural link to remember the adjective *usata* 'sick.' In learning *tawako* 'young woman,' if you knew *imilla* 'girl' and *warmi* 'woman,' then you could group 'young woman' with the topic group of descriptors for females by age group. You may have remembered a word just by visualizing it as it looked—like *cunalaycuti*, as a long (five-syllable), funny word for such a short word in English—'because.' You may have linked *puncu* 'door' to a classroom activity in which you had to get up, walk to the door, and open it. Finally, the word *inti* 'sun' may feel hot to you as you say it, or maybe the sun was streaming in the window at the moment you went about learning the word. Then the association would be to the sensation of heat.

There are other forms of association that we have not discussed which may also play a role in vocabulary learning. For example, it is possible to link a word to a certain person that you know. For example, one student reported learning the word for 'horizon' in Hebrew, *ofek*, by linking it to the name of his teacher, Aphek. Or you could remember a word just because you enjoy the sound that it makes. For example, I remembered the word in Hebrew for "motor vehicle bureau" because it sounded silly to me at that time: *misrad harishui*. (Now, having been submersed in the Hebrew language for the past 15 years, it no longer sounds silly!)

It is important to point out that associational links are often combinations of various types of associations together. For example, the Hebrew word for an appendix to a paper is *nispax*. I learned it by linking *nis* to "nice" (association through sound and meaning to a native language word) and *pax* to its Hebrew meaning, 'trash can' (association through the meaning of part of a word in the target language). Thus, *nispax* 'appendix' is a "nice trash can," that is, a good place to throw material that is not central to a paper.

VOCABULARY LEARNING STRATEGIES

Word Analysis

While traditional approaches to study skills point out the importance of attending to parts of words (i.e., the word base or root, prefixes, and suffixes) as a clue to their meaning (e.g., Yorkey 1970, Martin, McChesney, Whalley, & Devlin 1977), more current approaches would warn against relying on analysis of roots and affixes (Nation 1990, Chapter 10). The danger is that by analyzing a word according to its parts, you may arrive at a meaning that is either totally incorrect or at least inappropriate for the given context.

Clarke and Nation (1980) would suggest leaving word analysis as the last resort, after exhausting contextual clues—for example, determining the part of speech of the unknown word, determining the relationships between the unknown word and other words in the clause or sentence, and looking at the relationship between the clause or sentence containing the unknown word and other sentences or paragraphs. If there is still doubt as to the meaning of the word, then Clarke and Nation would recommend breaking the unknown word into its prefix, root, and suffix, if possible. Nation and Coady (1988) have even eliminated word analysis from their list of steps.

The Learning of Cognates

A potential supply of easy-to-learn vocabulary can be found through *cognates*—that is, words in two languages which are from the same source. In the case of true cognates between your native language and the target language, you only need to be alerted to the fact that the target language word is the same or quite similar to one in your native language. Of course, you need to be wary of false cognates, where two words look alike but mean different things in their respective languages. For example, in English a "tramp" refers both to a hobo and to a prostitute. In Hebrew, a *tramp* refers to a 'lift'—you give someone a *tramp* in your car. Of course, sometimes the existence of false cognates can actually help you remember the meaning of the target language word—by remembering the discrepancy in meaning between the words in the two languages.

Despite the existence of false cognates, the percentage of true cognates between various pairs of languages (those that are clearly related) is high. For example, it has been estimated that 10 out of every 11 cognates between English and French are true cognates (Hammer, n.d.). In other words, most of the words that look like cognates are, in fact, cognates. Listings of cognates across languages are available (e.g., Hammer, n.d.; Freedman 1985) and could be used to enhance vocabulary learning in a target language (see Keller 1978; Jahn, n.d.; Hammer 1979).

Using a Dictionary

One message that seems to be popular these days is not to rush to the dictionary. Although using the dictionary only as a last resort may be too extreme a position, there are advantages in not using the dictionary as a constant crutch. The dictionary is good for checking those words that keep coming up and that are not readily understood from context. It is also good for finding the meaning to unknown words that seem to be crucial to the meaning of the utterance. It can also serve to provide intermediate or advanced learners especially with a more finely tuned meaning or set of meanings for a word with which they have some familiarity.

Just as there are times when monolingual dictionaries supply synonyms that are as unintelligible to the monolingual learner as the word being looked up, likewise there are problems with bilingual dictionaries. For instance, it may be that the user erroneously refers to another meaning of the target word. And even if the meaning is the closest to the target word, it may be different enough to be misleading. In any event, it is considered good practice not to look up a word in the dictionary until the entire available context of the word has been scrutinized (whether the word was spoken or appeared in writing). Nation and Coady include looking in a dictionary as the last means of checking a guess, and the guess is only made if the use of the wider context does not provide the meaning (1988:107).

If there is a need to use the word in speaking without being sure of its meaning, especially in a given context, it is always possible to try it out and see how natives react. As suggested above, the most helpful dictionary for any given learners may ultimately be their own mental lexicon—that which they themselves create based on their own cumulative learning of the language over time.

STRATEGIES FOR PRACTICING WORDS

The Use of Flash Cards

The use of flash cards is always a trusty means of learning vocabulary. It gets words off of lists where they may stagnate—and into a form that is easily portable for study while traveling, while waiting on lines, or wherever. The vocabulary words are prepared on small cards (1½" × 3½"), usually made out of sturdy paper or cardboard. On one side of the card appears the word and possibly related forms. On the other side appears a definition of the word in the target language. Nation (1990) stresses that learning is more efficient if the target language word form is associated with a word in the native language rather than a target language synonym or definition. The learner may also wish to include on the card a minimal amount of context in which the word was heard or read. Ideally, the information on each card would be checked with a native informant before it is studied to make sure that the word is spelled correctly, that the meaning has been correctly interpreted, and that it is used correctly in a sentence.

Obviously it is impossible to get all the relevant information about the word onto these small cards. Rather, the card is to serve as a basic prompt—as an aid to remembering the word, along with one or several of its most basic meanings. You may also wish to note in the left-hand corner of the native language side of the card any mnemonic device your created to help remember the word. Then, in cases where you cannot remember the word any other way, you would consult that mnemonic. The following is an example from Hebrew.

| asur | 'prohibited' (adj.) |
| asur le'ashen bakita | 'No smoking in class.' |

Mnemonic keyword: "sewer." "It is forbidden to go into the sewer."

Stevick notes that flash cards can be used to greater benefit when a word that has given a wrong or incomplete answer is not put on the bottom of the pack, but instead is placed somewhere within six cards from the top (1982:77–78). In this way, the learner can build the total image of the word bit by bit without having to start from the beginning each time, since the image for troublesome words may otherwise have faded away by the time the learner returns to it. Stevick then recommends placing the word further back in the pack until it is well beyond the reach of short-term memory. As Stevick puts it:

> Using flash cards in this manner then becomes a process in which the learner observes his own learning, makes a series of simple but delicate choices, and lives with the results of his choices—something quite different from the dull mechanical routine which flash cards can be in the hands of some people. (1982:78)

Another suggestion regarding flash cards (in this case, in the form of index cards) is that the classroom teacher collect the cards once a week and correct them (Kramsch 1979). Teacher evaluation of the cards would be instead of verification by a native informant—a practical suggestion in foreign language situations where natives are not easily accessible. The teacher's role is to suggest that the learner substitute other words in place of obsolete or low-frequency words, and to make sure that the learner has chosen an appropriate sample sentence in which to place the word. It is also suggested that the cards be used as a vehicle for students to present their words to the rest of the class, as well as to exchange cards with other students in pairs as a vocabulary exercise.

Grouping

Whether the words appear on cards or are stored in some other format (such as lists in a notebook), one way to study them would be according to meaningful groups—so as to reduce the number of discrete elements that have to be learned (Oxford 1990). Groups could be based on the type of word—for example, nouns, verbs, adjectives, or function words. It has been suggested that learners could benefit from learning those 200 or so *function words* in a language that are hard to guess and that occur frequently —such as personal pronouns, determiners, auxiliaries, prepositions, and conjunctions (Hammer 1979). Groups could also be based on a theme or topic (e.g., words about the mood you are in) and could be arranged according to synonyms and antonyms—perhaps within that same theme (e.g., "happy," "content," "joyful"; "sad," "dissatisfied," "sorrowful"). In addition, you could group together words useful for realizing a particular speech act like apologizing (the equivalent target language words for "really," "very," "sorry," "didn't mean to," "let me help," and so forth).

Finally, you may wish to create separate packs of words that you wish to know productively in speaking and writing, and those words that you are content to have a receptive knowledge of—words that you would want in your receptive vocabulary for the purposes of listening and reading. For the former pack, you would want to advance to the point where you are using the side of the card with the native language translation as a prompt to recalling the target language word. In the latter case, you would simply run through the cards on their target language side, calling up the native language meanings for the words.

It is also possible to combine memory strategies through techniques such as semantic mapping (see Hague 1987:221-223; Oxford 1988; Oxford 1990), whereby the learner makes a graphic arrangement of concepts and attributes. The key concept is highlighted or centralized, and it is linked with subsidiary concepts, attributes, and so on, by means of lines or arrows showing relationships. This technique combines making associations, grouping, and visual imagery, as a diagram is used to show visually how ideas fit together. Thus, in the above example of "the mood you are in," it would be possible to depict a person in the center of the page without a face. Around the person would be sets of faces depicting certain general states (happiness, anger, fear, etc.) and groups of words that could be appropriate for each face.

It is important at this point to introduce a word of caution with respect to the learning of words by topic (associational strategy 4 above) and the use of other grouping techniques as suggested in this section. The potential problem is that which George (1972) called attention to in his book on error analysis, namely, the possibility that the learner will make *cross-associational errors* when learning two words that share semantic characteristics. The example of this that Nation (1990, Chapter 3) gives is of the learning of 'long' and 'short' in Samoan—*umi* and *puupuu* respectively. The argument is that if the two forms are learned together, there is a good likelihood that they will be cross-associated and therefore confused. This phenomenon happened to me with respect to two forms in Hebrew, *alul* 'liable to be' and *asui* 'likely to be'—where the first has a negative connotation ("He/it is liable to be of no assistance") and the second has a positive connotation ("He/it is likely to be of assistance"). I learned the two together and found them hopelessly cross-associated until I generated a mnemonic device to keep them apart—that *alul* has the double *l*'s also found in the word for 'negative' in Hebrew, *sh'lili*.

The issue that Nation raises is that teaching synonyms, opposites, and other associations together may have a detrimental effect on the results. He cites native language research such as that of Higa (1963) which found that some kinds of relationships among words help learning while others have a strong negative effect. Higa found that lists of words that were strongly associated with each other, for example opposites and free associates, were much more difficult to learn than a list of unrelated words. Even though this research was based on previously known native language words as opposed to unknown target language words, Nation is skeptical about suggestions for teaching new vocabulary in associative networks. My own feeling is that grouping can be valuable as long as it is done cautiously, perhaps building in mnemonic devices when needed.

Cumulative Vocabulary Study

Various experts stress the usefulness of cumulative vocabulary study—that is, explanation followed by planned repetition of the words in a variety of typical contexts (Barnard 1971). Some experts even advise overlearning of vocabulary—for example, learning only 10 words at a sitting, reviewing the last two when each new one is learned, reviewing the words once the same day and for the next two days (Prokop, n.d.). Holec (personal communication, 1986) refers to the period of discovery that the learner engages in once the word has been presented—and suggests that memorization of the word takes place after the presentation and discovery phases. Meara (1982) views vocabulary learning somewhat differently in that the period of discovery is a long, complex one, continually resulting in the incremental development of the learner's own "mental lexicon." This mental lexicon is seen as being in a continual state of flux. It can be characterized, for example, by somewhat tenuous semantic links between words and by cases of knowing a word but not being able to say what it means (but then having an "of course" reaction after getting the meaning from someone or checking the dictionary).

Thus, it is necessary to separate the act of memorizing a word from what it is that is actually being memorized about that word. So, for some words, the learning may seem to be almost automatic—for example, through a powerful associational technique—so that there is little need to review the word before being called upon to use it or to comprehend it in context (Nation 1990, Chapter 8). For other words, the learning process may be arduous at best and fraught with numerous misunderstandings while the details are being sorted out for the benefit of the learner's mental lexicon. It is precisely this lingering confusion that is not documented in the research literature at the level of processing, but just in terms of product—that is, the errors the learner comes up with. What is lacking is some vivid documentation of the Olympian effort that is made in producing even the most erroneous words and expressions. This is an indication of one's mental lexicon at work.

WHAT NATIVES KNOW ABOUT THE VOCABULARY IN THEIR LANGUAGE

An important message to the learner in this chapter is that we sometimes close off options when we learn new words. We do not allow ourselves to explore all the possible ways we could enhance our vocabulary learning. In fact, we may be unaware of the best or most suitable way for us to learn a particular word or words. It is true that we have a lot to learn when we truly "learn" a vocabulary word. When we use a mnemonic device, then, we are simply enabling ourselves to retrieve the target language word more easily. In actuality, there is a lot we would need to know to have mastery of the word.

One way of determining what there is to know about a word is to find out what a native knows about it. Perhaps these kinds of insights can serve as a benchmark and can give nonnative learners ideas concerning what to focus on. Here are some of the things that natives know to a greater or lesser extent (see Richards 1976, for a more complete description).

A. The frequency of the word in speech and writing, and acceptable collocations (i.e., words that can go with it—for example, fruit that is "ripe," "green," "sweet," or "bitter," but *not* "stale").
B. Limitations as to the use of the word:
   (1) Temporal—is the word out-of-date or too avant-garde?
   (2) Geographical—in what part of the country or world is the word used?
   (3) Social
      (a) By class—do people of a certain social status use the word more/less?
      (b) By situation—what is the resulting level of formality conveyed by using the word?
      (c) By job or profession—is the word restricted to talk within a given profession (e.g., law)?
   (4) Mode of discourse—is the word used more in speaking or in writing or both equally?
C. The syntactic behavior of the word—how can you use it grammatically in a sentence?
D. The common dictionary meanings of the word (denotations).

WHAT VOCABULARY SHOULD BE LEARNED?

Only a few suggestions will be offered here as to the selection of vocabulary to learn, as there are good discussions available concerning this issue (e.g., Bright & McGregor 1970). One approach to selecting vocabulary to learn is to select those words that are the most useful to you in your daily language needs. For example, if you need to speak the language on the job, perhaps you could draw up a list of the native language equivalents of those words that you need to accomplish your work most effectively.

The next step is to find one or more colleagues who might be willing to supply you with the appropriate target language forms. Very often such information is not directly obtainable from the dictionary since language develops so rapidly. Some of the words at work may not be in the dictionary or may have a different definition. It may be necessary to obtain an example or two of the word as it is used in context, rather than simply a translation equivalent—in those instances where misunderstandings about meaning could arise. It may be that the most useful dictionary for learning the target language is your own mental lexicon (mentioned above) which you yourself construct on the basis of your learning experiences and interactions with native informants.

One shortcut exercise for acquiring vocabulary in order to talk about some specialized area would be first to tape yourself talking about it in your native language. Then give the tape to a native of the target language and have him or her provide a rough translation in the target language. The translation might simply consist of a listing of the important words and phrases. Then take this information and learn it in a way that enables you to give your talk back to the native speaker meaningfully in the target language.

While you give your talk, have the native listen and offer comments and corrections (ideally after you have finished giving it so that the corrections do not disturb the flow; see Chapter 3 for more on corrections). This approach can serve as a quick means of giving you a working vocabulary for broaching a topic you may not have known how to discuss. Waiting around for the words to turn up in a language classroom might prove unfruitful since teachers cater to the common denominator and do not usually get into specific areas or domains of vocabulary.

Discrepancies may arise between what teachers expect learners to do and what they actually do; for example, a discrepancy may exist between what a teacher thinks students have jotted down about a word while taking class notes and what actually gets written down. While the teacher may expect that students have written down the word, one or more target language equivalents for it, and a sentence or two that it could be used in, the truth is that most learners feel themselves fortunate if they have written down the word in its correct spelling and possibly with an attempt to provide a *native language* equivalent for the word. There are usually no target language synonyms written down in the learners' notebooks unless the teacher has specifically given them, and there is also usually no example of the word in a sentence.

The explanation for this is relatively straightforward. Even if learners are given all of this rich, contextualized information about words, they do not tend to have time to write it all down, nor are they necessarily able to understand it all, or remember it all—even if they do understand it as it goes by them. Hence, what is left is a piecemeal set of notes that are sorely in need of verification by a native informant in order to ensure accurate learning of the material. Such verification of learners' recorded vocabulary (whether appearing in the learners' notebook, in vocabulary lists, or on flash cards) is probably a key strategy in the learning process. Otherwise, much time can be wasted learning what turns out to be misinformation— words with misspellings, mispronunciations, or misinterpreted meanings.

STAYING OPEN TO AVENUES FOR VOCABULARY LEARNING

In conclusion, then, remember that the mind may close off fruitful options to learning vocabulary based on justifications such as, "I have so many words to learn that I don't have time for gimmicks." The reality is that some of these activities—like learning words through association— can save an enormous amount of time. As has been pointed out, "the mind remembers what the mind does" (Rivers 1981a). Thus, if the vocabulary learner gives the mind only a meager embedding for a new word, that is what the mind will store and then attempt to retrieve. If, on the other hand, the mind concocts an elaborate web of associations around the word, the extra mental activity will most likely facilitate subsequent recall and retrieval of that word.

As noted at the outset of the chapter, this elaborate web of associations has been related to the theoretical notion of depth of processing (Craik & Lockhart 1972, Craik 1977). The simple rule is that the durability of memory traces depends on the depth of processing, or the degree of analysis af- forded the words in question during the various moments or stages when those words or some features of those words are input for the learner. It is your job as learner to ensure that there is ample depth to the processing of vocabulary, and to ensure that what is selected for input is accurate— something that may depend on verification by native informants.

Chapter *3*

Attending to Ensure Learning

This chapter will discuss techniques for paying attention more effectively primarily in classroom settings, although the principles could apply out of class as well. Not only is the primary focus on the classroom, but on the frontal classroom, since this seems to typify the way target language lessons are often taught in many parts of the world. The teacher stands in the front of the classroom and teaches the class. Much of the input to students comes from the teacher. Student participation is limited to responses to specific questions and exercises. In such situations the learners are attending primarily to the teacher and occasionally, it would appear, to fellow students as well.

You will get the most out of the material presented in this chapter if you are able to try it out in the classroom, starting with the exercise that follows. Much of the material in the chapter does not reduce itself easily to one or another exercise. Rather, it involves taking a new look at how you attend in language learning situations. As will be mentioned at the end of the chapter, the relatively simple activity of taping snippets of the target language, whether they be segments of a language class or conversations out of class, can provide extremely useful data for experimenting with the techniques mentioned in the chapter.

SELF-TEST OF ATTENDING

The following is an exercise by which you can check out your level of awareness and attending in the classroom. In order to do this, you are invited to use the short questionnaire that appears below. The way it works is as follows. If you are currently taking a target language course, you simply select one or more moments during a given class session and stop what you are doing in order to ask yourself the following questions:

1. What am I thinking about right now?
2. What are the thoughts that were "in the back of my mind" while I was listening to the class session just now?
3. If I was tuning out or having difficulty attending, was it because the material was:

too easy _____

too difficult _____

not interesting _____

too condensed _____

other _____?

4. If I *was* thinking about what was being taught, was I:

repeating the material to myself (orally or in writing) _____

paraphrasing the material in my own words _____

characterizing the material in some way (e.g., labeling it, looking for an example, etc.) _____

relating this material to some other material _____?

The purpose of this last question is to see how actively you are processing the content of the lesson—from simply repeating it (a potentially weak approach to remembering the material) to relating it to other material (a potentially powerful way to remember material, such as through associative links; see also Chapter 2).

Research that I have conducted using such a questionnaire has revealed that students apparently *intake* less classroom input than might be expected. The students do not seem to be attending to the instructional context in class at a level that will insure that language learning takes place (Cohen, 1983a). Attending to instructional content seems to range at any given classroom moment from about 25 percent to 85 percent, depending on the age of the learner and the interest value of the material, among other things. It appears that, on the average, 50 percent of students are attending to the content of a lesson at a given moment, and most are just repeating the material to themselves—rather than performing any higher order functions on the material (such as making analogies to other material already learned).[1]

ATTENTION

Since language learning is a function of memory and memory is largely a function of attending to language input, learners stand to gain from taking a look at their patterns of attention—that is, the amount of cognitive effort allocated to a given task. Different types of input may all vie for your attention simultaneously. A popular model for how we attend, "the capacity model," would in fact suggest that simultaneous input can be processed in parallel on a "space-sharing" basis (Kahneman 1973). In other

---

[1] For more on this research, see Chapter 7.

words, we can do some processing of all information available to us in our sensory memory. But since we seem to be limited to a single pool of processing resources, we have to set priorities, such that some stimuli get complete analysis and others only superficial analysis (Wingfield & Byrnes 1981:214–216).

The number of messages we receive, their complexity, and our purpose in processing them (i.e., the nature of the task) will determine whether and when we would choose to focus on them and whether our attention will be broad or narrow in nature. If the input is more complex and demanding, we need to analyze it more completely in order for it to be available to our conscious memory or awareness. On the other hand, cognitive activities that are sufficiently well-practiced and automatic (like, in our case, certain language drills and other more automatic activities) can undergo more superficial analysis and still be successfully processed. Thus, teachers who look to students' responses in mechanical drills (e.g., "John likes, we like, they _____ . . .") as a sign of whether those students are paying full attention may be deceiving themselves.

This capacity model provides another dimension to the *depth of processing* principle presented in Chapter 2—that is, the principle that if you really want to learn language material, it pays to analyze and enrich this material by giving it more attention. With respect to the learning of vocabulary, more attention would mean repeated exposure to the words so as to create associations or images to help fix the vocabulary items in memory. Yet before you make the effort to process material more deeply, you need to select the material that will receive this deeper processing. At times, you may use your processing resources primarily for one stimulus —an unknown word—at the expense of other stimuli which in the long run may prove more important to you. Perhaps the main point here is that your awareness as a learner is crucial to making choices about what to attend to in class based on your best estimate of what will have the greatest payoff.[2]

The question of concern to the language learner which emerges from a discussion of attention is: "Am I attending in class at a level that will ensure that language learning takes place?" For maximal learning to go on, you would be directing primary attention to the input, namely, the language instruction—such as the teacher's presentations, explanations, gestures, and words written on the board or in handouts; or another student's question and the teacher's answer.

In reality, there is other input competing with language instruction— namely, input from your mind regarding other academic or social issues; visual and auditory input from the classroom environment but irrelevant

---

[2]Unfortunately, sometimes this means listening with an ear cocked to what may later appear on a quiz, semester test, or final exam—whether or not this material has any redeeming value beyond the confines of the test. Ideally, both what teachers teach *and* what they test for would contribute to effective long-range language learning.

to language learning; and sensations from your body, such as aches and pains or states of hunger and thirst.

Teachers may well be heard to exclaim, "But I taught you that yesterday!" In these cases, the teacher is making the assumption that what is taught is necessarily learned. Yet, as we are seeing more and more clearly as research evidence continues to accumulate, language input is not necessarily language intake. Why is that? First, let us consider the kinds of input you are exposed to, then different ways you approach that input, and finally ways you could approach it that would enhance your language learning.

TYPES OF INPUT

There are at least five types of oral language that you are likely to be exposed to during your language learning—that is, five kinds of talk that are likely to be available to the average learner: the talk of media people on the air, the talk of native speakers to themselves, the talk of natives when addressing foreigners, the teacher's language in the classroom, and the speech of nonnatives during the learning period.[3] The following is a description of each:

1. *Commentator talk:* the language of TV and radio commentators, which is often read from a prepared text, so that there is little repetition, few false starts, and not much redundancy. If you are a beginner in the language, such talk will be most difficult to understand, even if it is in supposedly simplified language.

2. *Native speaker talk:* the language of natives speaking to one another with no attempt to simplify, slow down, or repeat for your benefit, except for the normal repetitions and repairs that are part of conversation.

3. *Foreigner talk:* the modified language that native speakers use with you in an effort to have what they say be more intelligible to you.[4] It may entail simplifying the verb tense or selecting a more common noun or adjective, or it may even mean dramatic reduction to telegraphese.

4. *Teacher talk:* the form of foreigner talk that teachers choose to use in the classroom—the language of classroom management and explanation. Such language is not necessarily grammatical.[5]

---

[3]The last three are based largely on distinctions made by Krashen (1982).

[4]The term *foreigner talk* is also sometimes used to refer to the talk that low-proficiency nonnatives produce, which has been subsumed here under category 5, *interlanguage talk.*

[5]Hatch, Shapira, and Gough (1978) reported on the phenomenon of ungrammatical utterances of target language teachers. They found that the teachers would adapt their speech not just by repeating, defining, slowing down, stressing, and filling in linguistic gaps, but actually by producing incorrect forms. Shoshana Blum-Kulka also collected videotaped data of teachers in Hebrew second language classrooms at the Hebrew University of Jerusalem in the late 1970s and found striking instances of ungrammatical utterances produced in an effort to be understood in the classroom.

5. *Interlanguage talk*: the speech of foreign-language learners—with all its developmental forms. *Interlanguage* refers to a language which you as a learner produce which may involve processes different from those in the native language and in the target language (Selinker 1972). It involves both transferring forms from the native language and extending forms within the target language, such as through analogy. When these processes produce errors, they are referred to as *negative transfer* and *overgeneralization*, respectively.

Although teacher talk and interlanguage talk may be somewhat problematic in that they provide a model which is not always acceptable (especially in the case of interlanguage talk), they nonetheless provide an important source of language input for the learner, especially for the beginning learner. An important reason for you to spend some time in a language classroom is that the teachers and the other students as well are likely to provide language input that is *comprehensible* (Krashen 1982, 1985a).

Particularly at initial stages of language learning, there are forms of language input that are far too difficult and frustrating—such as TV news broadcasts and rapid-fire conversations among natives of the language, where feedback from nonnative listeners is not of concern. Repeated exposure to such input would eventually lead to comprehension, but such an approach does not constitute a very efficient way to arrive at comprehension. A more efficient way would be through receiving exposure to input that is comprehensible. The exposure to comprehensible input has been found to stimulate learning.

While the classroom is a good place to obtain comprehensible input —especially in the initial stages of language learning, it would appear that learners do not usually take full advantage of the available input. In a study that I conducted with learners of Hebrew in Israel, a class of intermediate learners were videotaped in a lesson and then four of the learners volunteered to view the videotapes several days later and to answer questions regarding the lesson. At certain selected moments the tape was stopped and the learners were asked to retrospect as to what was going through their minds at that moment during the lesson. The study revealed that the students had what appeared to be a "pecking order" as to whom they listened to. For example, a learner who was said to be "too talky" was tuned out entirely and another one with a poor accent was tuned out partially.

This finding would suggest that learners are not necessarily letting all input become intake, but rather automatically deselecting some of the input according to largely predetermined criteria. In other words, learners only listen to some of what their fellow students say—according to whether they accept the accent that a fellow students has, whether they are willing to pay attention to a student who says a lot in class, or whether they have the patience to listen while a weaker student struggles to produce an utterance.

HOW DOES INPUT BECOME INTAKE?

When you are ready and willing to pay attention to input and to let it become intake, what is involved in the process? It begins with perception. You have to perceive the input, and in order to process it, must both identify its features and also discriminate between features that could be confused with each other—which includes features *not* in the given input. For example, you inquire in Hebrew regarding the whereabouts of an old friend you are trying to locate, and the people in the town tell you: *hu xaya kan lifney kama z'man* ('he lived here a while back'). You misinterpret their response because you incorrectly perceive the second word, *xaya* 'lived,' to be *haya* 'was.' Hence, you think your friend is still living there, was there a while back, and will probably be returning soon. This kind of misunderstanding happens frequently in target language listening. In this case, you incorrectly identified the first meaningful sound or phoneme of *xaya, x* (*xet*) as if it were *h* (*hey*), thus hearing the word as *haya* 'was' instead of *xaya* 'lived.'

Actually, there would have been another cue to help you discriminate the two words from each other. *Xaya* is accented on the first syllable and *haya* on the second. Yet when you are in the midst of conversing in a language where much of the input is a challenge to you, many cues to meaning go unnoticed. In other words, target language listening involves a selective process whereby not all features are processed by a given learner. Processing involves perceiving the sounds and determining the elements of meaning that are conveyed not only through the words and phrases, but through the stress that words receive and intonation pattern of the utterance as a whole.

Also, we know that learners differ in how rapidly they are able to process the information. It would seem that some learners are what I would call *speed listeners*—that is, they can process input quite rapidly, while others with similar background characteristics and language proficiency experience overload early on. Learners at the initial stages of learning and even more advanced learners who are slower listeners may find most or all of the input goes past them. Then there are the somewhat more successful listeners who relate frustratedly that they understood many of the meaningful units of the utterance as they heard them go by, but were unable to put them together in a meaningful way. The burden of this piecemeal listening on their memory was too great.

Actually, there are perhaps three levels of processing:

1. identification and selection of elements without retention,
2. identification and guided selection with short-term retention—understanding "everything" when hearing it but not remembering anything, and
3. identification and selection with long-term retention.

It is not so surprising that target language input seems to escape us. For one thing, our auditory memory span for foreign language material is only about 60 percent of what it is for our native language. If it is around 15 words per segment in native language, it is only nine words per segment for a foreign language (Rivers 1981b:174–175).

So, especially given the limits of our memory, we need to listen in a way that will help us perceive the meaning. What are some of the strategies that good learners use? Here are a few.

- Listening for key words. These are sometimes signaled by stress or by a pause before or after them.
- Tapping into the key topics and paying particular attention to these—what I would term *skim listening* during input on other topics.
- Listening just for the overall theme without worrying about the details.

Language teaching programs, such as that at the Foreign Service Institute, are beginning to include tasks such as having the learners hear one or two minutes of rapid-fire taped conversations between two natives early on in their training. The purpose is to get learners used to "overhearing" natural language—with its characteristic rhythm, intonation, pauses, contractions, and elisions—and to making an effort to understand the message at least globally (Stevick 1984).

If we are not able to catch all the data as they go by in an utterance, how then do we come up with meaning? Good learners play the game of probabilities, of inference. They use their world knowledge or *content sche-mata* for what is most likely being said, given:

1. the topic and their prior knowledge as to possible utterances for the topic,
2. the conditions under which the utterance appeared,
3. who the particular speaker is and what the speaker's perceived intentions are (Rivers 1981a:160),
4. the speaker's tone of voice and body language,
5. the context of the discourse in which it appeared, and
6. cues from prior utterances within the given discourse.

A general rule of thumb would be to seek input that is generally understandable—which reduces the options somewhat at the initial stages of language learning. In the next section, we will look at different types of input and focus on the classroom situation specifically.

INPUT AND THE CLASSROOM

Different types of learning may go on in the classroom, and various terms are used to describe the kinds of learning that go on. There is learning that seems more automatic and effortless—when you feel you picked something up as if through osmosis. It may never have been written down in your notebook. You heard it—or were even unaware that you heard it—and had it available when you needed to use it in an utterance. Then there is learning which comes less automatically, is more studied. It often involves repeated study of material through review of class notes, exercises, and drills.[6]

In order for the input to have maximum impact on your learning, you must be open to it. In reality, you probably find yourself being only somewhat attentive, and actually selective in what you attend to. For example, it is possible for you to attend only partially to well-practiced classroom routines—that is, those that are more automatic, such as when students take turns reading aloud or take part in verb drills. Your teacher may consequently get the false impression that you are engaged more fully than is actually the case.

In order to look good, you may purposely give the teacher the impression that you are engaged more fully than you really are. This may be done through continual nods of the head or vacuous eye contact. (Meaningful eye contact would be something else.) It may be done through asking questions now and again—possibly even questions that you actually know the answer to (as reported in a diary study, Bailey 1980). It may be done through counting ahead to find the line(s) that you will most likely be asked to read, so as to appear well-versed in the material when the time comes (Hosenfeld 1976). Sometimes these activities are performed almost instinctively so that you will not be singled out and possibly embarrassed in front of the other learners as being unprepared or ignorant.

IMPROVING YOUR LEVEL OF ATTENDING

This section proceeds under the assumption that you are willing to expend the effort necessary to attend successfully in class—regardless of whether the topics or tasks are to your liking. This is sometimes a tall order. Learners tune out in class because they are simply not interested in what is going on. But if you see teacher-fronted lessons in the classroom as an

---

[6]Krashen (1982) would refer to the more automatic learning as *acquisition* and the more conscious learning as *learning*. McLaughlin (1978) prefers the terms *automatic processing* and *controlled processing*. But this is a simplistic representation of the two theoretical positions. For more details on the acquisition-learning debate, see Gregg (1984) and Krashen (1985a).

opportunity to be exposed to comprehensible input that can be utilized in language learning, then you may wish to improve your attending patterns.

Unquestionably there will be moments in class when you will need to take a mental break—to stop paying attention. It is probably the case that most learners need to "come and go" from time to time. Such a pattern need not have a disruptive effect on learning, but if the interruptions are repeated and frequent, then this may severely limit the amount of intake and therefore limit the potential for learning. Thus, if you take a look at your patterns of attending in class, you may discover that you are not affording yourself the challenging level of intake which you are capable of handling.

Since there is a possibility that you may tune out in the classroom and thus lose the opportunity for learning, you may wish to consider using attention-enhancing strategies to reduce the likelihood that this will happen. One such attention-enhancing strategy to be employed during teacher-fronted lessons is to *respond silently to tasks requested of other students* in the class—not just to wait until it is your turn. In other words, you become in essence every learner in the class. Unfortunately, I have no research validating this technique, but I have had testimonials from learners over the years that this technique made them feel more engaged in the lesson. What it means in practice is that instead of using the time between your turns to prepare for your next turn, look up words in the dictionary, or do some other activity removed from that which the teacher is directing at the moment, you put all your efforts into performing to yourself the tasks requested of your peers. Then you check their performance as assessed by the teacher with your "silent performance."

Active listening and attending would also involve a *continual search for the meaning* in utterances. Good learners use a number of strategies in their search for meaning. As indicated above, they call upon their knowledge of the world and of possible topics for given contexts, the given speaker, and cues from prior utterances in the discourse. They also look for linguistic cues within the utterance itself, such as cues from the stress that individual words have received.

The point here is that good learners stay open to input, even if they do not understand everything. They are good observers of what is going on around them. When things are not clear, they may create interactions in which they can find out what they do not understand. For example, this may mean that learners raise their hand when something is not clear in order to obtain clarification.

In *small-group interactions*—which are becoming more common these days in language classrooms—there is a greater opportunity for learners to seek and obtain such clarification than in a whole-class session. Of course, sometimes they may not be sure as to what they should be seeking clarification about, because their role in the group has not been made clear or it is not a genuinely productive one. Moreover, small groups are not necessarily a panacea for genuine interaction because the nature of the activity that the small group is performing is crucial.

A review on the use of small groups for peer critique of writing, for example, found that teachers were too likely to impose rigid activities on the group participants so that the potential for dynamic group interaction to improve the quality of the essays was most likely diminished or lost (DiPardo & Freedman 1988). Assuming teachers do not impose strict controls on the groups but rather train the groups to function as semi-independent units, there are still different ways that groups can operate.

For example, small groups can be centered around *peer tutoring* such that, say, the members of a small group are to help each other complete a worksheet. The teacher serves as a major source of knowledge but encourages interpersonal communication, interaction, and mutual help. The group's score is based on the performance of all the members, and groups may compete with each other to increase the motivation of group members. The group could also function as a *discussion group*, perhaps having to generate a report which is then presented to the whole class. Here the teacher serves as a guide, consultant, and facilitator. A recent study comparing peer group and discussion group approaches to the whole-class method for teaching English as a foreign language, found that both of the group methods yielded significantly greater improvement than the whole-class method (Bejerano 1987).

Small groups have certain built-in advantages over larger classroom setups. Their size is more conducive to full participation—especially for students intimidated by large numbers. Furthermore, there is more of a need for students to participate because there are fewer of them and each may have an important role. Also, it is more likely that students in a small group will maintain a higher level of attention because their active role in group tasks would require it.

In a *one-on-one situation* with a native speaker, skilled learners may break in from time to time with a short summary of what they thought was said in order to check their comprehension. Research has shown, for example, that receiving input is not enough. Learners may really need to negotiate for meaning as well in order to make the incoming speech truly comprehensible (Long 1981).

The importance of negotiating for meaning cannot be overemphasized. Learners may, for example, use the technique of summarizing: for example, "Now, let me see. If I understood you correctly, I am to be at your place tomorrow evening at 7:30. Correct?" Or they may ask for a repetition of the utterance: "Excuse me. Could you repeat your invitation again? I want to make sure that I got it correct." Misunderstandings can result in embarrassing situations. For instance, during our first years in Israel, my wife and I showed up for dinner at the home of some Israelis one day too soon because I misunderstood the difference between *leil shabbat* (the evening when the sabbath begins) and *motza'ei shabbat* (the evening after the sabbath ends). I heard the part *shabbat*, did not understand the *motza'ei* part very well, and yet did not get it verified.

If you have access to a portable tape recorder, then it may be most helpful to record a portion of the lesson (e.g., when the teacher is telling an interesting story) or a talk with someone, and then to play it over to yourself several times later that day or another day. You will notice that your level of comprehension increases each time you play the tape. You may experiment by paying attention to different things each time. One time, for example, you may just focus on the general message, another time on specific vocabulary words selected by the speaker, and another time on the grammatical forms that are used. By taping speech, you are allowing yourself the "luxury" we have when reading a text or writing one—the luxury of being able to go back over the material.

So-called natural methods that rely on the absorbing of material through comprehension of meaningful input are in many ways dependent on the listener to attend successfully and to convert input into intake. As this chapter has indicated, there are tricks for enhancing such attending. It could be said that language learning really begins with such efforts.

Chapter 4

Speaking to Communicate

Speaking to communicate involves a number of dimensions. This chapter will deal only with four of them, with a view to the challenges facing the learner and to means at the learner's disposal for facilitating the task of speaking in a target language. The chapter will first detail the demands made upon the average learner in order to produce spoken utterances. Second, communication strategies which learners employ to assist them in getting their message across will be considered. Third, the correction of oral errors and its role in the learning process will be looked at. Finally, some time will be devoted to describing in detail what may be involved in producing a situationally appropriate utterance, such as an apology—with a concern for what the learner might wish to do in order to be more successful at producing speech acts such as apologies in a target language.

THE COMPLEXITIES OF SPEAKING

Successful speakers are willing to talk. They are also willing to make errors. It is not surprising that errors are made because in order to produce even a single sentence in a target language, a learner has to engage in a mind-boggling series of tasks. Let us break down these tasks for inspection in order to see just how complex the process is.

Planning an Utterance

First, you—the speaker—plan the utterance. This includes the following factors:

Selection of Elements   You need to call upon different types of knowledge you have about the language:

1. linguistic knowledge—how words, phrases, and sentences are formed.

2. discourse knowledge—how these linguistic elements are linked to one another to form meaningful text.
3. sociolinguistic knowledge—rules for when it is appropriate to use such forms.
4. content knowledge—what to say and how to say it (in terms of amount of information required, relevance, and clarity; Grice 1975).

Ordering of Elements   You need to know possible and preferable ordering of elements in an utterance. For this, you rely heavily on your discourse knowledge. Actually, both in the selection and ordering of elements, you need to draw on your *strategic knowledge*—your knowledge about how to organize the information most effectively to get the meaning across (Canale & Swain 1980).

Agreement of Elements   You need to know what has to agree with what in person, number, gender, or tense. For this, you rely heavily on your linguistic knowledge.

Pronunciation   You need to know how to pronounce the utterance so that it will be intelligible to the listener(s). It may take extra attention to do this, and there is the added pitfall that mispronunciation of some of the sounds may result in the speaker being stigmatized socially.

Executing the Utterance

Once you have cleared all the hurdles relating to the planning of the utterance, you must then tackle the equally awesome task of producing the utterance so that it is understood. This, too, involves various factors:

Time   First, there is the matter of rate of production, and the number and length of pauses. You may not know where it is appropriate to pause in a target language utterance and how to signal that you have not finished. This usually entails some way of filling the pause, which varies from language to language. The time it takes to get the utterance out is largely dependent on the ease of retrieval. Especially at early stages of language learning, you probably find the words and structures do not come to you quickly. Sometimes you remember them but then forget them just before you arrive at the spot where you need to insert them.

Avoidance of Slips of the Tongue   You have to be wary of producing speech errors which are the result of thinking one set of sounds or words and uttering another. The likelihood of such slips occurring is greater at the early stages of learning but remains problematic for advanced learners speaking certain target languages.

Self-Repair   Once you have spoken, you may see the need to retrace your utterance, rephrasing or replacing some or all of it.

It has been suggested that there are two general groups of speakers in a target language—the *planners* and the *connectors* (Seliger 1980). The planners plan their utterances before they talk. The connectors start executing their utterances before they have planned them completely, in more of an "on-line" fashion. Actually, individuals may do some of both. The point is that sometimes the planning and the execution are two separate phases, and sometimes they are integrated into one. Regardless of which approach a speaker uses, the task of producing an utterance is impressive. This difficulty in producing utterances helps to explain why certain modern methods for teaching a target language (such as Total Physical Response; see Asher 1977) do not require learners to speak at all for an initial period—until they feel comfortable enough in the language so that speaking is not an excessive burden.

Regardless of whether they start with a silent period, successful speakers are those who eventually end up talking more. By talking they increase the amount of "personalized" language input they receive from others. When you do not speak up, you get whatever input is available, whether or not it is at your level. Successful speakers may also be more *extroverted*—that is, they are more outgoing, more likely to look for opportunities to interact with speakers of the target language.[1] It was found, for instance, that Spanish-speaking twelfth graders who were more extroverted were also better speakers of English as a second language (Rossier 1975).[2] In a study of 78 adult language learners studying or teaching at the Foreign Service Institute, it was found that the more extroverted respondents also tended to have better affective strategies for learning a target language (Oxford & Ehrman 1989). In other words, they were considered to be better able to cope with their feelings and attitudes about language learning. They were also more likely to indulge in authentic language use.

---

[1]The research literature is not unanimous on this issue owing primarily to shortcomings in the different research designs (Kezwer 1987). Among the studies of classroom extroverts, there is the case study of Igor who dominated the turn-taking in his university ESL class—largely because of his inability to make himself understood (Allwright 1980). Extroversion may be a factor in the development of speaking as opposed to listening, reading, and writing, since it requires face-to-face interaction (Brown 1987:110). Yet research has shown that more *introverted* Japanese EFL learners attained better pronunciation in the target language in a classroom setting than did the more extroverted learners (Busch 1982).

[2]After controlling for IQ, general educational attainment, grade point average, and time spent studying in the United States.

to be better able to cope with their feelings and attitudes about language learning. They were also more likely to indulge in authentic language use.

COMMUNICATION STRATEGIES

Successful speakers also make wise choices about the forms they use and how they use them. They select forms in order to keep the conversation going. This often entails compromise. They may not find the exact word they want so they use another. In fact, a major trait of successful speakers is that they use strategies to keep the conversation going. Some of these strategies are dependent on native language knowledge and some draw on the target language. Because these communication strategies compensate for deficits the speaker may have, they have been referred to as *compensatory strategies* (Poulisse, Bongaerts, & Kellerman 1984; Poulisse 1989).

Strategies Based on the Native Language

Borrowing   You use a word from your native language, pronouncing it as you would in your native language. Sometimes, you may know or guess that certain borrowed words would be understood by the listeners. At other times, you just do not feel that there is any alternative so you insert the native language equivalent. For example, a learner inserts the English word "Kleenex" or "taxi" into an utterance in the target language with the knowledge or belief that the word will be understood.

Literal Translation   You perform word-for-word translation into the target language from your native language. Sometimes, you are unaware that you are doing this. Hence, an Israeli who says, *"They do not give me to play with them," is translating from Hebrew, where "give" and "let" are the same verb (*not'nim*).

Foreignizing   You use a word from the native language, with phonological and morphological adaptation to the target language. So, for example, when my son at age 10 wanted to say in Portuguese that a dog had fallen out of a window, he used *felía*, with its marking for imperfect tense, whereas the correct Portuguese form would have been *caiou* (Cohen 1989). Or a speaker of English who has difficulty finding a word for "insights" in Hebrew might simply take the English word "insights" and pronounce it as if Hebrew, possibly pluralizing it with the Hebrew plural, *-im*: /insaytim/.

Strategies Based on the Target Language

Use of a General Word   You use a *core* or semantically more general word (e.g., "animal" instead of "deer," "tool" instead of "hammer").[3]

Approximation   You use a word sharing certain semantic features with the appropriate word, at about the same level of semantic specificity (e.g., use of "lake" when "pond" is more appropriate, or "stone" when "rock" is called for).

Description   You describe the object in question. One form of description would be a *paraphrase*. If you do not know how to say something the way you would like to, you say it the way you can—that is, with the vocabulary and sentence structure you have (see Kramsch 1981a, Kramsch 1981b). It may mean rephrasing the utterance from the start. It may include finding a more general or core word (instead of supplying the precise word, "hammer," you would say "tool" or "instrument") or a synonym for the word you would like to use (instead of "to hammer in the nail," you say, "to drive in the nail"). It also could include the use of *circumlocution*. For example, if you do not know the word for "island" in a target language, you would describe with whatever vocabulary you have at your disposal that it is a tract of land surrounded by water (Blum & Levenston 1978:411–413).

Word Coinage   You make up a new target language word to communicate the target item (you create "airball" because you do not know "balloon").

Mime   You use gestures to replace or illustrate the concept you are trying to get across.

Appeal for Assistance   You ask the interlocutor to provide the missing word or phrase. Such appeals may be of two kinds: a direct request for the form or an indication that a target language form is missing (a pause, intonation, repetition, gesture) and that you need help. In these instances, you are using your interlocutors as partners, letting them provide you vocabulary or grammatical structures. As a communication strategy, the technique helps to engage you in dialog.

For example, you do not know the target language equivalent for

---

[3]Core vocabulary items are those that are more neutral or "unmarked" structurally, semantically, and pragmatically in the lexicon as a whole or in a particular field (Carter 1988:171–172). For example, "thin" is more a core word than "skinny," "slim," "lean," or "emaciated."

"steering wheel," and wish to make sure your listener knows what part of the car you hit when you had a car accident. So you provide the native language word or signal the concept nonverbally, and let your listener provide the target language word. You may not even use that instance as an opportunity to learn the word in the target language. That may not necessarily be your purpose. It may be simply to make sure that your listener is following your message. In this instance, you would be using a *communication* strategy and not a *learning* strategy. Of course, it would be possible for the two to be combined—if you were to make some systematic effort to learn the word for steering wheel as well.

Word Abandonment   You give up the search for a particular word upon realizing that the word is not forthcoming.

Discourse Planning Strategies

Avoidance   You do not know certain grammatical forms or lexical items in a target language, so you avoid using them. For example, you do not know the past tense very well or at all in some language, so instead of describing the action, you give the consequence. For example, rather than, "Cynthia gave birth to a 6-pound baby boy," you would say, "Cynthia is now mother of a 6-pound baby boy." Or instead of, "I would like two pounds of cherries, please," you would say, "I would like two pounds, please" (pointing to the desired fruit).

Topic Avoidance   You do not know how to say something in the target language, so you avoid that topic. For example, you are writing a friend a letter in the target language and want to describe a new project at work, but you realize that you do not have the necessary vocabulary. So you avoid the issue altogether.

Gambits

You may also turn to a word or phrase which you have learned and which you know serves to signal your turn in the conversation (Coulmas 1981). You may use one as an *opener*—to add new information ("Furthermore . . ."), develop something said by someone else, express an opinion ("In my opinion . . ."), and so forth. You can also use gambits as *links* to tie into what has just been said—for example, to disagree with the speaker and provide your own opinion: "*I think* the real problem is money, not time." You may also want to give your conversational partner feedback through a *responder* such as "Yeah," "Really," or "You're right." Finally, a gambit may indicate a desire for terminating the conversation: "Well, it was real nice talking to you" (Keller & Warner 1976).

These various communication strategies may *not*, in fact, be strategies for learning, but rather solely ploys for communicating, as indicated above. For example, a listener may be prompted to provide the learner with a word or two along the way, and the learner may make no effort to learn that word. The appeal is simply to make sure that the listener was following and to keep the conversation going. This in turn provides the learner with more input from which to benefit in the learning process. Learners who practice language by initiating interactions with the teacher and with fellow learners, thereby generating more personalized input for themselves, have been referred to as *high input generators*, and those who play a passive role in the language classroom and do little to get input directed at them have been termed *low input generators* (Seliger 1983:253). These labels can apply to behavior in nonclassroom situations as well.

There are times, of course, when the you may well make an effort to learn a word that is supplied—when there is (1) time for processing the word, (2) interest on your part, (3) a focus on new forms, and (4) adequate knowledge so as to know what to do with the form. A teacher-fronted lesson may provide more time for processing a word than a small-group session or one-on-one in that you are likely to be engaged in conversation for a shorter period of time, allowing more time for processing the input that has been generated.

If these strategies do not necessarily lead to learning of the forms in question, you might wonder why they should be used. Perhaps the main reason is that such communication strategies may well keep the conversation going and keep you in it, as suggested above. If you continue conversing, you are getting more of a chance to have input directed at you by an interlocutor. And in order to keep up a conversation, you may need to avoid certain topics, to use roundabout methods for discussing other topics, and to rely heavily on your interlocutor to fill in gaps where you cannot supply even an approximate word or phrase.

CORRECTION OF ERRORS

Successful speakers also have a selective concern for error correction. They want corrections—but at the proper moment and in a meaningful way. As detailed above, speaking a target language is such a taxing undertaking that you inevitably make errors. But what is perhaps *more* taxing is to successfully deal with incoming feedback concerning errors that you have made. Why is this? In order to understand this issue fully, let us look at the typical error correction situation in the classroom (remembering that it applies to out-of-class situations as well).

You have said something that the teacher has deemed incorrect. Let us say that you used the wrong form for subordination in the target language—for example, *"He wants I should come," instead of "He wants me to come." The teacher may give you a funny look, make a disapproving sound, correct the utterance in full or partially, say "no," or wait for other students to signal that an error was made. The main thing is that some indication is given that you have erred. The teacher may then require you to produce an acceptable form—either by giving you the task again, by asking you to say part of the utterance again, or by having you repeat the correct utterance. The teacher could also correct the form or have another student correct it, and move on.

Whatever approach is selected by the teacher, experts (e.g., Allwright 1975, Krashen 1982) would suggest that the correction of oral errors will probably have limited or no effect if:

- You are not focused on the *form* of your message (i.e., its vocabulary, grammar, or pronunciation) because you are too busy communicating the *content*.
- You do not have enough time to consider the correction since such consideration would be at the expense of the activity the class is engaged in.
- You do not have adequate knowledge of the area being corrected to benefit from the correction, and the teacher or peer doing the correction is unaware of this.
- You have too little knowledge about how the language works to know what question to ask to get clarification, or you ask for clarification but find that you do not understand the response.
- Your current level of proficiency is not high enough to understand the teacher's explanation of what you did wrong.

Oral corrections would be most likely to have an impact when:

- You are ready for them and have adequate knowledge about the structures involved.
- You have time to digest the corrections.
- You write down the correct form in a notebook—possibly in a special section for that kind of information.
- You verify the correct form with an informant (possibly the teacher) at a later time.

It needs to be pointed out that there is little research basis for these pronouncements. Efforts at assessing the impact of oral corrections have been limited. A major survey of studies on oral feedback (Chaudron 1988:136–153) focused almost exclusively on preferences that teachers and learners had for correction, on the errors that should be corrected, and on how they are to be corrected and by whom, primarily due to a lack of research concerning *the impact of the corrections on the learners*—that is, what learners actually do with the corrections, if anything.

Two studies that graduate students of mine did as seminar projects would suggest that corrections of oral target language utterances may not even be attended to at all—or only ineffectively, and that even repeated and blatant corrections may not "take." Alamari (1982), for example, looked at the way in which 26 adult advanced-level Hebrew second language learners in four classrooms related to their teacher's oral correction. She recorded each instance in which a learner was corrected, and then approached the learners at the break in order to ask them what they did when their oral language was corrected in class. Although all the learners said that they wanted to be corrected and almost all said they took teacher corrections seriously, about 20 percent reported not paying attention to the corrections and only 15 percent said that they wrote down the correction in their notebooks. Mostly, they reported repeating the correction to themselves. Such behavior would provide ample opportunity for forgetting the correction altogether.

Rosenstein (1982) conducted an interventionist study as teacher of a 100-hour university EFL course in spoken English. He collected two-minute segments of spoken language from each student in each of six class sessions (12 minutes in all) as a pretest and then another 12 minutes of speech as a posttest. An analysis of the transcriptions of the pretest allowed the teacher/investigator to assign each learner an overt error as a "public error" in need of eradication. He also assigned each learner a covert or "secret" error, one that that learner did not know about. He made sure that each covert error was another student's overt error in order to see if learners would learn from overhearing other students corrected on "their" error. The learners were corrected repeatedly on their overt errors.

Of the eight students for whom he had complete data, two showed significant improvement in their public errors and one in her secret error at the end of the semester. Another two students showed improvement in their public errors and one student in her secret error, but these findings were not at a level of statistical significance. The others showed modest or no improvement in their public and secret errors. Rosenstein credited the level of success attained to his general discussions with the learners as to why they made errors, individual discussions with them about their particular public errors and explanations for them, written assignments regarding the errors, and immediate correction of the public errors when occurring in speech. Yet his success was still only about 50 percent for public errors and perhaps 20 percent for secret errors.

The reason why at least half the students managed to emerge from the treatment with little or no improvement can perhaps best be found in the Alamari study: The learners simply were not paying attention to the corrections, not paying attention well enough, or paying attention but not efficiently recording the feedback that they received for future reference.

Another study, conducted at the University of California at Los Angeles, focused just on learners' ability to spot the oral language errors that they made (Schlue 1977). Three intermediate-level college ESL students were audiotaped for 15 minutes once a week. They then listened to their tapes for 45 minutes, over a 10-week period. It was found that the students were able to spot their own errors only 25 to 40 percent of the time. In other words, they were oblivious to at least 60 percent of their errors, with their attention to form decreasing the more they wanted to communicate. When they were able to spot their errors, they were able to correct most of these. Hence, the message to the learner and to the teacher would be to make sure that the learner is afforded an opportunity to perform on-line correction of errors while speaking. This means that the teacher gives the learner time to self-correct rather than providing immediate correction.

As it turns out, you may be able to self-correct perhaps half of the mistakes you make when you speak (Holley & King 1971). You simply need time to hear just what it was you actually uttered. Allowing this to happen is a matter for negotiation. In other words, if you are in a situation where a teacher or other speaker of the language corrects your errors as soon as you utter them, you may wish to request that they delay such correction. One way would simply be to let you finish your utterance or set of utterances, before they provide the correction. A study of first-, second-, and third-year college students of German found that if their teachers gave them from five to 10 seconds wait time in order for them to check out what they have said and to self-correct *before* the teachers jumped in to correct, the learners were able to spot and rectify more than half of their errors (Holley & King 1971).[4]

When you are given an opportunity to clear up any errors you can spot, you will usually find that these tend to be a result of momentary lapses and slips of the tongue due in no small part to the demands put upon you to plan and execute your utterances. The kinds of errors that are left, then, would be the more "serious" ones—that is, the ones that you do not spot as errors.

What actually makes speaking errors clear up the best seems to be more exposure to the language, which includes talking more to stimulate more exposure to language. The impression you get is that the errors have

---

[4]This study, which involved the use of videotapes, found that the teacher's pause and the nonverbal expectation of student performance created a class atmosphere conducive to student self-correction. The time interval did not produce tension and did not slow the tempo of the lesson noticeably. To the contrary, it was found that teacher correction, explanation, and restatement of the questions took up as much or more class time than extra seconds of silence.

cleared up by themselves. In fact, what happens is that you begin to think more like a native would. In part, this means thinking less in your native language with the result that you are less likely to carry over to the target language words and structures that are incorrect or inappropriate for the given context. While you continue to think in your native language, the kinds of errors you may make are those of *negative transfer*—the use of a native language pattern or rule which leads to an error or inappropriate form in the target language (Selinker 1972). Of course, there are also instances where two languages—particularly related ones—have similar words and structures, and so carrying over material from the native language would result in *positive transfer*.

Another source of error is that of generalizing from one instance in the target language to another. Often such generalizations are perfectly valid, but on occasion the generalization or analogy does not hold. Such errors are referred to as *overgeneralization* (Richards 1973). For example, you have learned, "He wants me to go," and by analogy, you say, "*He requests me to go." Such errors clear up as you begin to get more exposure to the variety of forms that a given language has and become aware of the exceptions in the language—the cases where the expected forms are not found.

Some learners find it counterintuitive to accept the premise that increased exposure to the target language will clear up numerous negative transfer and overgeneralization errors. They are convinced that they need to be corrected on these errors for anything to happen. The simple reality is that overt correction by others accounts for only a small portion of the correct target language we speak. This does not mean that we should discourage correction, but it does mean that we may want to think carefully about when, how, why, where, and in what fashion we receive it. The rest we learn by other means—mostly by increased exposure to the language in one form or another.

The capacity to acquire one's first language has been viewed by Chomsky and others to be largely innate in that every normal human being is born with an independent language faculty referred to as a *language acquisition device* (LAD) (Chomsky 1965). This LAD supposedly contains a knowledge of linguistic universals which are innate and which provide children with a starting point for acquiring the grammar of the language they are exposed to. The notion has been applied to target language learning as well in that certain "core" rules are posited to exist in all natural languages and that learners may find these rules easier to learn in a new language than the language-specific ones (Ellis 1985:14–15). A major challenge for the learner in learning a target language is that of sorting out the rules that function in that language and exactly how they function—whether this is done through formal or informal learning.

According to some scholars, we progress in a target language by testing hypotheses about how the language works, on the basis of inferences based on previous knowledge (Schachter 1983). According to Schachter (1984), for example, learners depend on *negative input* to verify hypotheses about whether their utterances are comprehensible, grammatically correct, or situationally appropriate. Such input includes not only explicit correction, but also confirmation checks (i.e., confirmation elicited by the speaker that the utterance was correctly understood or heard) and requests for clarification (new information or a rephrasing of what was already said). Such negative input could also show up as a failure to understand (with or without the learners realizing it). Our task as language learners, then, is to continually negotiate with our interlocutors to make sure that they have understood our intended message and that we have understood them.

SITUATIONALLY APPROPRIATE UTTERANCES: THE LEARNING OF SPEECH ACTS

As a learner, you have a need to determine the situationally appropriate utterances—that is, what can be said where and when. Successful speaking is not just a matter of using the correct words and forms. It means evoking whatever strategies are necessary for us to learn *what* to use them for, *when* to use them, and *how* to use them. It has already been suggested that there are powerful influences working against our appropriate use of target language forms, namely, how we do it in the native language. What appears to be a particular challenge for the target language learner are those patterned, routinized utterances that speakers use regularly to perform a variety of functions—the *speech acts*, such as apologies, complaints, requests, refusals, and compliments. The importance of such speech acts at truly critical moments in communication serves as a justification for providing a detailed discussion of one such complex speech act, that of apologizing, in this chapter. The correct use of speech acts may well be a result of both clever use of learning strategies and communication strategies.

In formal terms, a speech act is an utterance with a basic or propositional meaning (e.g., "I am hot" = the speaker is feeling hot) and an intended effect or illocutionary meaning (e.g., "I am hot" = the speaker is requesting that someone open the window). The fact that such utterances are routinized helps learning in the sense that much of what is said is predictable. For example, almost half the time that an adjective is used in a compliment, it is either "nice" or "good" (e.g., "That's a nice shirt you're wearing." "It was a good talk you gave."), with "beautiful," "pretty," and "great" making up another 15 percent (Wolfson & Manes 1980).

Notwithstanding the routinized nature of speech acts, there are still various strategies to choose from and often a variety of possible forms for realizing those strategies, especially in the case of complex speech acts such as apologies and complaints. As a target language learner, you may tend to respond the way you would in your native language and culture, and find that either the strategy used or the specific language forms (or both) is/are not at all appropriate in the target language and culture situation. In other words, you come to realize that speech acts are not necessarily translatable to other languages.

With regard to strategies for apologizing, for example, you forget an important meeting with your boss and in an apologetic call later in the day, you suggest an alternate meeting—unaware that you have violated a cultural rule in the target culture which stipulates that in such a situation the boss would be the one to suggest the next move, and not the offender. With respect to speech forms, you want to take a window seat on a bus and need to get by the person in the aisle seat. You say the equivalent of "Excuse me" in the target language and the addressee jumps up as if he or she had just stepped on your foot. You were unaware that in the target language there are other, more acceptable means of requesting access to the window seat: for example, "Is it possible to sit there?" or "May I get by?"

In short, you may fail to communicate effectively in one of those situations even though your command of grammar and vocabulary is fine. What is lacking is knowledge of how to execute the given speech act appropriately. One of the most important tasks in acquiring communicative competence in a target language is learning the rules of appropriateness or, in other words, learning to use the language in an acceptable manner. But although the learning of speech acts would appear to be an important priority for the language learner, the set of strategies and the language forms to be used in realizing each strategy are not always "picked up" easily. Blum-Kulka and Olshtain (1986) found that nonnatives needed at least five years for their speech act behavior to accommodate itself to that of natives.

In fact, speech act competence may need to be taught. One small study that a colleague and I conducted, demonstrated that it is possible to teach them. We gave three 20-minute lessons on apologizing to two groups of advanced English foreign language learners and found that the lessons influenced both their ability to rate utterances in terms of their appropriateness and their own ability to produce appropriate utterances (Olshtain & Cohen, 1990).

The intention here is to illustrate the kinds of information it would be useful to have in order to realize the speech act effectively. For this purpose, we will consider just one speech act as used by two language/cultural groups of speakers. The speech act will be that of apologizing, as realized by American English speakers and Israeli Hebrew speakers. For the purposes of this example, we will assume that you are a native Hebrew speaker in Israel learning American English.

An Exercise in Apologizing

The following is an exercise for you to see how versed you are in executing speech acts. In the following series of situations, you are to provide an apology. Pick a language you have learned as a target language and respond to the given situations in that language. Next, check your responses with a native speaker of the language, if possible. In fact, ask the native to respond to these same situations before showing him or her your responses. Then, compare the two sets of responses.

Situations:

1. You promised you'd buy your neighbor medicine for her sick child while in town, but you forgot. Your neighbor: "Did you get the medicine?" You:
2. You don't stop in time at a red light and bump into the car in front of you. The other driver and you get out and see that there is damage to the other car. The other driver is very upset. You:
3. At a library, you accidentally bump into an older person about 70 who is holding a stack of books. The person is startled, but unhurt. A few of the books fall on the floor. You:
4. You promised to meet a friend at a bicycle store to help him or her choose the right bike. You forgot the meeting. The next day, you see your friend. Friend: "Remember, we were supposed to meet at the bicycle store. I waited for you at the store for an hour. I didn't want to buy the bike without you." You:

As requested above, now compare your apologies to those of the native respondent. In what ways were your apologies like those of the native? In what ways did they differ? Now try these same apologies in your native language. Compare the way you apologize in the two languages. Notice the ease or difficulty in preparation and delivery. Notice what you know how to do in your native language that you may not know how to do in the target language.

An issue that arises is whether a nonnative speaker should be expected to deliver a speech act the way a native does. In many cases, your delivery will be accepted even if you violate certain rules for that speech act in that situation. In other cases, it may be accepted but would still stigmatize you. In still other cases, it may not be acceptable at all. Textbooks actually tend to be general in their coverage so as to cover a wide variety of situations. The problem is that the patterns taught may not be specific enough to help you "fine-tune" your speech act utterance for the given situation.

In the next exercise you will be given two situations and a number of possible speech act utterances for each. Rate the utterances according to whether they are acceptable, more or less acceptable, or unacceptable in American English.

Situations:

1. A student forgets to return a book to a professor. Student:

   a. _____ I'm sorry. I forgot it.
   b. _____ Oh, damn! I forgot it.
   c. _____ Sorry. I forgot.
   d. _____ Oh, I'm really sorry. I completely forgot.
   e. _____ Oh, well, I've had a lot on my mind lately.

2. A young woman bumps into your shopping cart at the supermarket and some of the groceries spill onto the floor. She turns to you and says:

   a. _____ Sorry.
   b. _____ Are you all right?
   c. _____ Please forgive me.
   d. _____ I'm sorry.
   e. _____ Very sorry.
   f. _____ Really sorry.
   g. _____ Oh, I'm really sorry. Here, let me help you.
   h. _____ I'm terribly sorry. Did I hurt you?

If you are a native English speaker, ask a nonnative to rate these possible responses as well. If you are a nonnative, have a native also do the rating. Then compare the two sets of responses. If you are a native speaker of a language, you should be able to notice from an exercise of this kind that you have attitudes about the acceptability of different utterances in given situations. For nonnatives, these judgments take longer to develop and may never reach a very sophisticated level.

A Description of the Apology Speech Act

Below are strategies for apologizing that apply universally to apologies in any language (Cohen & Olshtain 1981, Cohen, Olshtain, & Rosenstein 1986). The trick is knowing which one or ones to use in a given apology situation in a given language—as well as knowing which language forms are appropriate for realizing that strategy. The strategies are as follows:

An Expression of an Apology   The speaker uses a word, expression, or sentence containing a verb such as "sorry," "excuse," "forgive," or "apologize." Languages have certain words that are used to express an oral apology more than others. For example, in American English, "I apologize . . ." is found more in writing than it is in oral language. An expression of an apology can be intensified whenever the apologizer feels the need to do so. Such intensification is usually accomplished by adding intensifiers such as "really" or "very"—for example, "I'm really sorry."

Acknowledgement of Responsibility   The offender recognizes his or her fault in causing the infraction. The degree of such recognition on the part of the apologizer can be placed on a scale. The highest level of intensity is an acceptance of the blame: "It's my fault." At a somewhat lower level would be an expression of self-deficiency: "I was confused/I didn't see/ You are right." At a still lower level would be the expression of lack of intent: "I didn't mean to." Lower still would be an implicit expression of responsibility: "I was sure I had given you the right directions." Finally, the apologizer may not accept the blame at all, in which case there may be a denial of responsibility: "It wasn't my fault," or even blaming of the hearer: "It's your own fault."

An Explanation or Account   The speaker describes the situation which caused him or her to commit the offense and which is used by this speaker as an indirect way of apologizing. The explanation is intended to set things right. In some cultures this may be a more acceptable way of apologizing than in others. Thus, in cultures where public transportation is unreliable, coming late to a meeting and giving an explanation like, "The bus was late," might be perfectly acceptable.

An Offer of Repair   The apologizer makes a bid to carry out an action or provide payment for some kind of damage which resulted from his or her infraction. This strategy is situation-specific and is only appropriate when actual damage has occurred.

A Promise of Nonreoccurrence   The apologizer commits himself or herself to not having the offense happen again, which is again situation-specific and less frequent than the other strategies. These five major strategies which make up the apology speech act are available to speakers across languages, yet preference for any one of them or for a combination of them will depend on the specific situation within the given language and culture group. The following is an example of one such situation.

> You completely forget a crucial meeting at the office with your boss. An hour later you call him to apologize. The problem is that this is the second time you've forgotten such a meeting. Your boss gets on the line and asks: "What happened to you?"

If you are an Israeli Hebrew speaker, your culture may support two types of behavior in your reply. First, in this and similar situations you would emphasize the strategy of explanation—more than an American would:

for example, "Well, I had to take a sick kid to the doctor and then there was a problem with the plumbing. . . ." On the other hand, you would underplay the strategy of repair, because our research has shown that in the Israeli culture, it appears to be the boss who determines the next step (Cohen & Olshtain 1981). It would be presumptuous for the employee to suggest what happens next.

Perhaps equally as important as knowing which strategies to use when, is knowing how to modify these strategies in a given situation. Factors that may affect how you would deliver an apology in your native language (and ideally in the target language as well) include your familiarity with the person being apologized to (intimate to very formal) and the intensity of the act (its gravity, seriousness, or importance).[5] So, for example, let us take the following situation where the offense is relatively severe and the recipient is a friend.

In a cafeteria, you accidentally bump into a friend who is holding a cup of hot coffee. The coffee spills all over your friend, scalding his or her arm and soaking his or her clothing. You friend shouts, startled: "Oooh! Ouch!"

As an Israeli Hebrew speaker, you may appropriately select the strategy of expressing an apology, but in selecting language forms to realize that strategy, you simply say, "Sorry," a translation from the often used *slixa* of Hebrew. This would not sound at all like an apology to the ears of your scalded friend if he or she is a speaker of American English. Or you might say, "I'm very sorry," which would be a normal textbook answer, without being aware that in American English there is a difference between "very" and "really," with "really" implying more regret and "very" more etiquette. Thus, the apology may still not sound very sincere to your friend. Your friend is probably expecting something more like, "I'm *really* sorry. Are you O.K.?"

Not only could an intensifier play an important role, but even an interjection like "Oh!" could have an important role. In fact, there could be times when a well-placed "Oh!" and an offer of repair could take the place of an expression of apology in American English: for example, "Oh! Here, let me help get something on that burn and clean up the mess," as opposed to, "I'm very sorry that I bumped into you." Even Hebrew speakers with advanced skills in English do not necessarily have control over particles such as "Oh!" and their absence in the discourse leaves a gap that signals nonnativeness (Cohen et al. 1986).

---

[5]Other factors such as the relative authority that each of you has, your ages and sex, and the place where the exchange takes place may all play some role, but my research with Olshtain has suggested that these factors are of less importance.

Ways to Improve Speech Act Competence

There are essentially three ways for a target language learner to obtain the kinds of information that were presented above by way of illustration. One way would be simply to be submersed in the target language and culture long enough that appropriate means for executing the speech act "come naturally." Another way would be to obtain these means through a language textbook. The third way is to make a conscious effort to gather information from target language informants as to the appropriate forms.

Whereas the first method appears the most effortless, the fact remains that people can study a target language and use it for many years without acquiring competence in a host of speech acts. At times, the speech act may be low frequency, like knowing how to extend condolences to the family of a deceased person at the funeral. At other times, the speech act may be quite frequent (e.g., a complaint), and yet your realization does not come close to that of a native in the given situation. As for the second method, textbooks have not tended to do a very good job of teaching these forms because the writers themselves may not be too certain about what to teach. Only recently have such speech behaviors begun to be studied empirically in a handful of languages—and the results from such studies are beginning to be utilized by textbook writers (e.g., Bodman & Lanzano 1984). A basic problem with trying to learn speech acts in a target language classroom situation is that it is difficult to create cultural and contextual meaning in the classroom.

The third method, that of consciously gathering information from speakers, can be reasonably useful and informative. Successful use of native speakers as informants starts with consciousness-raising about what to ask. This section on apologies has probably heightened your awareness about the dimensions of apologizing. You would now have a better idea of what to ask a native speaker in order to complement the knowledge that you already have. Here is a possible checklist of steps to take to investigate how apologies work in the target language:

1. Ask a native how to apologize in situations from those involving only a minor offense (e.g., slightly bumping into someone or interrupting their conversation) to those involving a major offense (e.g., hitting their car or hurting them physically). Try to imagine situations which you could be in, or ones which you have been in if you have had experience with speakers of the language in the past.

2. Ask this native whether there would be any difference in each of these apologies depending on whether the person being apologized to is:

    a. of higher status (e.g., boss, parent, etc.), equal status, or lower status
    b. a friend/acquaintance or a stranger

3. If the native uses any intensifiers in the target language (such as the equivalent of "very," "really," and "so"), ask if any other forms could be substituted for those, and, if so, what the meaning of each would be.

It may seem easier to consult a textbook, but as stated above, even the more recent ones may not have such information, or if they have it, there is unlikely to be any indication as to how commonly certain forms are used for a given speech act. For example, the textbook may list a series of intensifiers, such as "so," "awfully," and "terribly," without indicating which are the most frequently used. Ideally, a conscientious learner might make use of all three means of obtaining the necessary speech act information—acquiring it naturally, attending a class, and asking native informants.

TOWARDS MORE SUCCESSFUL SPEAKING

This chapter has had as its major focus coaching you in the direction of more successful use of communicative language. We know how frustrating it can be to be taught a language in a way that virtually excludes the possibility of speaking it when that is our main purpose. It is difficult if not impossible to eliminate such courses. Sometimes teachers feel most comfortable teaching that way. Thus, the responsibility lies with you, the learner, to apply constructively whatever form of instruction you receive to your efforts at speaking successfully.

Essentially, more successful speaking appears to be based on a willingness to utilize strategies for executing utterances. The task of producing utterances in a target language is so demanding that it is almost a necessity to use communication strategies—strategies for utilizing the language you have control over, for avoiding that which you do not, and for engaging your interlocutors as coaches and assistants in getting your message across. Part of the challenge is to find ways of maximizing the benefits of correction from other speakers so as to have it not interfere with your thought patterns and yet contribute to your subsequent utterances. Finally, the use of language to accomplish speech acts such as apologizing needs to be kept in mind, since sounding appropriate in a target language is more than simply learning its vocabulary. As we have seen in this chapter, it also involves the learning of how to use the language in given contexts in order to accomplish your purposes without alienating your interlocutors.

Chapter 5

Reading for Comprehension

At a time when learners have been found to be lacking reading strategies for coping with target language texts (e.g., by Hosenfeld 1984), books and articles have appeared which emphasize for teachers and for the learners directly, practical techniques for reading more successfully (e.g., Hosenfeld, Arnold, Kirchofer, Laciura, & Wilson 1981, Dubin & Olshtain 1981). What is sometimes lacking in such training efforts is a commensurate emphasis on *what* the reading process is: what reading processes consist of, why learners are being asked to learn and practice reading skills to facilitate these reading processes, and the extent to which strategies can be utilized to implement reading skills more effectively (Scott 1986). For example, both learners and teachers could ask the question, "What strategies might aid the reader to employ the reading skill of skimming or that of inferring the meaning of a word from context more successfully?"

The treatment here will not be that of reviewing the skills involved in reading and prescribing teaching actitivities for developing these skills among learners, as can be found elsewhere (e.g., Nuttall 1982, Williams 1984, Grellet 1981, Dubin, Eskey, & Grabe 1986). Rather, this chapter will consider some basic aspects of the reading process from the vantage point of the learner and will then consider effective reading strategies in target language learning. It will give you, the learner, an opportunity to observe the reading strategies that you tend to use, and to become more aware as to the full array of options open to you for improving your reading in a target language.

INTRODUCTION

Why is it important to read well in a target language? There are many who cannot read foreign languages that they speak. They may manage to get along in the society all the same. Thus, we know that it is not essential to be able to read in order to understand and speak a language. Yet reading allows for one more channel of communication and for an important source of input. In some cases, people need to learn how to read only in the target language. As long as what is read is also understood, then reading can provide usable data in improving language skills. Skillful reading can accelerate language learning. Poor reading will simply frustrate you and discourage you from reading altogether.

Research has shown that the strategies you use in reading in a target language may be similar to the ones you use for reading in your native language. This may be good or bad depending on the kind of reader you are in your native language. For learners who are poor readers in their native language, the reading of target language material may produce similar problems, along with the difficulties associated with reading in another language. If the target language teacher trains such learners in the use of reading strategies, the learning of the target language may provide an opportunity for them to strengthen their reading skills altogether, which has been found to have a positive backwash effect on native language reading (Levine & Reves 1985).

It has been thought that readers decrease their use of strategies in target language reading once the level of language is beyond their language proficiency. It now appears that readers may read on—drawing on their reading strategies, but possibly with little or no comprehension because of the excessive linguistic demands (Sarig 1985, 1987).[1] In other words, rather than give up on a reading passage if it makes demands beyond their level of language, nonnative readers may well continue reading, drawing on their reading strategies to compensate for a lack of proficiency.

If it is fair to assume that average learners are also average readers, then they are likely to select strategies that promote comprehension some of the time and inhibit comprehension at others. There is a growing consensus that if these learners have greater conscious awareness of the strategies that they select, this awareness can lead them to genuine gains in reading comprehension.

It is really important for you to take the initiative to improve your reading rather than waiting for the teacher to spot your reading problems, diagnose them, and provide remediation. A problem for the teacher is that in the average language classroom, learners may *appear* to be good readers without being so. In other words, it is possible for you to keep rehearsing a line or two until called upon to read aloud, and to give the teacher the impression that you understand what you are reading when in fact you do not. It is natural for you to do this kind of rehearsing. It is a form of self-defense: to look good in the classroom—not to let the teacher know that you do not know. There are some classic examples of this reading without comprehension, such as that of the *bar mitzvah* boy in North America reciting a passage in Hebrew without comprehending it.

---

[1]In Sarig's study, the subjects were seniors in high school, reading in Hebrew as a native language and English as a foreign language.

This next section will describe what the act of reading entails—what you, the reader, need to be aware of.

READING AS AN ACTIVE SET OF SKILLS

What does reading in a target language call for? Actually, reading in a target language is in many ways like reading in the native language. First of all, it is not a "passive" activity as it has been labeled. Already several decades ago it became fashionable to view reading as a most active *psycholinguistic guessing game*—a process whereby you predicted what would come next on the basis of what you had already read, you sampled from the text,[2] and then confirmed or corrected your hunches about the predicted meaning of the text based on what the sampling of the text provided you (Goodman 1967).

More recently, reading has been viewed as a continual interaction of *identification skills*—that is, the recognition of words and phrases and the grammatical signals required for the simple decoding of the text, with *interpretive skills*—the higher-level cognitive skills that allow for the meaningful reconstruction of a text as a unified, coherent structure of meaning (Eskey 1986:13-14). In this interactive model, readers are seen to use their previous knowledge of form (the alphabet, words in context, rhetorical form) to identify the visual cues and their expectations about the conceptual structure of the text (culture, subject matter, pragmatics[3]) in order to perform a personal reconstruction of the meaning of the text.

Another way that reading has been described is as the perception of current text in the perspective of previous text already read and prediction of the text still to come (Beaugrande 1984). Your success at reading depends on how alert you are, how motivated you are to read the particular text, how good the fit is between what you are reading at a current moment and what you already read, your familiarity with the topic, and the complexity of the material.

In still another view, reading is seen as a dynamic interaction between the writer and the reader in which the reader creates meaning for the text (Candlin & Saedi 1981). The activities of the reader include retaining newly acquired knowledge, accessing recorded and stored knowledge, and attending to the writer's clues as to the meaning intended for the text. In this view, the writer is actually seen as writing to a moving target in the

---

[2]*Sampling* is used here to imply that the reader does not read every feature of every letter of every word, but rather focuses on certain features, certain words, perhaps certain phrases in order to get a sense of the meaning of the text.

[3]I.e., how people tend to use the language in writing.

sense that you are not the same reader in the middle of the text as you were at the outset. This is because you accumulate background knowledge from the text as you go along. This view emphasizes two approaches to understanding the reading process: the text-based approach with its emphasis on what the writer intended to write and how it was actually written, and the reader-based approach with its focus on what the reader brings to and gets out of the text.

THE PSYCHOLOGICAL PROCESSES INVOLVED IN READING

Reading is a set of skills about which we have various preconceived notions that are in some ways mistaken. One of them is that reading is somehow a passive skill. As pointed out above, this is not at all the case since reading calls for the reader actively to supply meaning to text on a continual basis. Scott (1986) points out some other mistaken notions regarding reading.

1. Whereas you may think that you remember sentences that you read, you most likely remember the meaning and not the exact words or the grammar. This explains why you may have difficulty identifying precisely which sentence you have read when presented with a set of similar sentences.

2. Whereas you may think that you are reading through a text without *regressions* (i.e., visual cycling back over words or phrases already read), you may actually be moving back and forth in the text more than you think—almost as you might do when observing a picture you have never seen.

3. Whereas you may think you are reading in a smooth, linear, word-for-word fashion, actually your eyes jump from one fixation point to another. This helps to explain why we do not necessarily notice repeated words or typing errors in a text. This is the sampling phenomenon referred to above in Goodman's (1967) description of reading as prediction, sampling, and confirmation.

4. Whereas you may think that you cannot understand a text with a number of unknown words in it, you may well find that it is possible to understand the text without using those unknown words and by guessing reasonably well the other words on the basis of the context and possibly through analysis of the words themselves (see below).

READING IN A TARGET LANGUAGE

What happens when the reading is in a target language? It appears that much of what the reader does is the same as when reading in the first language. However, reading is often slower and less successful. A study done some years ago revealed that the slowness is not because target language readers are making more eye fixations, or *saccades*,[4] per line, but rather because they are spending more time at each fixation (Tullius 1971, Oller & Tullius 1973). The finding was that the difference in the eye movement of university-level English as a second language students as compared to that of native readers was that the duration of their eye fixations was almost three times that of the native students.

Furthermore, when reading in a target language, you are usually confronted with far more unknown vocabulary than in the native language. Also, the sentence structure may pose an obstacle, though perhaps less than might be expected. Readers have been seen to use various tricks for overcoming unfamiliar sentence structure to get at the meaning of text. One such trick is to focus almost exclusively on vocabulary and to infer probable sentence structure based on the likely relationship of words.[5] In some ways it is like piecing together the syntax of a telegram on the basis of the few words provided (although the syntax of telegrams is usually not so complex).

READING GOES ON AT DIFFERENT LEVELS OF PROCESSING

When we read in a target language, we are performing operations at different levels, sometimes simultaneously. Let us look at these different levels in turn.

The Recoding Level

First, most readers engage in *recoding*—that is, the converting of written symbols into sounds—some or all of the time. It has been shown that words are recoded differently in a target language than in a native language. In your native language, you do not look at all the letters in a word. In fact, often you just sample certain features of certain letters in the word and on the basis of these features you can already identify the word. In English native language recoding, consonants have been found to be more

---

[4]According to Just and Carpenter (1987:26), eye fixations occupy from 90 to 95 percent of the time in reading and the average fixation in native language reading lasts about 250 milliseconds. The average duration increases with the difficulty of the text.

[5]On the basis of a series of studies with university-level readers of a target language, Ulijn (1981) concluded that whereas thorough conceptual analysis was needed in order to extract meaning from text, thorough syntactic analysis was not. He conceded, however, that complex syntax could cause reading difficulties.

important than vowels, the beginning of words more important than the end and the end more than the middle, and the tops of letters more important than the bottoms (Weaver 1980).

In a target language, readers need to take in more features of more letters in words in order to recode them (Meara 1982). And furthermore, the sampling process is more susceptible to error since their knowledge of the orthographic features of the target language may be somewhat inadequate. It is important to point out that the recoding level does not deal with meaning. It is possible to recode an entire text without knowing what any of it means. A Jewish child in the United States, for example, usually prepares for *bar mitzvah* by learning to recite a long passage in Hebrew without understanding its meaning very well, if at all. Likewise, it is possible to read without recoding to sound.

It should be pointed out that picture writing systems or ideographic writing systems pose distinct problems for readers used to an alphabetic system. Recent research, for example, found that native Chinese readers associate the Chinese character with a sound in order to hold single words in short-term memory for the purpose of identification. Advanced non-native readers were found to use both phonological and graphic processing, with an emphasis on the latter (Hayes 1988).

Decoding

Beyond recoding is *decoding*—the obtaining of meaning from words and phrases. Decoding can go on at each of four sublevels—those of grammar, information, discourse, and writer's intent. So, let us say we have the sentence, "Your alligator is bigger than my crocodile." You could process this sentence at all four sublevels and may need to do so in order to make any sense out of it.

The Grammatical Level   You may undertake a grammatical analysis of the text—that is, determine the grammatical categories that the words, phrases, and sentences fall into. You may consciously identify words by their grammatical function as nouns, adjectives, verbs, or adverbs. You may also analyze sentences for the syntactic role they play in that text. If we take the above sentence, you need to know that "your" is a pronoun, presumably referring to the addressee. "Alligator" must be identified as a noun and as subject of the sentence and "crocodile" as object. You then identify "is" as a copula verb and "bigger" as a comparative adjective. In reading in a native language, much of this analysis is performed automatically, as needed. In a target language, such analysis may be quite conscious and even labored if it is performed.

Informational Level   It is likely that you will read to extract information from the text—that is, to determine what the basic concepts or messages are that the text wishes to convey. To do this, you need to do enough analysis of vocabulary to distinguish known, possibly known, and unknown words. In the given example, the information is that the addressee has an alligator and that the speaker believes that this alligator is bigger than a crocodile which she or he apparently has. It is not known whether these are model animals or real animals, live or stuffed. It may help you to know that alligators and crocodiles are different reptiles with certain distinguishing features.

Again with reference to Chinese as an ideographic writing system, native readers were found to use graphic and semantic strategies for processing their text, with a focus on the overall meaning of the sentence, while advanced nonnative readers were seen to attend largely to the graphic features of the Chinese characters (Hayes 1988). The investigator surmised that the nonnatives were overwhelmed by the number of different possible distinctive features available in Chinese, while the actual characters had no more features than most English words.

The Discourse Level   At the next level up, you are dealing with the fit between portions of a text—that is, the grammatical and/or lexical relationships between the different elements of a text. This phenomenon is referred to as *cohesion*. Thus, in the context, "Your alligator is bigger than my crocodile," "your" and "my" play important roles in linking the two reptiles together in the given text.

Also at the discourse level, you could look for the relationships which link the meanings of the sentences in a text so as to produce an intelligible text. This phenomenon is referred to as *coherence*. The above sentence seems to be coherent. "Your alligator is bigger than my pride" causes us more difficulty if we are without the benefit of context. Possibly such a sentence would make sense with more context. In isolation it is incoherent. Another aspect of discourse concerns the function that the portion of text has in the text. "Your alligator is bigger than my crocodile" could constitute a complaint—a feeling by a younger sibling that the older one got a bigger model than he did. It could also serve as a compliment, intended to indicate how clever or skilled the poacher was in bagging such a large alligator.

The Writer's Intent   Finally, we have the author's intent—that is, attitude and tone. In an explicit, clearly written text, the author's intent may be easy to determine. In other cases, the author's tone may be quite subtle and require the ability to pick up on small cues to, say, irony, where the use of a certain word is ironic to the native reader and tends to be ignored by the nonnative reader (through lack of knowledge or awareness).

An accurate interpretation of the message about the alligator and the crocodile may depend upon awareness as to whether the sentence was intended to be neutral, funny, sad, sarcastic, cynical, or angry. Sometimes punctuation—like exclamation points—helps out. Sometimes intensifiers (e.g., "*too* big") or invectives (e.g., "your damn alligator . . .") indicate the tone. In order to reach this level, the reader is likely to pass through all or most of the other levels, however briefly, from recoding to decoding for grammar, information, and discourse.

TYPES OF READING

Many readers consider target language reading to entail starting at the first word of text and moving linearly and slowly through the text to the last word—if it is possible to get that far without collapsing from fatigue (most likely after many searches in the dictionary). Actually, successful reading in a target language, as in the native language, depends on careful selection of the type of reading that most suits the *purpose* for reading or the specific task at hand.

There are at least three general reasons why you read in a target language. First, you may read as part of a program of instruction. The teacher has you read a passage in order to learn the language. Second, you may read to get information of importance to you—sometimes it is with a specific application in mind, such as a description of how to work a new appliance. Third, you may read for pleasure. Your reading could, of course, be motivated by some combination of these three.

There are also different ways you can read. You can read in a manner that Pugh (1978) has termed *receptively*, whereby you read to take in the entire piece in an unhurried fashion—its aim, the organization of ideas, and identification of the most important areas. This type of reading could also be referred to as "inclusive." In this form of reading your purpose is to discover everything or nearly everything that the author seeks to convey. You can also read for the *main points* or for *detailed comprehension*. In the case of reading an insurance policy before signing or reading a verbal math problem, you may read for detailed comprehension. In reading a lengthy editorial about an upcoming election, you may read just for the main points.

In addition, you can read *responsively*, using the author's material as a prompt for your own critical reflection. This type of reading is often most gratifying—when the reading of someone else's ideas stimulates your own thinking. This type of reading may not occur when reading material for instructional purposes—that is, if the material was written with the intention of teaching basic structures and vocabulary rather than that of stimulating thought. Of course, even material written to be thought provoking may fail to stimulate responsive reading. And by the same token, it is also possible to read responsively while reading receptively or reading for main points. The different types of reading can be combined in any given reading session.

A type of reading that is often referred to but rarely discussed and drilled in depth in target language reading textbooks is *skimming*, whereby you do a rapid overall inspection of the text—with periods of close inspection—in order to get a sense of the content and organization of the text. You may well be calling upon skimming as a means for determining what material deserves a second, less hurried reading. The main purposes of skimming are:

1. to get the gist—that is, a basic impression of what is written,
2. to identify the type of text and its status (e.g., fact, opinion, a report, hearsay), and
3. to determine whether it is relevant to your needs.

Nonnative readers fear that if they skim, they will miss something. Yet by not skimming you may well miss more because you read less and not necessarily with more comprehension. Slow, belabored reading may be less productive than skimming, perhaps yielding identical results although the latter takes, say, a quarter the time.

Speed reading is another form of rapid reading, in this case systematically trained for. Speed readers are usually taught how to make rapid on-line inferences, using their previous knowledge as much as possible and sampling from the text as little as possible. When compared to skimmers, it has been found that the speed readers sample from text more uniformly (Just, Carpenter, & Masson 1982). Another way of referring to speed readers is as *systematic skimmers*. But speed reading does not become automatic. It always calls for a continued effort and may simply be an inappropriate form of reading in the given instance.

Other forms of rapid reading include *scanning*—the locating of a specific symbol or group of symbols (e.g., finding a name or date in a text) and *search reading*—attempting to locate information when you are not sure of its form. For example, someone has told you that there is an article in yesterday's newspaper about a topic of keen interest to you but you do not know how long it was or what part of the newspaper it appeared in. You do not even know if it is part of a larger article under another name.

Yet another form of reading is *oral reading* as recitation—a process different from that of silent reading (Leu 1982). Oral reading implies a linear recitation of a text with the main purpose in the classroom usually being to indicate to the teacher whether the reader understands the text, and not as a means for training students in the art of oral recitation (e.g., for use in the media or in theater).

Actually it is a problem endemic to many classrooms that students are called on to read out loud. The problem is that oral reading is a specialized form of reading. Sometimes in conjunction with such oral reading, the teacher performs a *miscue analysis* on the product of such reading to check for additions, deletions, substitutions, and transpositions of portions of text while reading aloud. Usually, such checking is not done rigorously, such as with the aid of a tape recorder in order to play back and systematically assess the recitation.

Except at the initial stages of language learning, when teachers may wish to know whether students have correctly perceived the basic sounds of the language, oral reading is self-defeating. For one thing, if you read orally, it does not really reflect the way that you read naturally in a target language. Whereas in oral reading you are obliged to read linearly and to keep moving through the text (possibly with little or no comprehension), in silent reading you skip words, regress, and pause.

INTERFERENCE FROM NATIVE LANGUAGE IN TARGET LANGUAGE READING

When we read in a target language we have certain expectations about the way language works based on our native language. These expectations may not be met in the target language, particularly if it is quite different in structure from our native language. Take the following two examples from the research literature. Farsi speakers processing English relative clauses in reading may ignore the referential function of the relative pronoun. Thus, they have been found to read, "He [A] saw the man [B] who said . . ." as "He [A] saw the man [B] and he [A] said . . ." (Cowan 1976). Likewise, native Chinese, Japanese, Korean, and Persian readers have more difficulty correctly interpreting English sentences with subordination or negation than do Spanish-speaking readers (Rickard 1980).

It appears, though, that target language readers make adjustments for interference from their native language and are able to understand text even when theory would say they will make interference errors. Why is this? In part it is because nonnative readers do not rely as heavily on syntactic structure as may have been thought. Rather, learners seem to focus on syntactic structure in their search for meaning when they find that their focus on the conceptual aspects of the vocabulary in the text is insufficient or when the syntax is particularly complex or hard to follow (Ulijn 1981).

It may be that certain types of syntactic structures are simply complex and hence predictably problematic in a given language, regardless of what the native language is. For example, *heavy noun phrases*—long groups of words performing a single grammatical function, whether as subject of the main clause, subject of a subordinate clause, or object of a preposition—

have been found to be problematic for readers from a variety of language backgrounds in English as a foreign language. Research that colleagues and I conducted found heavy noun phrases to be among the few structures that were predictably problematic for students in reading university-level texts (Cohen, Glasman, Rosenbaum-Cohen, Ferrara, & Fine 1979). The following is an example of a heavy noun phrase (the 16 words in italics) serving as the subject of a subordinate sentence introduced by "that."

> Thus, it was conjectured that *such treatments as holding cells in buffer after irradiation before placing them on nutrient agar plates* might function by inhibiting normal growth processes while repair systems completed their task. (Hanawalt 1972:84)[6]

READING STRATEGIES

Reading strategies are those mental processes that readers consciously choose to use in accomplishing reading tasks. According to this definition, all levels of strategies, from overall, global ones, such as guessing new words from context to more specific ones, like performing interparagraph analysis to guess words, are all considered "strategies," as opposed to referring to the more specific ones by some other term, such as "technique" or "tactic." Such strategies may or may not facilitate successful comprehension of text. In addition, strategies can be distinguished from skills in that a *skill* is an overall behavior or general class of behaviors, while a strategy is the specific means for realizing that behavior. For example, skimming would be a skill, while reading the first sentence of each new paragraph would be a strategy for realizing this skill.

Strategies are distinguished from other cognitive processes through the element of choice. In the case of a strategy, you have made a choice —at some level of consciousness—to use that particular reading process. These strategies fall on a continuum from those you are paying total attention to in any given reading event to those on which you are not placing your attention at that time. If your attention were called to these latter strategies, it is likely that you could describe them because you are aware that you are using them, but just not attending to them.

For example, you may be attending to the strategy of summarizing each paragraph as you are reading a given text. You may have to keep reminding yourself to do it in this given instance. In contrast, you may be making predictions about what will come next in the text almost automatically. Nonetheless, if you were to be asked to describe your reading strategies, you might well point out that you were anticipating what would

---

[6]For the details of this study, refer to Chapter 8.

come next based on what you had read in the text and on your knowledge of the world. Although you were not attending to your strategy of prediction, you were sufficiently aware of it to be able to mention it when asked to describe the reading strategies of which you were conscious.

One purpose of a book like this is to encourage you to be more alert to *how* you are performing the language tasks that you are performing. You may be consciously or subconsciously aware of certain reading strategies, but may not have your attention focused on those strategies. At times, this makes no difference. The strategies function fine. At other times, there may be a need to pay careful attention in the realization of the strategy. For example, skimming a passage will probably produce more useful results if strategies for successful skimming are kept in mind, such as looking for key words and phrases and organizational markers, without getting bogged down in detail. At times, a low level of processing may be enough to detect the relevance of information in skimming. At other times, skimming means slowing down to disentangle a series of complex points.

Recent research has shown that reading strategies are not in and of themselves "good." It depends on *who* is using them, with *what text*, at *what point* in the text, under *what circumstances*, and with *what purpose* in mind. In other words, a strategy may work well for a given reader on a given task with a given text or point in a text, and not work well for that same reader with a different text. Why is this so? Part of it is a matter of judgment and care. For example, you may choose the skill of skimming, but your strategy for employing this skill is to read so rapidly that meaning is lost, you skim so laboriously that you defeat the purpose of skimming, or you jump around so erratically that you are not left with usable impressions as to the content and organization of the text.

In addition, you may perform a number of reading strategies appropriately—using good judgment and care—only to find that the use of *one* strategy ineffectively in a given instance causes a breakdown in comprehension. There are no easy formulas because readers differ as to the strategies that they choose to use and as to the frequency with which they use them (Sarig 1987). However, there are basic principles to be applied and their application starts with an awareness of the options. For example, some target language readers make the mistake of trying to read all texts as if they were the same. So, they read both a portion of a science textbook and of a short story in the same word-for-word fashion, stopping frequently to look up words.

Key Reading Strategies

Although there are probably no inherently good reading strategies, there are a series of general strategies that do seem to come up time and again as strategies that have merit for readers in various texts under differing circumstances. Some of these strategies will be listed below. This list is drawn from the work of researchers such as Baker and Brown (1984a, 1984b) in native language and Hosenfeld (1977, 1979, 1984) and Hosenfeld et al. (1981) in foreign language.

Clarification of Purpose   Successful reading starts with a clarification of purpose. The reader needs to establish why the text is being read. Then it is possible to determine what type of reading to use—skimming, receptive reading, responsive reading, and so forth.

Organization of Text   Readers may look for the ostensibly important aspects of the text by seeing how the text is organized. It usually includes a rapid skimming of the text, taking note of any subtitles, figures, tables, pictures, and other features. It may mean jumping to the end to see if there is a useful summary, discussion, or conclusion. The reader may go so far as to outline or map the main sections of the text in list form or graphically. This effort to get a sense of perspective as to where the text is going can be most helpful as a prereading activity. All the same, the search for text organization does not always prove useful, particularly if there are few or no subtitles or if the writer drifts from theme to theme even when using subtitles.

Reading for Meaning   Reading for meaning involves the activation of networks of real-world and rhetorical information for the purpose of interpreting texts. These sources of background information have been referred to more technically as *schemata* (Anderson & Pearson 1984, Carrell & Eisterhold 1983). Such schemata have been classified according to three basic types.

1. *Content schemata*—systems of factual knowledge, values, and cultural conventions.
2. *Language schemata*—grammar, spelling and punctuation, vocabulary, and cohesive structures.
3. *Textual schemata*—the rhetorical structure of different modes of text—for example, recipes, letters, fairy tales, research papers, and science textbooks.

When you approach text on the basis of prior content, language, or textual schemata you may have with regard to that text, this is referred to as *top-down* reading (Carrell 1988). For example, you may note that the text is an article reporting on a piece of research in an academic journal. This realization would be likely to activate certain *textual schemata* regarding research papers. In other words, you would most likely apply your prior textual schemata to the reading of this research paper. You would also be likely to hold certain expectations with respect to *language schemata*—types of terminology that appear in your article (e.g., "research hypotheses," "factorial analysis," and so on) and patterns of cohesion that are likely to be found (e.g., the mention of key concepts in the abstract of the paper, elaboration of these concepts in the review of literature, and reference to them in the findings section and in the discussion). Finally, you notice that the article is, say, a study of the reading skills of trained apes. This topic would immediately signal certain *content schemata* or an awareness of the lack of them. In other words, you may come to the realization that you are lacking the relevant content schemata.

When you focus exclusively on what is present in the text itself and especially on the words and sentences of the text, this is referred to as *bottom-up* reading. Such reading is also referred to as "text-based" or "data-driven" reading. Successful readers usually display a combination of top-down and bottom-up reading. In fact, it has been suggested that readers may use top-down reading to compensate for deficiencies in bottom-up reading, and vice versa (Stanovich 1980). In other words, a reader who has poor word recognition skills may rely on top-down reading to provide meaning for that portion of the text.

Particularly in a target language, you may do a host of busy bottom-up reading activities—like word analysis, use of a dictionary, and analysis of sentence structure—without coming away with a clue as to what the sentence means. Such a situation can be avoided by using texts that are not too far above the level of proficiency you have in the language. And when you tackle a text that is clearly above your reading level, it is crucial for you to compensate for the lack of bottom-up knowledge by using top-down reading, invoking whatever content, textual, and language schemata can be of help in answering the question, "What does this text mean?" At times, the use of such knowledge makes a positive contribution. At other times, the procedure will lead to distortions in the text.

Let us consider the following example of distortion caused by top-down compensation for deficiencies in bottom-up vocabulary knowledge. The example is taken from research by Laufer and Sim (1983). Within a text by Margaret Mead that the reader had to interpret, there was the following sentence:

> This nurturing behavior, this fending for females and children instead of leaving them to fend for themselves, as the primates do, may take many different forms.

One reader read 'nurturing' as 'natural,' 'fending' as 'finding,' and 'leaving' as 'living.' The reader's interpretation of the sentence was as follows:

> Instead of living natural life, natural behavior, females and children find many different forms of life.

The reader substituted other words that were known instead of the unknown words and built meaning around these substitutions.[7]

Focusing on Major Content   In attempting to determine what a text means, you are called upon to identify the major content as distinguished from trivia. This means sorting the key items from others which may be familiar to the reader but not of prime importance or relevance. This is easier said than done. Sometimes you recognize more of the vocabulary for the content than would be considered trivial and do not recognize the words that you suspect are dealing with major issues. Perhaps these would be the instances in which you would use your dictionary (number 5 below), see if the context holds any clues to the meanings of these potentially important words (number 6 below), or check with a native language reader (if available).

Parsimonious Use of a Dictionary   One mistake that nonnative readers make is to overuse the dictionary. Not only does dictionary use distract the reader away from the text, it also may yield erroneous results. It has been shown, for example, that readers misuse dictionaries and that dictionaries themselves are misleading (e.g., Neubach & Cohen 1988). A good rule of thumb is to use a dictionary sparingly. Then, if the dictionary is used, you may wish to have some effective system for recording the outcome if you do not have one already. It is often the case that learners keep looking up the same words over and over because they forget what the entry was immediately after finding it.

In addition, there is the problem of type of dictionary. Bilingual dictionaries are misleading because languages often do not have direct equivalents. Monolingual dictionaries can be more helpful in truly understanding the meaning of words, but then the user needs to be versed enough in the language to understand the definition. Learner dictionaries are a potential aid, but such dictionaries may also have the drawback that they lack more advanced vocabulary or have simplified definitions that confuse the user.

Judicious Use of Context   In recent years there has been a push to have readers use context more and dictionaries less in figuring out the meanings of words and phrases. Yet a problem exists in determining what is or should be meant by *context* (Carter 1987:166). Is it "a stretch of naturally occurring text," and if so, how much—a phrase, a clause, a sentence? A further distinction can also be made between *grammatical context* (i.e., the occurrence of certain forms as context due to obligatory or optional grammatical relationships) and *conceptual context* (i.e., contextual material based exclusively on meaningful—not grammatical—ties).

---

[7]It should be pointed out that the reader was a native Hebrew speaker and the fact that Hebrew is read without vowels might have contributed to the substitutions.

It is true that sometimes the immediate or the broader context of an unknown word is rich in clues that will assist you in decoding unknown or unfamiliar words; that is, the text is characterized by (1) relatively few difficult words, (2) a topic that is familiar to the reader, (3) syntactic patterns that are easy to process, or (4) typographical clues like italics and sub-headings (Haynes 1987). Yet at other times the text seems to provide no assistance whatsoever. There could be a number of reasons for this. For one thing, it may have too many unknown words in it. For another, the context may itself be too limited—not enough clues to the meaning of the word in question, especially in the immediate context of the surrounding words, phrases, and sentences. Furthermore, it has become clear that, for many nonnative readers, using context means using the word or words immediately preceding the word and possibly following it, while the real clues to meaning may have appeared much earlier in the text or will appear much later. A reader who is more skilled at using contextual clues may look for such clues at a greater distance from the word in question.

It is unlikely that a reader relies exclusively on the context, but rather indulges in a simultaneous back-and-forth checking of the word and of the context. At times, the dictionary is also brought into this back-and-forth checking—moving from each dictionary entry to the text at hand to see if a definition seems to fit. It may be that the reader has some vague notion of what the word means from previous encounters or from repeated en-counters in the text at hand, and this notion accompanies the reader during the search for contextual clues. What may be confusing the reader is that the word has multiple meanings as well, and it is not clear which meaning is implied in the current context. The fact that a word may be a cognate of a native language word would also interact with contextual information—either to help or further confuse the situation. If words are *true cognates* (e.g., "sweater" in English and *sveter* in Hebrew), then it is a help, but if the words are *false cognates* (i.e., different meanings in the two languages) or *deceptive cognates* in that they have only partial overlap of meaning[8] (Nash 1976), then the reader may erroneously interpret the mean-ing of the word.

Reading in Broad Phrases   Readers need to break out of the word-for-word habit that accompanies them from their grade school days. In the early stages of native language reading, youngsters are often drilled in oral reading, whereby every word must be read aloud. This kind of training—plus whatever similar drills the target language teacher uses—inadver-tently predisposes readers to read word-for-word even in their silent, pri-

---

[8]For example, the word for "plumber" in Hebrew is *instalator*. In English, it is possible to refer to a "plumbing installation" but not to an "installer" as a plumber, so there is semantic overlap of the two words.

vate reading. It would appear that more successful readers tend to read in broad phrases. They take in groups of words at a time. This is a technique that certain speed reading courses train for—getting readers to take in more information on each sweep of the eyes. It is true that in a target language it may not be so obvious where the natural breaks are between phrases. This is a skill that needs to be acquired, and one current attitude is that the best way to acquire this ability to read in phrases is by increasing the amount of reading (Krashen 1985b).

Ongoing Summaries   It is not uncommon for the reader of a target language to have the feeling of understanding a text as it is going by, but to arrive at the end of a section or of the whole piece without remembering anything. This phenomenon is not so surprising in that reading in a target language is like trying to watch all the acts in a three-ring circus simultaneously or to cook a meal on five burners simultaneously without neglecting any of the dishes. The truth is that the mind has to perform mental gymnastics in order to extract meaning from a target language text. An aid to retention of what is read would be to make ongoing summaries every few lines. This strategy helps to keep the meaning of previous material fresh while continuing on to new material. Sometimes this summarizing is assisted by readers continually generating questions about the text as they read along.

What does it mean to make ongoing summaries? Ideally, you would identify the topical information (i.e., main ideas or key concepts) or generate it if none appears explicitly in the text, distinguish superordinate from subordinate material (possibly substituting superordinate terms for lists of terms or sequences of events), and identify redundant as well as trivial information—so as not to include it in your ongoing summaries (Kintsch & van Dijk 1978, Brown, Campione, & Day 1981, Brown & Day 1983). In addition, you might make sure that each minisummary sounds coherent. If the ongoing summaries remain in the form of thoughts or verbalizations, then it may not be so important that they be well formed. If they are written down, however, then the form that they take may be of more importance, although the distinction is made between *private* (writer-based) and *public* (reader-based) summaries, with the former written to be read only by the person doing the summary and not by some outside audience (i.e., teacher or other) (Hidi & Anderson 1986).

Although it is easy enough to stipulate that summaries are to involve the reduction of content to main ideas and supporting ideas, research has shown that nonnative readers have difficulties doing this task effectively —even after training. It would appear that the most difficult task in summarizing is that of *reconceptualizing* material at a higher level of abstraction—that is, transforming concepts from the more specific and local to a more general or *macrolevel* (Sarig 1988).

A study by Holmes (1986), for example, found that six English as a foreign language (EFL) graduate students read in a linear and compartmentalized manner when asked to summarize a text, rather than globally so as to extract the main ideas. Consistent with Holmes' study, a study with five EFL graduate students revealed the major summarizing strategy to be that of word level processing, with the summaries often reflecting a focus on only part of the text. The interpretation of the text was found to be based upon the words that the subjects had learned (however effectively) and collected up in reading the text, and upon previous knowledge (Gimenez 1984). A case study that I conducted with five EFL graduate students (Cohen, in press) also found the respondents did not have a good sense of balance with respect to how much to delete in written summaries. They were either too vague and general or too detailed.

Making Predictions   Part of the problem of reading in a target language is that when such reading is too slow and plodding, it is also tiring and possibly boring, even if the topic appears interesting. One way to overcome this problem is for you to keep actively predicting what the writer is likely to be writing about in the next portion of text. Making predictions is a way to stay alert. It often speeds up the reading process itself as it stimulates your curiosity to know what is next. It may help to have certain "preview" questions in mind when reading a text, or as is suggested in the SQ3R[9] technique, the reader could generate ongoing reading questions by turning each heading and subheading into a question, using words such as "who," "what," "when," "where," "why," and "how" (Robinson 1970, Jolley 1985).

Looking for Markers of Cohesion   A text has a series of words and phrases that tie together the ideas, namely, the cohesive links which form a part of the discourse level mentioned above. These link words include discourse connectors (e.g., "whereas," "however," and "furthermore"), pronouns and *contextual paraphrases* (i.e., words or phrases that are synonymous in the given context; see also Chapter 8). A wise reader looks for these markers to aid in the reading process. Such markers indicate who or what is being referred to and the function of the reference (e.g., to add information or to provide a contrast).

Unskilled readers miss these cohesive markers and may well come away with a series of disparate ideas without any links between them. Some nonnative readers, for example, seem to skip over what may well

---

[9]SQ3R is a process intended to promote active reading, whereby readers survey the text (S); turn the headings and subheadings into *wh* questions (Q); read the text, recite (i.e., state aloud) the answers to their questions along with the main ideas and answers to questions asked by themselves or by others (3R).

be critical discourse markers like "unless" or "thus," consequently arriving at interpretations of the text that are inaccurate.

The problem of contextual paraphrase is more subtle but can be equally confusing. Let us say that our text deals with the electoral process and refers to voting one time as "voting," another time as "balloting," and a third time as "a referendum." The reader who is not sensitive to such stylistic license may assume that the writer is talking about three distinct activities, when in reality the intention is to refer to the same concept in a stylistically varied way.

Strategies for Dealing with Strategies   Usually the use of any of the above strategies is enhanced by the overlay of strategies for dealing with strategies. In other words, there is a set of strategies for supervising our strategy use—often referred to as *metacognitive strategies*. These include *planning* which strategies to use, *monitoring* how effective their use is, and *assessing* how effective their use was. When readers recognize that there has been a failure to understand a portion of text, then they can also select one or another fix-up strategy.

Thus, let us say that you choose the strategy of generating ongoing summaries. If engaged in auto-supervision, you would first plan how to incorporate that strategy into a given reading task, would then check to see how it was working, and afterward would assess how it worked. Just going through the motions of using a particular strategy may be of little value. It is more beneficial both to use the strategy and to perform auto-supervision regarding the success of its use as well.

Classifying Reading Strategies

There are actually many possible reading strategies to choose from. A recent doctoral dissertation on the topic found that a group of 10 high school students used approximately 130 different strategies in reading Hebrew as a native language and English as a foreign language (Sarig 1985). A useful contribution of this work was to classify these many strategies into four basic types. They include:

1. *Support strategies*—types of reading acts undertaken to facilitate high-level strategies—for example, skimming, scanning, skipping, marking the text, and using a glossary.
2. *Paraphrase strategies*—decoding strategies to clarify meaning by simplifying syntax, finding synonyms for words and phrases, looking for propositions or basic ideas, and identifying the function of portions of the text.

3. *Strategies for establishing coherence in text*—the use of world knowledge or clues in the text to make the text intelligible as a piece of connected discourse—for example, looking for organization, using context, and distinguishing the discourse functions in the text (such as introduction, definition, exemplification, and conclusion).
4. *Strategies for supervising strategy use*[10]—conscious strategies for checking on the reading process as it takes place—for example, planning, ongoing self-evaluation, changing the planning and executing of tasks, identifying misunderstandings, and remediating when reading problems are found.

Given this classification scheme, a strategy such as skipping over an example in a technical text can be viewed from different categorical perspectives. At the psychomotor level, the skip is purely a matter of physically jumping over the examples. At the paraphrase level, the skip may be a move to avoid getting sidetracked—to keep the focus on determining the author's meaning. At the level of coherence, you could have detected that the example was unnecessary reading because you already knew the material contained in it. At the level of auto-supervision, you could check to see if the skip does in fact enhance the reading of the text. Obviously you need not be functioning at all these levels at once, and in fact, the work of Sarig and others has shown that the poorer nonnative readers are involved mostly at the psychomotor and the paraphrase levels, while the better readers use more strategies concerned with establishing coherence in text, as well as more strategies for *supervising* the use of support, paraphrase, and coherence strategies.

HOW CAN YOU FACILITATE YOUR TARGET LANGUAGE READING?

There are certain activities that you can indulge in so that reading becomes more pleasurable. Some of these are enhanced by the assistance of another person—be it the teacher or a peer. Before reading a new text, it is helpful to have some introduction to it, such as an explanation of the topic. Such a discussion would supply you with the content schemata for interpreting the text. It is also helpful to have several reading questions posed before starting to read so that there is a purpose for reading (as mentioned above). These questions could be posed by you yourself or by an instructor or peer. It may help to have certain vocabulary words defined in advance. Also, it is helpful if the topic is one that you are motivated to read about.

---

[10]The translation of these four types of strategies actually appeared as *technical-aid moves, clarification and simplification moves, coherence-detecting moves,* and *monitoring moves* (Sarig 1987).

In addition, it could be useful for you to find out what is actually difficult for you in reading the given type of text. It may be that you need special kinds of vocabulary—not necessarily technical words. It has been found that sometimes nontechnical words and nontechnical words used with a technical meaning in a given text are more problematic for nonnative readers than the technical words (Cohen et al. 1979). For example, a biology student reading an article on DNA molecules in a target language may know quite well what technical terms like "zygotes" and "ciliated protozoans" mean, but may not be familiar with the technical meanings in genetics of the seemingly nontechnical words "recognition" and "specificity." Likewise, the reader may lack a series of specialized nontechnical words in the target language that could be crucial in extracting meaning from text. Such groups of words include, for example, time sequence or frequency, such as "eventual," "succeeding," "ensuing," "preceding," "consecutively," "subsequent," and the like.

It may also be that certain types of syntactic structures are predictably problematic for you, such as the heavy noun phrases mentioned above (i.e., groups of words performing a single grammatical function, whether as subject of the main clause, subject of a subordinate clause, or object of a preposition). If these are problematic structures for you, you might be on the lookout for them and process them with care so that they do not cause you to lose track of the meaning of the text.

Another especially problematic area in academic reading is that of markers of cohesion. There are not that many of these in any given language, so readers could master them in a relatively short time. All the same, they are not usually taught thoroughly and learners try to pick them up, often unsuccessfully. Hence, readers may not have mastery over seemingly easy cohesive markers like "thus," "unless," and "however."

GATHERING VERBAL REPORT DATA ON READING STRATEGIES

The following are a series of exercises to assist you in eliciting verbal report data on reading strategies both from others and from yourself. The first set of exercises train you in data gathering and then the two subsequent reading tasks are intended to give you an opportunity to perform verbal report data collection and analysis of data in pairs.

In order to start this first exercise, each participant is to have a partner. One is to be the reader/informant and the other is the investigator.

Practice in Thinking Aloud

Reader Describe out loud all the steps that you go through as you actually perform one of the following tasks *with your eyes closed:*

  a. tying your shoelaces
  b. combing/brushing your hair
  c. determining how much change you have in your wallet/purse (i.e., how many coins and what denominations).

Investigator Make sure that the reader verbalizes his or her actions aloud and that every step is included. Coach the reader in doing this if the process is not being described clearly enough.

Minitraining for Investigators in Categorizing Reading Strategies

Investigator The following is a minitraining in the categorizing of reading strategies. Please familiarize yourself with the following four categories of reading strategies (adapted from Sarig 1987).

  1. *Support Strategies*—types of reading acts undertaken to facilitate high-level strategies—for example, skimming, scanning, skipping, marking the text, and using a glossary.
  2. *Paraphrase Strategies*—decoding strategies to clarify meaning by simplifying syntax, finding synonyms for words and phrases, looking for propositions or basic ideas, and identifying the function of portions of text.
  3. *Strategies for Establishing Coherence in Text*—use of world knowledge or clues in the text to make the text intelligible as a piece of connected discourse—for example, looking for organization, using context, and distinguishing the discourse functions (e.g., exemplification, definition, conclusion) in the text.
  4. *Strategies for Supervising Strategy Use*—conscious strategies for checking on the reading process as it takes place—for example, planning, ongoing self-evaluation, changing the planning and execution of tasks, identifying misunderstandings, and remediating when reading problems are found.

Practice in Thinking Aloud While Reading

Reader Read the following two brief definitions in such a way that you have a clear idea of what they mean. You are to think aloud as you read—that is, share with the investigator whatever thoughts come up as you read. For some, this means mumbling the words of the text and voicing aloud any thoughts you have as you are reading. For others, it means reading silently and then providing an oral recap each time there is a natural pause in the reading process.

Self-observation while reading refers to the inspection of specific reading behavior, whether while the information is still in short-term memory—that is, introspectively—or after the event—that is, retrospectively (usually after 20 seconds or so). Retrospection can be immediate (e.g., within, say, an hour of the event) or delayed (a few hours, days, or even weeks after the event). It appears that the bulk of the forgetting occurs right after the mental event. Thus, data from immediate retrospection may only be somewhat more complete than data from delayed retrospection.

The term *self-revelation* refers to a learner's report that, unlike self-observation, is not based on inspection of specific reading behaviors. Rather it consists of "think-aloud" stream-of-consciousness disclosure of thought processes while the information is being attended to. The data are basically unedited and unanalyzed.

Any given verbal report of reading behaviors may have different types of data in it. For example, a given verbal report may include:

1. the readers' retrospections about specific reading behaviors,
2. introspections where behaviors are analyzed as soon as they are performed (e.g., "I just made an effort to guess the meaning of that word."), or
3. think-aloud data (e.g., "The word *assiduous* probably means 'industrious' in this context, but I am not really sure. . . .").

Reading Strategy Task 1

Reader   Read the following essay by Bertrand Russell rather rapidly and provide verbal report data while reading. After reading it, state the gist of the text to the investigator (in two or three sentences).

Investigator   While the reader is reading the Russell text, make note of any strategies that you observe within one of the four categories. You may wish to use abbreviations for each strategy:

1. support strategies [SPT]
2. paraphrase strategies [PARA]
3. strategies for establishing coherence in text [COH]
4. strategies for supervising strategy use [SUPER]

How to Avoid Foolish Opinions
by Bertrand Russell[11]

To avoid the various foolish opinions to which mankind is prone, no superhuman genius is required. A few simple rules will keep you, not from *all* error, but from silly error.

If the matter is one that can be settled by observation, make the observation yourself. Aristotle could have avoided the mistake of thinking that women have fewer teeth than men, by the simple device of asking Mrs. Aristotle to keep her mouth open while he counted. He did not do so because he thought he knew. Thinking that you know when in fact you don't is a fatal mistake, to which we are all prone. I believe myself that hedgehogs eat black beetles, because I have been told that they do; but if I were writing a book on the habits of hedgehogs, I should not commit myself until I had seen one enjoying this unappetizing diet. Aristotle, however, was less cautious. Ancient and medieval authors knew all about unicorns and salamanders; not one of them thought it necessary to avoid dogmatic statements about them because he had never seen one of them.

Many matters, however, are less easily brought to the test of experience. If, like most of mankind, you have passionate convictions of many such matters, there are ways in which you can make yourself aware of your own bias. If an opinion contrary to your own makes you angry, that is a sign that you are subconsciously aware of having no good reason for thinking as you do. If someone maintains that two and two are five, or that Iceland is on the Equator, you feel pity rather than anger, unless you know so little of arithmetic or geography that his opinion shakes your own contrary conviction. The most savage controversies are those about matters as to which there is no good evidence either way. Persecution is used in theology, not in arithmetic, because in arithmetic there is knowledge, but in theology there is only opinion. So whenever you find yourself getting angry about a difference of opinion, be on your guard; you will probably find, on examination, that your belief is going beyond what the evidence warrants.

A good way of ridding yourself of certain kinds of dogmatism is to become aware of opinions held in social circles different from your own. When I was young, I lived much outside my own country—in France, Germany, Italy, and the United States. I found this very profitable in diminishing the intensity of insular prejudice. If you cannot travel, seek out people with whom you disagree, and read a newspaper belonging to

[11]Excerpt (pp. 135–139) from An outline of intellectual rubbish. In B. Russell, *Unpopular essays*. London: Allen & Unwin, 1950, 95–145.

a party that is not yours. If the people and the newspaper seem mad, perverse, and wicked, remind yourself that you seem so to them. In this opinion both parties may be right, but they cannot both be wrong. This reflection should generate a certain caution. . . .

For those who have enough psychological imagination, it is a good plan to imagine an argument with a person having a different bias. This has one advantage, and only one, as compared with actual conversation with opponents; this one advantage is that the method is not subject to the same limitations of time and space. Mahatma Gandhi deplored railways and steamboats and machinery; he would have liked to undo the whole of the industrial revolution. You may never have an opportunity of actually meeting anyone who holds this opinion, because in Western countries most people take the advantages of modern technique for granted. But if you want to make sure that you are right in agreeing with the prevailing opinion, you will find it a good plan to test the arguments that occur to you by considering what Gandhi might have said in refutation of them. I have sometimes been led actually to change my mind as a result of this kind of imaginary dialogue, and, short of this, I have frequently found myself growing less dogmatic and cocksure through realizing the possible reasonableness of a hypothetical opponent.

Be very wary of opinions that flatter your self-esteem. Both men and women, nine times out of ten, are firmly convinced of the superior excellence of their own sex. There is abundant evidence on both sides. If you are a man, you can point out that most poets and men of science are male; if you are a woman, you can retort that so are most criminals. The question is inherently insoluble, but self-esteem conceals this from most people. We are all, whatever part of the world we come from, persuaded that our own nation is superior to all others. Seeing that each nation has its characteristic merits and demerits, we adjust our standard of values so as to make out that the merits possessed by our nation are the really important ones, while its demerits are comparatively trivial. Here, again, the rational man will admit that the question is one to which there is no demonstrably right answer. It is more difficult to deal with the self-esteem of man as man, because we cannot argue out the matter with some non-human mind. The only way I know of dealing with this general human conceit is to remind ourselves that man is a brief episode in the life of a small planet in a little corner of the universe, and that, for aught we know, other parts of the cosmos may contain beings as superior to ourselves as we are to jelly-fish.

Reading Strategy Task 2

In this task, you will be asked to read a passage and provide brief *written* answers to three questions about it. If English is not currently your dominant language, then write your responses in the language you are dominant in. If possible, find a partner to do the exercise with, as you were asked to do in the previous exercise. If that is not possible, then use a tape recorder and let the tape recorder be your partner. As you read the text and answer the questions, you are requested to report your thoughts as you read—to think aloud as much as possible.

Indicate to your partner or to the tape recorder the strategies that you are using to read the passage and the thoughts you are having about the text as you read and answer the questions. Your partner is to take notes on the major strategies you use and the insights you have. If you tape it on your own, listen to the tape and take notes as to strategies and insights. After the exercise, you are to see what you learned about your reading strategies. Your partner may also wish to indicate what he or she learned about the reading process while being in the role of the investigator.

You are now asked to read an article from *New Scientist* (14 August 1986) dealing with nuclear disaster at Chernobyl as the passage upon which you are to provide verbal report data. Proceed according to the instructions given above.

The passage:

Chernobyl: The Grim Statistics of Cancer

Two American physicists have drawn a rough but grim outline of the spread of cancer that could result from the fallout from Chernobyl. They expect tens or even hundreds of thousands of tumours, and possibly several thousand deaths from cancer during the next 30 years. Experts in the US government's nuclear agencies accept the findings.

The estimates have been made by Frank von Hippel of Princeton University and Thomas Cochran of the Natural Resources Defense Council, an environmental group. They calculated the following consequences from all routes of exposure:

- 2000 to 40 000 cases of thyroid tumours from inhalation of iodine-131. Only a few per cent of these tumours will be fatal.
- 10 000 to 25 000 cases of potential thyroid tumours from iodine absorbed from contaminated milk.
- 3500 to 70 000 cases of cancer from all sources of caesium-137. About half might be fatal.

Von Hippel and Cochran will describe their research in the September issue of the *Bulletin of Atomic Scientists*. "There is a lot of uncertainty in the figures," von Hippel stresses.

The calculations start from an estimate of contamination of land and the level and duration of contamination of the air.

The pattern of fallout is derived from models made by Helen ApSimon and Julian Wilson of Imperial College, London (*New Scientist*, 17 July, p. 42) and the Lawrence Livermore National Laboratory in California. When combined with data on population densities and standard coefficients for the amount of radioactivity absorbed by human bodies, a "population dose" can be established. For direct inhalation of iodine-131, that figure is 8-150 million person-rads; for contamination with iodine-131 via crops and food, it is 50-900 million person-rads; and for caesium-137, it is 5-84 million person-rads.

Finally, these dose calculations are multiplied by a "dose-consequence" coefficient, which translates a given dose into a figure for the likely increased incidence of death or tumours.

ApSimon and Wilson calculated that the accident at Chernobyl released 15 to 20 megacuries of iodine-131 and 1 to 2 megacuries of caesium-137. These amounts correspond to 20-25 per cent of the reactor's inventory of these two radionuclides when the accident occurred.

Scientists are still tabulating how much radioactivity fell where. The maps drawn by ApSimon and Wilson, unlike those made in the US, take into account weather patterns and rainfall over central and western Europe. Rainfall brings radioactivity down to Earth, increasing contamination.

The measured concentration of caesium-137 in Stockholm averaged about 1 becquerel on 28 April. There were hot spots, however, such as at Simpedvarp, on the Swedish coast about 200 kilometres south of Stockholm, where values of 190 becquerels were reported.

For the 200 million people in Eastern and central Europe who were most exposed to Chernobyl's cloud of radioactivity, the extra dose would be about the same as that received by the generation of humans exposed to the peak of global fallout from atmospheric nuclear tests during the early 1960s.

If, before the accident, the lifetime risk of cancer in an area was 20 per cent, it would now increase to perhaps 20.005 per cent. The high numbers of tumours and cancers are not a result of heavy doses of radiation, but of the sheer numbers of people exposed to a low dose.

The moral, perhaps, is that in the aftermath of the accident, governments (who should be concerned about the risk of deaths among entire populations) should have panicked more, while individuals need not have panicked as much as they did.

Now answer the following questions in writing.

1. What does the article tell us about "caesium-137"? About "becquerels"?

2. What is the role of wet weather right after a nuclear disaster?

3. How does the article relate the size of the dose of radiation from the Chernobyl incident to the expected number of deaths in Europe?

The following is a list of questions for you, the reader, to ask yourself about how you did the task.

1. Did you read the text first or go right to the questions? Actually, starting with the questions may well be a more efficient means of answering reading comprehension questions than reading the text first (Cohen 1984, Kennedy, Kenyon, & Matthiesen 1989:83–84).

2. What support strategies did you use? For instance, did you underline words and if so, which ones? Did you read through the text in linear fashion or jump around?

3. Did you use strategies for simplifying the text through paraphrase?

4. Did you attempt to establish coherence in the text, such as through content schemata (knowledge of the topic) or textual clues (organization, context, discourse functions)?

5. Were you aware of supervising your use of reading strategies—that is, planning the strategies, monitoring their use, and evaluating the results of your reading?

6. Did you vary the type of reading you used? For instance, did you skim certain portions and read others in depth?

The following are possible answers for the three questions.

1. Caesium-137 is one of the two radionuclides that the reactor has. A becquerel is a measure of the concentration of caesium-137.

2. Rainfall brings radioactivity down to earth, increasing contamination.

3. A high number of tumors and cancers is not a result of heavy doses of radiation but of the sheer numbers of people exposed to a low dose.

Did you miss any of these or come up with other answers that you feel are acceptable? Take a look at how you came up with the answers you arrived at? Can you see a link between the way you read and the results? Did you gain any insights about how you read in such exercises? What would you say are the strengths and weaknesses of such an approach? If you are a native English speaker, you had certain natural advantages over a nonnative reader. It would be valuable for you to repeat the same exercise with a text in a language you are learning.

TOWARDS MORE EFFECTIVE READING IN A TARGET LANGUAGE

We see, then, that target language reading is not a passive activity at all, but rather quite active—requiring an ability to derive the maximum from the text itself (bottom-up reading) while bringing the maximum to the text from world knowledge (top-down reading). We also see that there are different levels of processing involved—from the most basic recoding level to high-level decoding for the author's intent. We have noted that one challenge of reading is to match the reason for reading with an appropriate type of reading (e.g., skimming, receptive reading, etc.).

Not only are there various strategies that can be employed to enhance reading, but there are also strategies for handling the strategies—that is, strategies for supervising the planning, execution, and assessment of any given reading effort. The chapter ended with sample verbal report exercises, intended to give you a firsthand glimpse at what it means to become more aware of how you read. Such exercises are valuable in sensitizing learners and teachers as to individual differences and similarities in reading target language texts.

Chapter 6

Writing As Process and Product

In some language learning methods, the learner does not write in the early stages. In some methods, the learner never writes extended prose, just isolated sentences. In other methods writing is a central part of study. When learners work on their own, writing may or may not be of concern. This chapter is intended for learners who have a need to develop their writing skills in the target language. The discussion is meant to provide some ideas regarding strategies for the target language writer.

While the process approach to producing written text is described here in some detail, the emphasis is on the kinds of *feedback* that writers can receive concerning their written work and what to do about this feedback—how to utilize it most effectively. A technique called "reformulation" is singled out as a means for improving writing in a target language, both because this technique is largely neglected in the literature and because I have conducted a series of studies indicating that it has promising features as a means of improving a nonnative writer's style. As the emphasis on reformulation demonstrates, this chapter actually focuses to a certain extent on writing issues "around the edges" of those raised elsewhere in the literature on target language writing.

Assuming that the teacher assigns writing tasks in class, such tasks may have a variety of different instructional objectives or purpose, regardless of the rhetorical function of the task (e.g., to report, to describe, to explain, or to convince), and this purpose will influence how and what we write (Raimes 1987b). One purpose for writing in the classroom is to have you *imitate* some model of writing by, say, copying a series of sentences. Particularly at early stages of language learning, this may give you a sense of how to write the language. At more advanced stages, imitation would be intended to help you become familiar with certain grammatical and stylistic forms. Another purpose for writing is to *train* you in the use and manipulation of linguistic and rhetorical forms. Thus, a teacher or textbook may have a series of sentences for you to complete or generate as a way of practicing writing in the target language. For example, you may have to transform a series of sentences from present tense to past tense, or from statements into questions.

A third purpose for writing in the classroom would be to *reinforce* some material that has already been learned. You may have read an article and now are writing a summary of it in the target language to help solidify your initial learning of the vocabulary. A fourth purpose for writing would be to improve your writing *fluency*. The purpose here would be to engage in writing without worrying about accuracy of language form. The task could be that of making entries in a journal (to be discussed below) or of writing freely for a designated time period without concern for grammar or spelling.

A fifth purpose would be that of authentic *communication*, whereby the writing is intended to impart new information to somebody else, with the assumption being that the writer really wants to impart that information and that the reader is genuinely interested in receiving it. Aside from imparting information, communicative writing may represent an effort at persuasion, an attempt to provoke thought and stimulate discussion, or a statement of a request. We see that in order to be authentic, the fourth and fifth purposes for writing, fluency, and communication would imply more than writing as a drill. Writing would be as a vehicle for self-expression in some areas. Still another purpose for writing would be to *learn* how to integrate all the purposes—imitation, training, reinforcement, fluency, and communication—with the emphasis on improving the whole performance, not just one of its aspects.

The above purposes are stated more in terms of what teachers may wish to use writing for—such as for drill or communication—than in terms of what students may wish to get out of a given writing task. Cumming (1989a) describes three specific kinds of learning that students may wish to derive from their writing.

1. Assessing and seeking out improved uses of language—searching for words that produce the best phrasing.
2. Testing functional hypotheses about appropriate language usage while writing—attempting to match their expressions to target language norms for producing grammatical structures in writing.
3. Comparing cross-linguistic equivalents—using writing as a way to try out hunches about ways that native language words and phrases are represented in the target language.

Not only can we write for different instructional purposes and personal learning goals, but we can also select different types of writing consistent with our purposes. Types of writing include: *expository* writing—to explain or inform, *persuasive/expressive* writing—to convince, *narrative* writing—to relate a series of events, *descriptive* writing—to offer a sensory impression of an object or feeling, and *literary* writing—to create exemplary text (in the form of a novel, poem, ballad, etc.). Usually, writing for a given purpose may entail the use of several different types. For example, a lesson intended to train learners in the use of past tense may require that the students write a narrative in the present tense and then change it to the past tense. Likewise, a lesson meant to emphasize communication could involve the writing of a letter meant to persuade a company to change its hiring policies.

The message to you as a learner here is that if and when you feel that your writing skills are not developing as desired, you might look to see if your exposures to writing have been limited to one purpose for writing (e.g., simply for training and not for fluency or communication) and/or to one type of writing (e.g., narrative). It may be that you have not had adequate exposure to writing for the purposes and types of writing that you actually need in the target language. You may have to find such exposure out of class. For example, you may need to write office memos in the target language, yet the classroom may not provide you any training in how to do this. The issues to be raised in this chapter are intended to be relevant to whatever purposes you have for writing and to whatever types of writing as well.

THE PROCESS APPROACH TO WRITING

The traditional approach to the teaching of writing has been the so-called *product approach*. Many learners and teachers alike feel that the major or only focus of this approach is on the finished product of writing—which sometimes is not so finished. This emphasis on product also puts emphasis on the grade. The underlying assumption of this approach is that learners are capable of turning out finished products the first time around. Yet it has become apparent to many educators that this approach of one-draft submissions discourages learners from taking their writing seriously because of its focus on instant products and on the grade that the writer receives.

In recent years, the *process approach* to writing has been introduced as another option. This approach emphasizes the notion that writing is a process whereby the finished product emerges after a series of drafts.[1] The process approach puts emphasis on an incubation period in which the written piece takes shape. The writer's awareness of writing processes is heightened, and the work comes to a teacher for appraisal only at the point when the writer is prepared for such appraisal. The composition has usually gone through several rounds of peer edits and self-assessment *before* it reaches the teacher for assessment.

[1]For an example of a process-oriented textbook for writing in English as a second language, see Raimes 1987a.

Along with the focus on process, there has been a commensurate de-emphasis of grammar and mechanics. While grammar and mechanics may have importance for certain types of writing, they are now being de-emphasized somewhat as evaluators of nonnatives' written work take a broader communicative perspective in their assessment. It has been observed that a learner's motivation to write can be negatively affected by a teacher's untimely or exclusive focus on surface issues of form (e.g., grammatical concerns, spelling, and punctuation).

Furthermore, popular models of writing are now emphasizing that writing is not properly characterized when it is seen as a linear set of stages, starting with prewriting, then writing, and then review. Writing is seen rather as one continuous process which is *recursive* in nature (Flower & Hayes 1984). In other words, writers go back to go forward. In addition, writers are seen to differ as to the manner in which they return to previous stages or issues in their efforts to plan, generate, and evaluate written text.

If we focus just on the initial phase of writing, for example, we will note considerable differences across writers. According to Arndt (1987), there are, at one extreme, *outliners*, who need a whole session just to plan out what they will write, and, at the other extreme, *listers*, who write quantities of text without concern for how they fit together.[2] The basic distinction here concerns the extent to which writers generate their texts on an on-line basis, as opposed to planning or prewriting before they write for most or all types of writing. Furthermore, writers differ in terms of how they review their writing, if at all. Review, resulting in major revisions and/or minor edits, may take place frequently in little spurts, at the end of a large chunk of text, at the completion of the draft, or according to some combination of the three.[3]

The extent to which conscious monitoring of the writing—such as goal setting and evaluation of progress—takes place depends on the writer and on what is being written. The goals that these writers set deal with both the *what* of writing (what content, in what structure, for what audience) and the *how* (brainstorming to generate ideas, jotting down notes during writing, and determining when to take breaks).

One of the frustrating aspects involved in the actual writing down of your ideas in your native language is attempting to capture your thoughts on paper before they get away. Such a task is all the more difficult in a target language when major or even minor gaps in language proficiency exist.

Then, once the piece of writing has undergone a few drafts and is

[2]A description of her study appears in "Further Readings" at the end of Chapter 8.

[3]The advent of word processing on microcomputers has had an impact on writing in many ways, and one of them is that writers who used to do extensive planning are now entering text directly into the computer with little or no preplanning—for better or worse (Nichols 1986, Haas 1988).

ready for assessment, the issue is one of what to assess. Evaluation can be a real challenge in that there are numerous things that could be evaluated: *rhetorical structure* (clarity and unity of the thesis), *organization* (sense of pattern for the development of ideas), *register* (appropriateness of level of formality), *style* (sense of control and grace), *economy* (efficiency of language use), *accuracy of meaning* (selection and use of vocabulary), *appropriateness of language conventions* (grammar, spelling, punctuation), *reader's understanding* (inclusion of sufficient information to allow for the meaning to be conveyed), and *reader's acceptance* (reader's agreement, if so desired).[4]

One of the noteworthy features of the current process models of writing is that they are based on writers' verbal report protocols, often in the form of think-aloud, stream-of-consciousness data. In other words, they are based on writers' ongoing accounts of what they are doing while they are in the process of writing: a description of the writing act based on the writer's notes, the writing itself, the way in which the writer reads and rereads what has been written, and meta-comments that the writer makes about the writing. Such descriptions are more authentic than intuitively based ones. As with the reading act, it is possible to obtain insights as to what effective writing strategies may entail on the basis of descriptions of how writers write. These descriptions can provide less successful writers with strategies which may prove beneficial for them depending on their language proficiency and learning style.

STRATEGIES REVEALED THROUGH PROCESS ANALYSIS

The painstaking description of how writers write has revealed certain insights about what effective writers do and do not do. These insights apply as much to target language as they do to first language. The following are some of these.[5]

1. *Going back to go forward.* Writing is seen as an activity that builds on itself. The context for writing, then, is to a large extent the text that has been created so far. Thus, the successful writing goes back over what was written to determine where to go next. In effect, this recursive procedure underscores the importance of reading in the writing process.

2. *Repeating key words and phrases.* Good writers are concerned that ideas within their text be clearly connected to one another (i.e., be cohesive), an important reason why good writers reread what they already

---

[4]These categories are based largely on Freedman and Clarke 1988.

[5]These insights are based on the work of Sommers 1982, Perl 1980, Smith 1982, Jones 1983, Jones & Tetroe 1987, Gaskill 1983, Zamel 1983, Connor 1984, Scardamalia & Bereiter 1986, Cumming 1989a, 1989b, and Raimes 1987.

wrote before continuing—to make sure that ideas are linked clearly. Successful writers have been observed to link up their ideas through the deliberate repetition of key words and phrases, rather than relying on apparent or actual word equivalents. The problem is that the reader—particularly the nonnative one—may not perceive that two words or phrases are meant to be synonymous in a given context. Good writers are also concerned to use conjunctions and referential pronouns wherever the use of such discourse markers help to clarify the meaning of the text.

3. *Using advanced or emergent planning (or both)*. Expert writers either have a plan thought out in advance for how to produce the given text or make workable plans as they go along—drawing on their knowledge of effective written discourse. (Inexperienced writers tend to work in overly small planning units, writing one phrase at a time, and then asking themselves what to say next.)

4. *Postponing major revision until the ideas are written down*. Major revisions are postponed so as not to interrupt the process of translating ideas into written words. For example, if writers perceive an inconsistency between sections of a text, a lack of balance, or a contradiction, they make a mental or written note of the problem but finish working on the current section before dealing with that dissonance. Thus, upper-level revision is performed when it does not disrupt the flow of ideas. Likewise, lower-level editing for grammar and mechanics is postponed until an appropriate moment, as it may be an unwelcome distraction to deal with such matters while attempting to compose text. If words are not known, then the writer may leave a blank, perhaps with a circle around it, or write in the native language word temporarily.

5. *Making decisions by assessing different aspects of writing in conjunction*. When necessary, effective writers are able to make decisions by assessing two or more aspects of their writing together (e.g., the content of a given section and the most appropriate discourse markers or connectors to convey the points cogently).

6. *Searching extensively for the "right words."* When it is deemed appropriate to look for words or phrases, expert writers indulge in a memory search and subsequent analysis of the material retrieved. The writers generate alternative language choices, assess their qualities, and choose among them according to the context and their intentions.

7. *Distancing self from text*. Good writers know that they need to step back from their text—perhaps leaving it for several days or weeks—to have the proper perspective as to its worth. Writers caught up within their text may not see its strengths and weaknesses so readily. Furthermore, better writers are able to keep their ideas and their expression of them separate.

8. *Keeping in mind the goals and the audience*. Good writers stay on purpose as they write and revise—making sure that what they write is consistent with their aims for writing. They also remain mindful of the intended

audience for the piece. First, assuming that some or much of their first draft was writer-based (i.e., written in order to get the ideas down and possibly meaningful only to the writer; Flower 1979), they then make the piece reader-based or reader friendly. Second, they adapt their style so that it is, among other things, at the appropriate level of formality. Good writers know how to move from oral text or spoken discourse into the written mode, transforming the text into the appropriate form for written discourse.

9. *Writing multiple drafts.* It is also the case that good writers produce multiple drafts of what they are writing. A draft may mean anything from a partial or total rewrite to a more modest revision to small-scale edits.

FEEDBACK ON WRITTEN WORK

One of the most problematic areas in the domain of writing in a target language is that of feedback to the writer—whether it be from teacher, tutor, peer, or self. Let us first consider oral conferences and written comments from the teacher.

Conferencing

Conferencing, the term used to describe one-to-one consultation between teacher and student during the evolution of a composition, has become one of the buzzwords of writing (Graves 1983, Calkins 1986, Harris 1987). The concern for conferencing sessions is based on the position that an interactive session can help to clear up matters that cannot be handled by written feedback alone. There is, in fact, some research evidence that spoken feedback has advantages over written feedback (Rose 1982). Yet a major problem is that teachers need to find the time to conduct such interactive sessions. One large-scale study in Europe, for instance, found that most teachers do not have time for extensive individual conferences (Freedman 1987), but, even when they do take place, the reality of such teacher-student interactions may fall short of what experts would recommend.

For instance, whereas the intention of such conferencing is to provide an opportunity for genuine interaction, teachers have been found to dominate conferences, depending on the task, its duration, and its purpose (Scardamalia & Bereiter 1986:797, Sperling & Freedman 1987, Sperling 1988). One study comparing native with nonnative writers found that nonnatives, especially the low achievers among them, were simply responding with "Yeah" or "Um-hmm" in order to keep the teacher talking and to keep from having to get more involved themselves (Ferris, Ferris, Hared, Kowal, Lapp, & Patthey 1989).

In some cases, the teacher's oral response about feedback in conferences has even been found to have as its purpose little more than helping
to decipher the handwriting of the teacher—which may not be the student's
problem (Sperling & Freedman 1987). Hence, we can surmise that conferencing is a technique that can be of benefit to learners when conducted
appropriately—that is, when there is continual attention to the students'
internalizing the planning, evaluating, and other processes that go on in
the writing conference (Calkins 1986).

Written Feedback

While teachers may spend hours marking student papers, the question
has been raised as to whether such written corrections make a difference.
Marzano and Arthur (1977), for example, studied 24 tenth-grade English
as a native language writers assigned to three treatments and found that
students did not read the teachers' written comments or read them but
did not attempt to implement the suggestions and correct the errors.

In a follow-up study with 141 American university students who received one of four correction treatments while studying German as a foreign
language, Semke (1984) found that corrections did not significantly increase
writing skill. The learners' achievement was enhanced by writing practice
alone. In fact, for those students whose purpose for writing is to learn how
to shape and reshape meaning in an effective way, the teacher's red marks
may serve as a distractor, shifting the focus away from communication and
excessively onto the form of the message (Sommers 1982).

A recent survey that I conducted with over 200 college students from
New York State who were studying English as a native language, English
as a second language, and three foreign languages (French, German, and
Hebrew) indicated that perhaps 20 percent of the students paid little or no
attention to the written feedback that they received from their teacher on
the last composition that they had written (Cohen 1987a).[6]

Since there appear to be moments when feedback works and others
when it does not, let us first take a look at factors which may need to be
operating for feedback on written work to have a positive effect.

When Written Feedback Works

The following are conditions that appear to be necessary or advisable
for feedback on written work to have an impact on you, the writer.

[6]See Chapter 8 for more details on this survey.

1. When you are knowledgeable enough about the area of the comments/corrections. If you have the knowledge necessary to understand a correction or receive an explanation that provides the missing knowledge, the feedback has some chance of having an impact.

2. When the feedback is in an area which you deem important for your immediate or long-term needs. If you are particularly concerned about vocabulary for a specific domain of behavior or about complex syntactic structures that you tend to use frequently, for example, you may be more mindful of feedback in those areas and more likely to benefit from it.

3. When the feedback is clear. Ironically, often the marginal comment "not clear" is not clear. The same can be said about the comment "awkward." Also, some teachers use symbols which their students may not be sure of because (a) the students lost their list explaining the symbols, (b) certain symbols have multiple purposes, and (c) some symbols do not adequately describe the nature of the problem.

4. When you have strategies for dealing with the feedback. Learners who have systematic approaches for handling feedback may well remember the feedback more successfully than those who do not. For example, if you create your own learner's dictionary with meaningful definitions, translation equivalents, and examples, each vocabulary correction or suggested alternative could be added to it. If you have a notebook for grammar rules and rhetorical devices (e.g., means for signaling a definition, an example, or a sequence of points), you could also update this notebook based on the feedback that you receive. If feedback is not clear, good learners may determine what is not clear and check with the teacher, another native speaker, or a classmate, in order to obtain clarification. Further clarification may still be needed to determine what should be written instead of what was written.

SPECIAL MEANS OF GETTING FEEDBACK

There are various means whereby you can ensure that your written work receives substantial feedback, whether you are studying in a classroom, in tutorial, or on your own. One way is to provide yourself the maximum amount of feedback for self-assessment. Sometimes simply writing the second or third draft of an essay will clear up certain existing problems in choice of content, organization of ideas, selection of vocabulary, grammar, or mechanics (Raimes 1983:149–150).

Cooperative Learning

Another way to ensure ample feedback is to elicit the support of nonnative peers in the classroom, usually within a structured framework. For example, learners may be requested to form working groups and to take turns reading each others' papers (Cramer 1985). They may be asked to focus on just one area or another, such as on content and organization of ideas. Sometimes learners pass their papers around so that each participant reads all other papers; sometimes one learner reads his or her paper aloud to the rest of the group while they follow along using photocopies (Moore 1986). Although learners tend to favor teacher feedback over peer feedback, peer feedback is not necessarily any less valuable (Chaudron 1983, Zhang & Jacobs 1989) and researchers have suggested using it more (e.g., Cumming 1985).

It would also be possible for you to form your own writing support groups which meet outside of the classroom framework. You would lend each other support in areas where you feel more confident. You could also identify issues which you are not sure about—areas that need to be checked by a teacher or by some other knowledgeable person.

Two other means for getting feedback are through dialog journals and through reformulation. The remainder of this chapter will be devoted to these techniques, with the bulk of the attention on reformulation, as it is a technique with potential that has been little utilized.

Dialog Journals

For some years, students have been keeping journals or diaries of their learning experiences. There is nothing new about that. More recently, however, a new twist has been introduced in the writing of journals. For one thing, journals have been transformed into vehicles for dialog between teacher and student. This may not be all that new either, since some teachers have used this technique, as well as the technique of teachers and students writing letters to each other for some time (Rinvolucri 1983). What is most innovative are the uses that such "dialog journals" are being put to and the ground rules concerning their use.

First of all, a major use of the dialog journal is to give you a vehicle for expressing any queries that come up while you are in the process of writing a composition or some other exercise. In other words, if you are struggling over the choice of a vocabulary word and finally write down a word without being sure that you are correct, you could note your uncertainty in the journal. Likewise, if you have trouble with a syntactic structure or discourse function (like giving an example or making a contrast), you can write down the nature of your difficulty. What usually happens if such concerns are not recorded is that you soon forget that they were genuine concerns—ones that may have resulted in much deliberation before any action was taken.

It is also possible for you to include other kinds of information besides queries about linguistic matters. You could write down your reflections on the assignment and perhaps indicate alternative ideas that you did not include in an essay, but that were likewise of concern to you. It would also be possible for you to include reflections on how the class is going— both academically and socially.

Ideally, these students' comments would be written in the target language to allow for practice in using the language for truly functional purposes. The teacher then collects these dialog journals from time to time (perhaps from five students per week depending on the size of the class). The teacher's responses would be in the target language exclusively if at all possible. This provides the learners with a source of exposure to written language ideally at a level that they can understand.

Teachers are to operate under one basic constraint with respect to dialog journals—namely, they are not to *correct* the language. They are simply to respond to the queries—writing their responses directly into the dialog journal, in the space provided by the learner. For this reason, the preferred format is to have the students write their essays and exercises on one side of their notebook and their queries on the other side. When they write their questions, they are to leave some lines blank for the teacher to answer.

Actually, one of the logistical problems that teachers have in giving feedback on compositions is that there is no room on the page to write the comments that they would like to. Dialog journals solve the problem—at least with respect to responses to the queries. Teachers are still expected to provide comments as always on the exercises.

The following are some special features of such dialog journals.

1. *The students generate the topics for discussion, the issues of concern to them in the course, and specifically with reference to a given task.* Furthermore, they can write their comments according to their own proficiency level, and in their native language if need be and if the teacher understands it.

2. *The teacher responds to each learner's queries individually.* This personalization of the learning process is most well-received both by learners and by teachers. Both groups have reported finding themselves feeling more closely in touch with the other (Kreeft & Shuy 1984, Staton, Peyton, & Gutstein 1986).

3. *The writing is truly interactive in that the learner and the teacher enter into an ongoing written dialog.* A learner once remarked to me that she found it far more interesting to read her teacher's replies to her comments in the journal part than to read the teacher's comments on her assignments. Nevertheless, the teacher's feedback to the students on their assigned work is *also* taken more seriously by the students as a result of the dialog journal interaction (Porat 1988).

4. *The writing is functional in that a genuine message is communicated.* Part of the above learner's interest in the journal derived from her perception that "real communication" was taking place rather than just a class exercise.

5. *The context is nonthreatening.* The moment that learners know that their performance in the journal will not be corrected, they become freer in the expression of their thoughts. The learners open up and feel more a part of the class, and likewise the teachers feel that they are contributing more.

The following are a few of the entries from a dialog journal between a sixth-grade ESL student, U Chal, and his teacher (from Kreeft & Shuy 1984:194).

STUDENT: I don't know what is valetines?
I can't do the report, I don't know how to start the report?

TEACHER: Valentines Day is when people buy or make heart shaped cards to give to each other. We will make a Valentine in class.
In language we talked about how to make a report. The first thing you need to do is to decide on what your report will be on. It should be on some form of ocean life. Then you begin finding books and information on the subject.

STUDENT: Can we do more than one ocean life? What test is the test we going to do tomorrow?

TEACHER: Yes, you can make more than one report. Do you like making reports? What is your report going to be on?
The test is called CTBS test. It will help me to know what you need to learn before you go to junior high.

STUDENT: Yes, like to make reports if fun to make and at the same time we learn more about life in the ocean.
I am doing the report about White Sharks then when I finish I am going to do about Dophins if I have time.

TEACHER: Dolphins or porpoises are unique mammals. They seem to have a language.

STUDENT: I know and I read that scientist was stunding about dolphins language. Last year when I was in Brazil I was in the beach and I saw a dolphin dead on the sand and when I touch the skin is like sofet and ten when I eat the lunch and I go to see the dolphin some birds were eating the dolphin.

TEACHER: The dolphins have even been trained to do undersea work for the Navy. They seem to have an intelligence. The birds help to clean

the beach by eating the dead animals. The dolphin's skin has no scales—
we expect an animal that looks like a fish to have scales.

Do you like doing reports? Our class seems to be deeply involved.

STUDENT: I liked to do the reports is best than do the report in a
paper. . . .

The preceding sample demonstrates how the dialog journal can be a
vehicle for expression of concerns regarding how to do homework assignments as well as ideas about content issues—both those that are specifically
related to school assignments and those that are not. As pointed out above,
such a journal could also have on-line commentary by the learner while
performing a given task. For example, U Chal could make entries into the
journal while in the process of writing up his report on white sharks—
entries deal with the format of the report, the handling of content, and
matters of language.

The maintaining of a dialog journal is most appropriate for learning
in a classroom setting, although it could be utilized by individual learners
if they can find a native speaker of the target language willing to be their
partner. The journal not only creates closer ties between learner and teacher
but also serves to heighten the learner's awareness of learning strategies.

Reformulation

Another special means of obtaining feedback is through reformulation.
This technique is primarily, though not exclusively, for intermediate and
advanced target language writers. Even after spending much time on a
piece of writing, an advanced nonnative writer may have the uncomfortable
feeling that a native would not have written it that way. In other words,
even though the content may be well thought out, the writer may have
the decided feeling that the form is not altogether acceptable. The piece of
writing could be a business letter to an important company, an article
intended for a popular magazine, a memo to a boss, or a professional
research paper intended for publication in a foreign language journal. In
all such cases, the content may be excellent, the basic grammar and vocabulary may be free of glaring errors, but the overall effect may be that
of a nonnative-sounding piece. It may sound stylistically awkward.

The technique of reformulation, to be described below, speaks to those
learners with a basic curiosity about how they compare to natives in the
language forms that they use in their written self-expression—their selection of vocabulary, their choice and ordering of sentence structures, and
the extent to which they tie these forms together effectively (i.e., cohesively
and coherently) in their writing. The technique is meant especially for

learners who are interested in seeing the kinds of revisions a native writer—whether teacher, peer, or other—would make when revising what they have written. These learners may find that some or even many of the revisions are not the result of an erroneous form being replaced by a "correct" one, but rather a *less* appropriate form being replaced by a more appropriate one within the given context.

In other words, the issue is really one of *style*, an area for which learners in a target language classroom may not receive much guidance. In beginning classes the teacher often emphasizes basic vocabulary and grammatical problems, but even at the more advanced levels there may still be a lack of emphasis on the more refined aspects of form. A recent survey of college students, for instance, revealed that grammar and mechanics constitute the bulk of teacher comments on student compositions in different foreign languages at the various class levels (Cohen 1987a). There is a growing tendency to treat writing as a creative process of discovery, with ongoing revision prompted by the teacher and by the writers themselves, but it is probably fair to say that many target language classrooms still do not reflect this trend.

In this section on reformulation, we will first look at the typical writing feedback situation. Then we will discuss alternatives to this situation, including reformulation, which will be our main focus. Several examples of reformulation will be given and then a suggested learner's exercise will follow. We will end with a discussion of some of the possible benefits from using such an approach, whether within the framework of a classroom setting or on an individual basis. From here on, we will assume that you are on intermediate or advanced target language writer and potential user of the reformulation technique.

The Typical Target Language Writing Situation   In a typical classroom situation, it well may be that the extent of feedback that you receive on written work is quite limited. For one thing, the teacher may not have enough time to give all the learners extensive feedback on their compositions and other writing assignments. Second, teachers may feel that they do not wish to spoon-feed learners. For this reason, the feedback may not only be limited in quantity but also reduced to certain symbols indicating approval or disapproval, and the existence of erroneous forms—without provision of the correct or appropriate forms for the given context. The nonnative writers are left to figure out the correct forms. Even if clues are given as to what these forms might be, as pointed out above, these clues may be too telegraphic to be helpful—for example, "awkward" (Hayes & Daiker 1984).

Third, the teacher may not correct for fear that the learners in the course are not advanced enough to understand the correction—that it will be over their heads. Fourth, the teacher may not correct because it is difficult to do so. For one thing, it may not be clear to the teacher what the writer intended to write. But even if the intention is clear, correction of one thing may actually require the correction of something else as well. In other words, when teachers start changing vocabulary or sentence structures, these changes now make other parts of the writing sound awkward to them. Such a phenomenon may discourage teachers and other reviewers from getting into what may amount to a partial or complete edit of a piece of writing.

The result of this situation is that you often receive correction of words here and there, with occasional suggestions as to alternate words and phrases. This constitutes partial feedback, and such feedback may well be low-level, focusing on basic vocabulary, grammatical forms, and mechanics (spelling and punctuation), rather than on higher-level phenomena—such as stylistically more appropriate lexical choices, syntactic structures, and markers for linking ideas within the text (markers of cohesion). The situation produces target language writers who reach intermediate-level writing stylistically, but do not advance beyond that point.

If, in fact, you receive little corrective feedback regarding the form of your written work, you may think that you are writing acceptably. Thus, you not only receive limited incentive to improve your target language writing style, but also receive little assistance in how to go about such a task. It may be that repeated exposure to well-formed writing will contribute to your own production of such prose. However, if acquisition of writing style takes place, it may take a long time—years, in fact. This volume is concerned with strategies for reducing the amount of time it takes to achieve more nativelike proficiency.

Alternative Means of Feedback for Target Language Writers   Corrective feedback techniques used in the classroom may include the approach whereby the teacher writes typical errors on the board and you are asked to identify them and to explain what the correct forms should be. Sometimes the teacher discusses one or more sample papers, for example, as a means of pointing out how to write and how not to write. You may be given one or more papers with clues as to where there are problem areas (e.g., Witbeck 1976). A drawback to the approach of using _typical_ errors is that it may not be individualized enough. You may have the reaction that you would never produce the kinds of incorrect or inappropriate forms that your teacher or you are identifying in the writing of your classmates. Thus, the impact of this kind of feedback on your own writing may be limited.

Another approach calls for more extensive revision than the nonnative writer usually conducts (Anderson 1981). Often nonnatives write only one or two versions of something, since they may feel that it is a strain to produce even this much in a target language. Yet extensive revision by the very same nonnative writer may clear up some (perhaps many) of the inappropriate forms. You are sometimes encouraged to conduct such extensive revision in stages, so that the effort does not seem so overwhelming.

For example, you may be asked to revise first for overall content and organization, then for effective means of connecting sentences and paragraphs cohesively, and then for vocabulary. Next, you may be asked to edit for grammar (correct use of inflections and syntactic structures) and for mechanics. One problem with this approach is that you may not always be aware of what needs to be revised or edited. You may use some forms only because you do not have in your knowledge base alternate forms to use. Thus, even after you have performed extensive revision, a significant amount of the written work may still not sound nativelike.

Yet another approach calls for repeated practice in writing rapidly (Brière 1966, Shaw 1982). In this approach, learners are encouraged to write freely and at a fast pace—the rationale being that an outcome of such writing will be both greater quantity and a more nativelike product. The approach is based on empirical evidence that as you write more freely, you gain confidence in your target language writing—confidence which leads to greater success at error-free writing.

In a replication by Shaw (1982) of Brière's (1966) study, intermediate-level EFL college students in Mexico were given six minutes to write rapidly during each class session. They were assessed for total number of words and the grammaticality of what they wrote. The students who engaged in rapid writing in class were compared to those who wrote once a week in class under untimed conditions. It was found that those in the rapid writing group showed significantly better results after a college semester than did those writing under untimed conditions. The study demonstrated that those learners having to write rapidly had not only become quicker, but had become more confident in their ability to write fluently and accurately.

Such an approach may well be part of what is needed to accomplish breakthroughs in target language writing at the intermediate and advanced levels. It is important to point out that such a technique is not meant to replace the beginning- and intermediate-level emphasis on more basic issues in writing, including structure. Rather, it is intended as complementary—providing the extra push once learners have studied the basics of writing in a target language.

The *reformulation* approach (based on Levenston 1978) is offered here as an alternative which personalizes the feedback that you receive, so as to motivate you to want to pay attention to the feedback that you receive. The feedback itself can be potentially quite beneficial and of immediate relevance and usefulness. How useful it actually is depends on your ability to implement the insights gained from the technique. For some writers on some points, feedback concerning the correct or more appropriate form will make an immediate and lasting impression. With respect to other points, it may take some extra attention (possibly in the form of exercises or drills) for the feedback to have a lasting impact.

The way in which nonnative writers go about learning the correct or appropriate forms may vary from one learner to the next. Some keep lists of points to remember, possibly categorized in some way. Others simply keep their earlier writings handy and refer to them when writing something new.

Let us now look at how this technique works.

The Reformulation Technique   This technique is characterized by the following stages:

Pre-Reformulation Tasks
1. You first produce a text, usually a short paper of 200–300 words. You are encouraged to revise this paper as many times as you and others may see fit until it reflects your thoughts accurately and is considered as well formed with respect to grammar and mechanics as is possible.

2. You then give the paper to a competent native writer—for example, a teacher or other native reviewer—at least once or twice for feedback, according to whatever system the reviewer wishes to use. One currently popular system is that of an open, developing dialog between the writer and the teacher, as discussed above.

3. Upon receipt of the reviewer's comments, you revise your paper based on the feedback received. This version is referred to as a *reconstruction* in that it has been corrected so as to reflect what the writer means to say. Note that a complete rewriting of the essay may be optional, particularly when the feedback is minimal and rewriting would just be an extra, non-productive chore.

Reformulation Tasks
4. At this point, a competent native writer is asked to rewrite or *reformulate* the entire paper or a portion of it (say, the first 100 words, since the beginning of the paper is often written with extra attention). Sometimes this reformulator is a classroom teacher, but usually a friend or acquaintance. It may be advisable to find someone other than the teacher to do the reformulating because the teacher is perhaps too close to the text already, having gone over it one or more times for correction and other comments.

If you are learning a language in a community where that language is spoken, then finding a reformulator should be no great problem. In contexts where few native writers are available, there is more of a problem but not an insurmountable one. Sometimes it is possible to befriend tourists and have them help you out. There may be visiting students at the local university or high school. There may be natives of the target language at your place of work or living in your neighborhood. When no local natives are easily accessible, perhaps you could send your essay abroad and have the reformulation written in a "pen pal" fashion.

When all other options fail, then perhaps you would turn to a non-native who is nonetheless a proficient writer in the target language, but then some of the effectiveness of the technique is lost. The problem in using nonnative reformulators is that they may well be lacking control of various stylistic niceties such as appropriate ways to realize rhetorical functions such as definition and exemplification, nuances in vocabulary usage, and preferred syntactic patterns. Since some of the rhetorical structures may be culture-bound (Kaplan 1983, 1987), even the most advanced non-native writer might not know how to write consistently appropriate target language reformulations of them.

Once an appropriate person has agreed to perform the reformulation, this reformulator is told to rewrite the paper so as to preserve as many of your ideas as possible, while expressing them in his or her own words so as to make the piece sound nativelike. Clearly, it is not always possible to preserve every idea—either because the original idea was not that clear to begin with or because the very use of a different word or phrase shifts the meaning to some extent. Yet the reformulator is expected to stay as close to the original ideas as possible, so as to ensure that the essay still reflects your work and not that of the reformulator.[7]

The native writers are encouraged to rewrite not simply a sentence or two (as a conscientious teacher may do), but actually to rephrase the entire paper (or part of it) so that it reflects their style, their approach to expressing those ideas. Their reformulation should reflect as clearly as possible what it was that the nonnative wished to write. This rephrasing or reformulating marks a departure from the best teacher edit of such a paper. It is important for the reformulator to stick relatively close to the original paper in ordering of ideas and in sentence structure so that you will still feel that it is *your* paper—only now it has been reformulated. This feature is, in fact, a special source of motivation in that you most likely are curious to see how your own piece has been dressed up to sound nativelike.

It is in this spirit, then, that the reformulator is encouraged to select words, phrases, and grammatical structures that are appropriate to the writing situation without being overly erudite or obscure. Reformulation is intended to challenge your knowledge to some extent, but not excessively. You need no more than an average writer to do the reformulating for you and do not want a reformulation that is too polished. The reformulator's purpose is, in fact, to shift the form of the message to a form

---

[7]This procedure, then, guards against the likelihood of plagiarism whereby the ideas of the essay—not only vocabulary and structure—would be replaced by those of the reformulator.

that is more stylistically in keeping with the approach of an *average* native writer, not that of a professional.

5. With the help of a native or on your own, you then compare your original corrected version with the reformulated one. You are encouraged to do this in several passes. First, you compare discourse functions in your version and the reformulated one. Then, you compare the means of linking one idea with another cohesively and its effect on the coherence of the text. Next, you compare the selection of vocabulary, and, finally, the choice and ordering of syntactic structures. Let us look at what these step-by-step comparisons might consist of:

Discourse functions   In comparing discourse functions, you are looking for the native's approach to questioning, defining, hypothesizing, asserting, qualifying statements, and other speech acts. In other words, you check whether the native writer used some other means than you did for signaling a certain purpose in each section of text. If, for example, you have written a letter of apology, in what ways does the reformulator's written apology differ from the way you wrote it, plus corrections?

Cohesive links and overall coherence   In comparing markers of cohesion, you are concerned with ways that the native writer linked together ideas —within and across sentences and paragraphs—to form a text. Such ties or connectors consist of grammatical forms such as *conjunctions*—either combining ideas together ("and"), contrasting them ("whereas"), showing one causes the other ("so"), or giving a time sequence ("then"), and *referential pronouns*—personal pronouns ("he," "it," "they," etc.) and demonstrative pronouns ("this," "that," "they," etc.). Such ties are also indicated by the use of vocabulary items—for example, by the repetition of the same noun, by the use of a synonym, or by the use of a more general or more specific word. For instance, after "voting" is introduced in a paper, it could be referred to by a pronoun ("it"), by the repetition of the same word ("voting"), by a synonym ("balloting"), by reference to the general event ("an election"), or by reference to a specific activity ("casting a ballot").

In comparing coherence, or global rhetorical organization, you are checking to identify ways in which the ideas may have been written more intelligibly than they were in your corrected version. For instance, you could check whether the reformulator identified the topic (or topics) that you are writing about more clearly. You could also see if the reformulator changed the order of presentation of ideas. The ideas may flow better in a different order in the target language. In addition, you could also see whether any ideas have been enhanced by the addition or elimination of words or phrases.[8]

Selection of vocabulary   In comparing the choice of vocabulary words and phrases, you are to pay attention to whether the native speaker used

---

[8]For more on the assessment of coherence in writing, see Canale 1982, Bamberg 1984.

more precise words, more concise phrases, more/less formal words, and collocations (i.e., restrictions on how words can be used together). Pay particular attention to collocations such as prepositions used with particular verbs, verbs used with particular nouns (e.g., "to *perform* an operation"), and adjectives with nouns (e.g., "The fruit is *ripe*"). Frequently, the changes that the reformulator has made are slight, representing subtleties of vocabulary use. Sometimes, a tightening up of the use of vocabulary may result in the possible removal of redundant or irrelevant material. Sometimes vocabulary associated with spoken language is replaced by vocabulary more suitable for formal written language.

Choice and ordering of syntactic structures   In comparing syntactic structures, you check for whether the native altered structures—for example, by changing some of the elements. You also see if structures—clauses, sentences, or clusters of sentences—have been reordered or replaced by others. If so, you note what structures were used in place of the ones in your version. It is possible to observe whether the native used more or less complex structures to convey the same meaning. You can see the techniques natives use to avoid repeating the same structure over and over. You will see structures that you already know but have failed to use, as well as those that you do not know. By noting new grammatical patterns and imitating them in your own writing, you are likely to acquire them (Sanaoui 1984).

So what then is reformulation? It is basically a refinement. It is intended to *complement* the feedback that you currently receive regarding your target language writing. It is certainly *not* meant to replace other forms of feedback. In other words, it does not suffice as a diagnostic tool for determining areas of writing difficulty. It is simply a personalized way of receiving extensive, largely indirect feedback. The issue we are raising here is whether current forms of feedback are sufficient, or whether a further step such as reformulation is desirable, at least once or twice as a potentially diagnostic tool. How diagnostic the reformulation experience is will depend both on the quality of the reformulation (i.e., native but not overly elegant) and on the thoroughness of the comparison that you make between the reconstruction (i.e., the original with feedback incorporated) and the reformulation.

Furthermore, when nonnatives go about composing text, they often rely on forms which they feel confident with. In other words, you may avoid those forms which you either do not know or do not know well. When teachers provide feedback, their comments generally relate only to the language forms that you *chose* to use. Thus, you do *not* get feedback regarding alternative, possibly richer avenues for expressing your ideas. Reformulation is a means for providing this potentially enriching input. The challenge put to the reformulator is to provide a native version that is more or less within range of the nonnative writer, without it being at the expense of accurate communication.

   Examples of Reformulation   We will now look at two examples of reformulation from EFL students. The first is a text written by a Hebrew-speaking high school student who was an intermediate learner of English as a foreign language (EFL). The paragraph was taken from an essay on the subject "Television." We will also look at a paragraph written by a Hebrew-speaking EFL student as an exercise in an English department course in writing at the university level. The paragraph was part of an essay on life at the Mount Scopus campus of the Hebrew University.

   Here is the original version of the first example.

> The TV is important in our life. In our free time we looked at TV program. The TV is served us at a lot of subjects. The littel box showes us the new in every day. It learn us geographi English and all the lecon of school. Sometime we look at a good movie at the TV or dicution with important people.

In this case, as part of the revision process, the teacher had the learner explain orally or reconstruct, in his native language, what he had meant to say, in order to know what kind of feedback to give. Then the teacher provided feedback and had the student revise the essay. The resulting version looked as follows:

> TV is important in our lives. In our free time we look at TV programs. TV offers us programs about a lot of subjects. This little box shows us the news every day. It teaches us geography, English, and all the other school subjects. Sometimes we look at a good movie on TV or a discussion with important people.

The reconstructed version no longer has glaring errors in verb forms ("looked," "is served," "it learn us"), article use ("the TV," "the lecon of school"), prepositions ("at a lot of subjects," "in every day," "look at a good movie at the TV"), vocabulary ("served us," "learn us," "the lecon of school"), cohesion ("*this* little box" instead of "the little box"), spelling, and punctuation.

   The thing is that the paragraph still does not sound very nativelike. Now that the surface mistakes are cleaned up, we begin to notice that the style is somewhat awkward. The vocabulary is not quite right, and the sentences are short and not totally tied to one another. Let us now take a look at this paragraph after it was reformulated by a native writer.

> TV plays an important role in our lives. We spend much of our free time watching TV programs, partly because TV provides us such a

variety of different types of programs. This little box brings us the news every day. It also teaches us geography, English, and other school subjects. From time to time we can enjoy a good movie or watch an interview with important people.

In the reformulated version, we can observe refinements in vocabulary use: "important role" for "important" (to be more explicit), "provide" instead of "served"/"offer," "a variety of different types of programs" instead of "a lot of subjects," "brings us" for "shows," and "watch" for "look at." While some of these changes are by no means required, they may well improve the essay stylistically. It can be quite useful for the nonnative writer to see that there is more than one way to say the same thing. As noted above, whereas some learners will perceive stylistic differences on their own, others may need the guidance of a native writer.

There are changes both in vocabulary and syntax, like "We spend much of our free time watching . . ." for "In our free time we looked at . . ." We notice that the second and third sentences were joined by means of "partly because," to provide more of a cohesive link between the two ideas. In the last two sentences we note the use of "also" and "even" respectively, to provide ties between those sentences and the preceding ones in the paragraph. It is possible that the corrected version, before reformulation, was lacking such cohesive ties because the person doing the correcting was focusing on surface errors at the sentence level. We could also ask whether the corrector made more than one pass through an essay while correcting.[9]

Now let us look at the second example, a four sentence paragraph from an essay by a university EFL student.

One of the severe problems of the social life on campus is the problem of the relationship between Arabs and Jews. It is well known that the mixture of the two cultures causes tension between students, and it especially effects students who live in the dormitories of the university. In my opinion this problem would not have been so severe if unreliable sections from the Students Union did not deliberately wake students to act violently. I therefore suggest that an immidiate change of the group which dominates the Students Union will be done by free elections on campus.

The teacher in this case was a teacher of stylistics and thus paid more attention to such matters as well. Her corrections were as follows:

[9]Sometimes, a second pass through an essay helps the assessor to see things that were overlooked the first time around. Yet when teachers have a stack of papers to grade, they may not feel that they have the time to go through a paper more than once.

1. "social problems" for "problems of the social life"
2. "better structure than coordination?"—marginal comment regarding the second sentence
3. problem with the word "effects"
4. "university dormitories" instead of "dormitories of the university"
5. "why a past idea 'would not have been'?"—marginal comment regarding the third sentence
6. another word for "sections"
7. deleted the plural *s* in "Students Union" in both places it appeared
8. comment about tense and choice of verb in "did not deliberately wake"—suggested "did not provoke"
9. spelling of "immediate"
10. marginal comment, "Structure!" with regard to "will be done" in the last sentence—suggested "to make a change."

The student incorporated the teacher's corrections into a revised version, and the paragraph in question came out as follows:

One of the severe social problems on campus is the problem of the relationship between Arabs and Jews. It is well known that because of the mixture of two cultures, tension exists between students, especially those who live in the university dormitories. In my opinion members of the Student Union provoked students and encouraged them to act violently, therefore I suggest that these members must be changed through free elections on campus.

As in the previous example, we see that surface mistakes have been cleaned up. There are now no glaring verb tense errors, for example. But if we look closely, we notice several vocabulary problems—"the mixture of the two cultures," "these members must be changed." Also, in the first sentence the noun "problem" is repeated, rather than a demonstrative pronoun, producing somewhat awkward cohesion in English.

The following is a reformulated version.

A serious social problem on the Hebrew University campus is that of relations between Arabs and Jews. It is well known that cultural and political differences between these groups lead to tension and conflict within the student population, especially among those who live in contact with one another in the dormitories. In my opinion, members of the Student Union provoke violence among students. For this reason, I suggest that these members be replaced through new campus-wide elections.

We note that in the last sentence "for this reason" provides a more specific cohesive marker than "therefore." We also note that the awkward phrases have been replaced: "cultural and political differences between these groups . . . those who live in contact with one another . . ." for "the mixture of the two cultures," and "I suggest that these members be replaced" for "these members must be changed." The awkward repetition of the noun "problem" in the first sentence is avoided by use of the demonstrative pronoun "that"—"A serious social problem . . . is that of . . ." With regard to syntax, the second sentence is simplified by eliminating a further subordinate clause introduced by "because of" after "It is well known that . . ."

By reading the reconstructed and then the reformulated versions of this passage on student relations in close succession, we can gain a sense of what reformulation is all about. The reconstructed text communicates the ideas more or less but it lacks the impact of the reformulated version. Whereas the first may have a stigma attached to it, the second flows smoothly. Motivated learners can use even a short passage such as this as a means for diagnosing the level of stylistic ability that they currently have in the target language, and can also receive useful information as to where their deficiencies may be.

It must be made clear, nonetheless, that some, if not many of these changes are matters for discussion. Regarding such changes, it is no longer a matter of correct or incorrect, but rather one of style. The very operation of comparing a nonnative and a native version stimulates such discussion—discussion which may play an important role in the development of mastery in writing in a target language because it increases the writers' awareness of key issues.

An Exercise   To make this approach to feedback on writing more real for you, you are requested to write a short essay or to select a short essay that you have already written in a target language. If you are required to produce target language writing in a specialized area, such as business correspondence, medicine, or law, you may wish to prepare as an exercise a piece of writing reflecting the field. If your interests are in more general writing, perhaps one of the following topics would be of interest to you.

My View of the "Good Life"

The Influence of the Personal Computer on My Life

The Perfect Mate for Me

The Best Friend I Ever Had

The Scariest Thing That Ever Happened to Me

Now have a friend, colleague, acquaintance, or whomever, correct it for surface errors. At this point, the essay may be rewritten, eliminating these errors, before giving it to a reformulator, but this is unnecessary. In fact, some students feel that there is too much busy work if they must rewrite the essay before it goes to a reformulator. Of course, an argument in favor of rewriting before submitting it for reformulation is that you then have yet one more opportunity to edit the piece before it undergoes reformulation. As word processors become more common, it may well be that the target language learner saves the initial and subsequent drafts of the composition on microcomputer diskettes, which all but eliminates the drudge work of tediously copying over material that is not in need of revision (Bridwell-Bowles, Johnson, & Brehe 1986).

The reformulator should preferably be someone other than the person who corrected the essay, so as to provide a fresh perspective. Ask the reformulator(s) to read the entire piece of writing through and to make sure that they understand the basic message and thoughts contained in the piece. Ask them to reformulate the essay in their own words, making sure to preserve content and order of ideas. They are to add or delete content sparingly.

When you get the reformulated version back, you are to compare the two versions—the corrected original and the reformulation. This comparison can be carried out under the guidance of the reformulator, with the help of some other native writer, or alone. As indicated above, it is suggested that the comparison be done in steps, first comparing for discourse functions (e.g., defining, asserting, questioning, apologizing, or complaining), then for cohesion (linking of ideas) and coherence (global rhetorical organization), next for vocabulary use (precision, conciseness, and formality), and finally for syntactic structures (alteration of elements within a structure, ordering, and replacement). It is possible for you to obtain insights about matters of style without outside guidance in doing the comparison. The very exposure to nativelike writing can be a rich source of usable input. However, a number of learners would need the assistance of a native to benefit from such a comparison.

Discussion Concerning the Reformulation Technique   The technique of reformulation has much promise, although it is not free of problems. It is important to find a native reformulator who writes reasonably well. But even if the writer is only average, you are still getting a model of native language input, which in itself is important. In learning how to say things correctly or appropriately in a target language, we frequently find ourselves turning for assistance to any native we are speaking to, regardless of whether the person is a qualified language teacher. In learning how to write, we could also utilize our native speaker resources more fully by requesting reformulations of written work from natives around us—in our place of employment or in our neighborhood.

Perhaps a more crucial issue is that of assistance for learners who are unable to make a meaningful comparison between the two versions on their own. There is then a need to elicit the cooperation of either a classroom teacher or another native who is capable of explaining differences. Very often natives cannot really explain why one form is more appropriate than another. They will simply say, "It sounds right."

There is also the issue of whether *nonnative* teachers or other non-natives with high proficiency in the target language are capable of doing a competent job of reformulating. It would be predictable that even a teacher with near native proficiency would lack some of the stylistic subtleties of the language that the reformulation technique can tap and draw attention to. Thus, it would pay to find a native reformulator, not necessarily a teacher. Of course, nonnative teachers may also benefit from having their own writing reformulated.

Notwithstanding potential problems, there is much to be gained from giving the technique a try. For one thing, there is an opportunity to obtain deeper feedback than in the simple correction of surface errors, which is often what learners receive as feedback on their essays. You become exposed to new idioms and more varied ways of expressing ideas of relevance to you, the learner. The reformulation actually illustrates to you an appropriate way to express in writing the ideas that you intended to express.

Notetaking

Notetaking is one other form of writing that may assist you in your efforts to become a more successful learner. What are some of the ways that learners take notes in language class? Some years ago, we asked 19 American college students to describe how they organized their notebooks on the basis of six weeks of study in an intensive Hebrew as a second language course (Cohen & Aphek 1979). The students were given a questionnaire in which they were to indicate the ways in which they classified vocabulary (if at all) and wrote out grammar rules. What emerged from a content analysis of their answers was the following composite description.

Minisurvey of Notebook Organization   A popular pattern was to enter all material in one notebook in a straightforward, chronological fashion—that is, in the same order that the material appeared in class. However, some students indicated other approaches, such as separate sections for vocabulary and grammar, or one side of the page for vocabulary and the other side for grammar. One or two students noted that they kept separate notebooks for class notes and for homework.

Organization of Vocabulary Entries.   Students who had a separate vocabulary section from the outset or who rewrote vocabulary in a separate notebook, varied in their handling of these words. Some listed them by topic group, others alphabetized them, others listed them by form class (e.g., verb, noun, etc.), and some even subclassified words within form classes (e.g., verbs by conjugation).[10]

Organization of Grammar.   Grammar rules tended to be entered chronologically, sometimes with a box around them to set them off, sometimes rewritten onto a special page. For example, verbs might be displayed by conjugation, in past, present, future, possibly all in the first person singular.

A source of variation concerned the level at which the rule was represented. Some students would just include a sample of language which illustrated the rule, others would have an explanation accompanying this example, and others would have not only the example and an explanation, but a listing of the exceptions as well.

Insights from the Minisurvey.   This survey noted that although language learners vary in how they take notes, the differences may not be so great. It was found that the basic notetaking patterns were similar. Much of the variation appeared to be a matter of rigor, consistency, and systematicity —the extent to which learners organized their material.

Unfortunately, the author's work did not get beyond the survey stage to try to link certain notetaking patterns to success at learning. For example, while vocabulary could be classified in a number of imaginative ways beyond simply appearing in chronological order of appearance in class or even alphabetized listing, what kinds of learners might benefit from this kind of imaginative listing? What kinds of learners might benefit from rewriting grammar rules into a special section such that exceptions to the rule appear alongside the rule as stated, and under what circumstances?

Insights About Notetaking from the Literature   Just as there are teachers who insist that the learners put their pens and pencils down during portions of the lesson and simply listen and interact, so there are learners who take minimal notes as a matter of course. Part of their learning style is not to take notes. Gilette (1987) described one such successful intermediate learner of French who was clearly a good attender. By the same token, there are learners who take copious notes. An impressionistic observation that I had from hours of observing elderly learners of Hebrew in intensive study was that some were using notetaking as a defense mechanism so as not to be called upon in class. In other words, their message to the teacher was, "Don't call on me because I am too busy taking notes to attend to your request right now."

The literature on notetaking tends to deal with the taking of lecture

---

[10]The students were not asked whether they then made flash cards for any of these words (as described in Chapter 2).

and reading notes,[11] rather than with notetaking in target language lessons. That literature on notetaking in the content subjects would suggest several things. One is that terseness benefits target language learners in notetaking more than writing everything down. It was found that both native and nonnative notetakers who compacted the greatest amount of spoken discourse into information units, used abbreviations and symbols, and were attentive to information-carrying words, were most successful at a test of retention concerning a video program (Dunkel 1988). While no time was given to review the notes before the video in that study, other research has constituted that if learners do not review their notes, the notes will be of only marginal assistance in the learning process (Carrier & Titus 1981). A further addition to this issue of review is evidence that it may be more beneficial to review your own notes than to review those of someone else (Barnett, Di Vesta, & Rogozinski 1981).

In keeping with the approach of this book, a prescriptive list of how to take notes will not be presented. Instead, the message to the learner is that you need to determine what works best for you. For example, does it pay for you to write down as much as you can in a lesson or should you just listen? If you do write things down, do you perhaps write down too much or the wrong things (e.g., writing down grammar rules you would never review, but omitting words you may need at some future point)? Or do you write too little so that you cannot reconstruct the issue afterwards? Do you spend any time going over your notes and do you attempt to bring order to them—beyond the chronological listing produced through class sessions? It would seem that the starting point is for you to describe to yourself how you take language notes and then to determine if your approach supports your needs as a learner.

LOOKING FOR BREAKTHROUGHS IN WRITING

This chapter started by calling attention to a process approach to writing, whereby awareness is placed not only on the written product, but also on the process that took place in order for the learner to come up with a written product. The major shift in thinking is that good writing—especially in a nonnative language—is a product of more than one draft. It is enhanced by the judicious use of a series of strategies, such as not getting bogged down in matters of form until the basic ideas have been written.

We looked at the issue of feedback and considered conditions for it to be of benefit. Then we focused on two special instances of feedback. The

---

[11]The split is between the "how-to" books which usually do not have any empirical basis underlying their recommendations (e.g., Casey 1985 and Chibnall 1987 on lecture notes, Deese & Deese 1979 on reading notes as well), and the research studies which provide recommendations only cautiously (e.g., Carrier & Titus 1981).

first, dialog journals, emphasizes two of the purposes for writing that were presented at the outset, namely, fluency and communication. The dialog journal focuses not on form, but on the message, with the extra purpose of actually communicating unknown information to someone else in writing. Such an approach constitutes a departure from the traditional role of target language writing which often consists of dealing with predetermined topics in a predetermined way.

The second, reformulation, provides nonnatives an opportunity to imitate the writing style of a native—as learners begin to utilize some of the native writer's words and phrases in their text and incorporate into their own writing ways that the native writer accomplishes speech functions and the syntactic structures used to do so.

It would be hoped that one or another of these techniques could assist you in attaining new levels of writing proficiency in the target language that you are studying.

Chapter *7*

Research on Vocabulary Learning, Attending, and Speaking

    This chapter will summarize research which I have conducted or supervised, dealing with vocabulary learning through mnemonics, attending in the classroom, and speaking for communicative purposes (i.e., the use of speech acts). Studies alluded to in Chapters 2 through 4 are described here in detail. The material is meant for readers who would like to see the extent to which the suggestions for language learning presented in this book have a research basis. This chapter and the next will also end with an annotated "Further Readings" section, to direct the motivated reader to studies conducted by other researchers which deal with issues related to those raised in these chapters.

    As was noted at the outset, one of the features of this book is that the material in the previous chapters is based on empirical research. The studies were for the most part conducted on small groups of learners in order to allow for in-depth analysis of learning processes. Furthermore, the studies were carried out under classroom, not laboratory, conditions, in order to assess patterns of learning in a typical, not a rarefied, laboratory environment.

VOCABULARY LEARNING THROUGH MNEMONICS

    Research on target language vocabulary learning has generally involved one-shot studies rather than longitudinal ones, where subjects are engaged in experimental tasks which are not necessarily part of regular classroom activities (e.g., Atkinson 1975, Ott, Blake, & Butler 1976). When learning by association is assessed under laboratory conditions, then the types of associations are often restricted. A colleague, Edna Aphek, and I felt that what was needed were longitudinal studies on target language vocabulary learning that would be based on a realistic classroom activity

—such as finding native language glosses for new words appearing in a text. We also wanted to open up the research to the total array of possible associations that the learner might make.

With these interests in mind, we undertook a preliminary pilot investigation of learning through word association among seven learners of Hebrew as a second language at the Jewish Theological Seminary's summer course in Jerusalem. This longitudinal study was conducted over 40 days. We found that words learned through association were generally retained, as indicated by performance on a series of three recall tasks. Furthermore, students produced a number of types of associations.

The 100-Day Descriptive Study

With the experience from this initial study, we then set out to investigate the topic in greater depth and over a longer time frame (Cohen & Aphek 1981). We subdivided the basic research question regarding vocabulary learning and the use of association into the following specific questions: When asked to learn new vocabulary from a written text in class, what do students do? Do students make associations? If so, what kinds? How successful are these associations over time? Does student proficiency affect success? Are there differences in types of associations across class level? Does degree of contact out of class have any effect on words learned through association? Of what benefit are associations which are supplied by teachers? To what extent does seeing new vocabulary in context help in the recall of these words, as opposed to encountering these words in lists?

Procedures   Seventeen students studying intensive Hebrew at the Jacob Hiatt Institute of Brandeis University in Jerusalem (nine beginners, six intermediates, and two advanced) took part in this study. They were given seven different tasks, spanning approximately 100 days. The following is a listing of tasks by day.

> *1st day*   The learners were given a passage in Hebrew to read, according to their level, and told to underline words that they did not know, both as the teacher read the passage aloud and then as they read it over to themselves. The teacher provided an English gloss for each word underlined. The students were given class time to learn these words and were asked to write in the margin the learning aid (if any)—such as association with the structure of the word, association with another word in Hebrew or with a word in English—they had used to learn each word.
>
> *2nd day*   The learners were given the same text with individualized underlinings of each word that students had indicated that they did

not know. They were requested to supply English glosses for those words.

5th day   There was a review of results on the vocabulary task, and then each learner's personalized words were presented in list form for which students were to provide English glosses.

7th day   There was a review of results on the lists, followed by a list of 10 words of common difficulty to the majority of the group, for which the students were asked to supply glosses.

17th day   The learners received a new passage with common words in their original forms. Students were to supply glosses and indicate frequency of contact with those words out of class ("no contact," "some," "frequent").

90th day   The learners were administered the same individualized word list as on the fifth day. They were to provide English glosses and to indicate frequency of contact with the words.

100th day   The same text was administered as on the second day, this time with each student's individualized words deleted, and English glosses were written over the deletions. Students were to supply the missing words in Hebrew.

Findings   In most instances, students simply tried memorizing the words that they did not know. As an aid to memory, some students rewrote the Hebrew word on the bottom of the page along with the English gloss. The number of words that students requested glosses for (in Task 1) ranged from 11 to 40. The mean percentage of correct glosses across all tasks was 75 percent. In other words, in three-quarters of the cases, students were retaining new vocabulary words over time, whether through straight memorization or through the use of associations.

Six of the nine beginners, five of the six intermediates, and both advanced students reported the associations that they used. It was perhaps surprising that even with only 13 students reporting associations, as many as 11 different types of associations were tallied. And it must be remembered that these were only those associations that students made when given a specific classroom task—such as associations for words glossed in a text. In other words, if students were learning words in conversation out of class, there could have been other associations as well—such as by touch, smell, taste, tone of voice, or by identification with a person or with an event.

The following are the categories of associations that appeared:

1. Associating Hebrew words to English words with a similar sound, such as *memaher* 'he hurries' to "hare"; *lazuz* 'to move' to "snooze"; *imunim* 'training' to "ammunition."

2. Associating part of a word to an English word by sound and meaning, and the other part to a Hebrew word by sound and meaning, such as *benatayim* 'meanwhile'—*ben* to *beyn* 'between' and *tayim* to "time."

3. Associating sound and meaning to an English phrase, such as *benatayim* to "been a long time."

4. Associating Hebrew words with other Hebrew words by sound, such as *tsava* 'army' to *tsena* 'leave'; *rexov* 'street' to *raxok* 'far'; *ramzor* 'street light' to *or* 'light.'

5. Associating Hebrew words to proper names, such as *maxane* 'camp' to *Mane* (the name of the street that the Jacob Hiatt Institute was located on).

6. Associating to another language through meaning; such as *tox* 'inside' to *tuchus* (Yiddish for 'backside').

7. Associating to structure, such as *lifney* 'before' to *lifamim* 'sometimes'; *seder* 'order' to *lesader* 'to order.'

8. Associating by one or more letters, such as *masait* 'truck' by [m], in that vehicles often begin with [m] in Hebrew; *maxane* 'camp' by the picture of [x], *xet* [ח] in Hebrew, because it looks like a shelter; *be'emtsa* 'in the middle' by the Hebrew [m] in the middle.

9. Associating with a frequently seen sign, such as *la'atsor* 'to stop' with the sign *atsor* 'stop' in busses.

10. Associating with the place in the text where the word appeared.

11. Associating by making a mental picture of the word.

After charting so many associations, we then were curious to know which of these types of associations were actually successful in the sense that the learner was able to provide a correct gloss in English on the tasks in which the word appeared. We were also curious as to whether contact with these words out of class made a difference. The following are illustrative examples from five of the students—a beginner and four at the intermediate level, in that order.

1. After learning *maxane* 'camp' through the Hebrew letter *xet* [ח] looking like a shelter, a student got it wrong in Task number 2, the text with personalized underlinings. But then it was correct in the three subsequent tasks in which it appeared, twice in list form and once in a passage. She reported no contact with the word out of class.

2. A student who made association to the [m] in vehicles got *masait* 'truck' correct three times, once in text and twice in list form, and then wrong the last time it appeared in a text, when she had to supply the Hebrew for the English gloss. In this last trial, we note that the source of her association, the [m], had been removed. This student had two completely successful associations over time, while reporting no contact with either word out of class: association by sound within Hebrew (*ramzor* 'street light' to *or* 'light'), correct all four times that it appeared, twice in text and twice in list; and associations to English and Hebrew sound and meaning (*benatayim* 'meanwhile' to *beyn* 'between' and "time"). She also made a structural association to *magía* 'he arrives,' which was glossed wrong twice (both in lists) and then glossed correctly in text twice and in list once. In this instance, the learner reported some contact with the word out of class.

3. A student who associated *be'emtsa* 'in the middle' with the [m] in the middle of the word, got this word correct in all tasks in which it appeared (three times in text, twice in lists). She reported some contact with this word out of class.

4. A particularly weak student got the four words that he made associations for correct in all tasks in which they appeared. He reported frequent contact with the first three and no contact with the fourth. His associations were *la'atsor* 'to stop' to the sign on the bus, *atsor* 'stop'; association by sound from Hebrew to English (*memaher* 'he hurries' to "hare"); association of a word with a picture (*nixnas* 'enters' to a picture of "going in"); and *yeshiva* 'meeting' with the Yiddish *Yeshiva*.

5. As a final case, a student made several structural associations, one of which was successful in producing the correct gloss all four times that it appeared, although she reported no contact with the word out of class (*yeshiva* 'meeting' to *lashevet* 'to sit down'), and the other (*mehanisiá* 'from the trip' to *linsoa* 'to travel') reflected inconsistent results—that is, incorrect in a text, then correct in a list, then incorrect in a list.

If general conclusions can be drawn from these results, it is that by and large *if* learners, whatever their class level or individual proficiency level, used some associational patterns for learning vocabulary, the words were retained successfully over time. The frequency of contact with words out of class did not necessarily affect the results one way or another. In other words, students who made successful associations retained words even if they had no contact with the word out of class.

When we looked closely at vocabulary learning performance by individual students at each of the three levels, we noticed fluctuation in performance from task to task. This fluctuation prompted a further analysis: calculating the average performance on the three tasks involving contextualization of vocabulary versus the average performance on the three tasks involving lists. These results showed that at the *beginning* level, tasks involving lists were easier (average 84 percent correct) than were tasks with contextualized words (average 69 percent correct), whereas at the *intermediate* level, tasks with contextualized words were easier (average 77 percent correct) than those with lists (average 70 percent correct). This finding may suggest that only once students have some background in the target language are they able to benefit from having vocabulary in a context; that until that time, the appearance of words in isolated lists simply means fewer distractions (i.e., from material that only confuses them because they cannot understand it very well, if at all).

As can be seen from the findings, on occasion a word was glossed wrongly in one or more tasks directly following learning, but then would be glossed correctly in later tasks. It is possible that this is an artifact of the research design, namely of presenting tasks which repeatedly use the same vocabulary. Students may need repeated exposure to words and occasional review of their meanings to learn them correctly. It may also be that there is a settling process or residual learning whereby students sort out all the various stimuli they are exposed to, and that this takes time.

The 35 Day Mnemonic Training Study

In a follow-up study (Cohen & Aphek 1980), the benefits of training students to make associations that best suited their needs were explored, and the role of these associations in the retrieval of the new vocabulary words over time was looked at. In our previous study, we had assumed that if a word that had been learned through association was recalled successfully, then the original association was responsible. We now wanted to determine to what extent such an assumption was well founded—What was recall actually based on? So, for this study our questions were: What is the role that an initial student-generated association plays in the retrieval of vocabulary items over time? Do students generate new associations for these items to help retain them over time? Do students stop using an association in recall, and if so, what happens to their recall of the word? What is the effect on vocabulary retention of student's proficiency, type of task (word list, words in context), and degree of contact with words beyond the study?

Procedures   The subjects were 26 native English-speaking students (23 males, 3 females; average age 23) studying at the Jewish Theological Seminary of America, Neve Schechter, Jerusalem. Ten were in an advanced class, eight in an upper-intermediates class, seven lower-intermediates, and one a beginner.

The study was conducted longitudinally for five weeks. The students were first administered a Baseline Measure of Hebrew Vocabulary and Reading Comprehension. This test was constructed to assess knowledge of vocabulary in context and overall comprehension of short texts. At the end of the week they were given a short training session (10 to 15 minutes) on how to learn second language vocabulary through the aid of associations. Each student received a copy of a list of associations and was given an example of each type of association on the list (essentially the nine-point list presented in Chapter 2).

In the second week, the students each received a reading passage in Hebrew at their respective level. The reading passages were selected such that each would include vocabulary deemed difficult at one of the four student levels. The teacher read the passage through and helped the students vowelize words that they did not know how to pronounce (since, as is usual in Hebrew texts, the words were not vowelized). The students were then asked to underline any words that they did not know. A researcher supplied the students with appropriate first language translation equivalents for those words from a master list of glosses determined ahead of time.

The students were asked to select 20 of these new words and to make associations for them (using the list of suggested associations). The students were then asked to describe in writing the type of association that they had generated for each vocabulary word. On the average, students selected only 15 words. They found associations for almost all of those words. As in the previous study, students reported using a wide range of associations.

Several days later, the students were given a Hebrew word list, representing the words that they had chosen to learn, with the words appearing in the same inflectional forms as in the original passage, but in a scrambled order. They were to supply English glosses for these words. They were also asked to write down the association, if any, that they had used in recalling the translation equivalent. Students received feedback concerning their performance on this task.

A week later, students received a second passage in Hebrew, which included almost all of the words that at least one student had gotten wrong at that level. Some effort was made to inflect the words differently (e.g., different tense, person, number, and/or gender). This passage was also read to them. Each student then had to supply English glosses for the underlined words, which represented the student's own set of initially known words. Students also wrote down the association, if any, that they used to recall each word. Students also received feedback as to their performance on this task.

During the fourth week, students received the first passage again, but this time with the students' individualized words deleted and replaced by native language glosses. Students had to write in the target language form and indicate the associational pattern that they had used in recall, if any.

In the fifth week, the students were again given their individualized lists of Hebrew words. In this task, they were to take target language words (in base form) and write a sentence for each word. The students were also asked to indicate how frequently they had come in contact with each word outside the context of the study—"frequent contact," "some contact," or "no contact."

Findings   Most students reported using the original association 46 percent of the time, with a high average rate of recall, 86 percent. They reported using a new association only 13 percent of the time with an average rate of recall of 78 percent. They reported no longer using an association 31 percent of the time and had an average rate of recall of 61 percent. Finally, for the 10 percent of occasions where no association had been used either at the time of learning or for recall, the average rate of recall was 72 percent.

Thus, it was found that students most frequently reported using the association that they had originally generated in order to recall the word in subsequent tasks and that their performance *when using this aid* was the best. Almost as successful a strategy was that of using a new association, although they did this infrequently. The average correct recall for cases where no association at all was used placed this strategy third on the list. These students were, however, a subgroup to begin with (N = 11) and only a few of their words were learned this way (4 out of 17). The second most utilized retrieval strategy, ceasing to call up a previously formed association, was also the retrieval strategy yielding the *least* success in terms of percent of correct recall.

These findings suggest that the creation of associations and the continued use of these associations over time (at least for a period of a month) is helpful in recall tasks. In addition, it was found that ceasing to call up these associations may lead to incorrect recall. Furthermore, creating *new* associations along the way was also seen to be helpful in promoting correct recall.

The words for which associations were not found were analyzed to see if there were any distinguishing characteristics of such words that would make the task of finding an association more difficult or unnecessary. It was found that these words often had a root that was not easily identifiable or a complex morphological structure.[1] For example, in the case of the word *sharui* 'in a state of' (masc. sing.) only three of the six students who selected it were able to find an association for it. It is a word that has a root which is not easily identifiable, making structural association somewhat difficult.

With regard to the relationship between individual proficiency and success at recall through association, we found that performance on words for which associations were used correlated significantly with performance on the Baseline Measure of Hebrew Vocabulary and Reading Comprehension (r = 0.56, p < 0.01, N = 23). In other words, if students were more proficient at the outset, they were also more successful at using association in recall tasks. This finding runs counter to the finding from the earlier study described above—that is, that individual proficiency did not seem to influence the ability to derive associations that would be helpful in recall over time. The current finding is reasonable in that one would expect increased proficiency in a language to aid in generating at least certain types of associations (e.g., as through sound and structure within the target language).

---

[1]One-third of the nonassociated words were in construct form with a preposition, which is a common phenomenon in Hebrew. Thus, the words were more complex, making for greater processing difficulties, particularly for students whose native language does not have prepositions appearing as bound morphemes.

This second study did corroborate the first one with respect to two other issues, namely, the relationship between learners' proficiency and performance on contextualized tasks, and the effect of contact with the word outside the study. The more proficient learners were better able to use context to their advantage in recalling a given word. Correlations between proficiency and performance on the second reading passage (requiring an English gloss for a Hebrew word in the context of a Hebrew passage) and on the first passage with deletions (requiring the original Hebrew word in the context of a Hebrew passage when given an English word) were both high ($r = 0.64$, $p < 0.01$).

It was also found that the degree of contact outside the study with words learned through association did *not* correlate significantly with average overall performance on recall of those words ($r = 0.13$). This finding, as in the previous study, would suggest that associational learning helps fix words in memory such that there may be no special need to come into contact with the words. However, it must be remembered that students received feedback after each task, so that the contact with the words within the context of the study was high.[2]

Student Reactions to the Study   We also asked students to share with us their reactions to the study when it was over. Of the 18 students who responded, most had positive things to say about the line of research in general, and at least half indicated some direct pay-off to them personally. For example, students felt that the study had alerted them more to the process which they use or could use to learn vocabulary. There were also several students who said that they had not applied the associational method beyond the study itself. There was one student who reported already being aware of how he learned vocabulary and who therefore felt he had learned nothing new. Perhaps it is a finding in itself that only *one* student reported being so in touch with how he learned vocabulary.

Students actually received only limited training in how to make associations, both because of our desire to interfere only minimally with the daily workings of the language classes and because of an interest we had in determining how *little* need be said about associations. The students were simply given a list of associations and then given examples of each type. No exercises or drills were presented along with the list. As it turned out, at least half a dozen students expressed a desire to have more training in this area and for a longer period of time. One student even suggested making it central to a course, since, as he put it, "After all, vocabulary is half the battle." Students suggested that more thought be given to devising

---

[2]It is also possible that students' judgments as to frequency of contact outside of class were not accurate.

easy ways to train students to associate and to developing exercises to accompany such approaches.

Issues to Be Researched with Regard to Mnemonic Associations

The quasi-experimental studies that have been reported above offer generally favorable findings regarding the use of associations. While true experimental studies tend to be extremely favorable with regard to the benefits of mnemonics (see Cohen 1987c), the problem is that results obtained under laboratory like conditions may not hold true for a natural context in which learners are called upon to recognize and use the words that they have learned. In fact, the form of assessment most common in research studies is that of written tasks. The question remains open as to how well learners can use vocabulary learned through association, particularly when under time pressure to use one of their associated words in speaking or to understand one when they hear it in a natural environment.

Another issue in need of investigation under nonlaboratory conditions is that of the lag time involved in retrieving a second language word or its native language meaning when a mnemonic device is being used. Although the literature suggests that such lag time is minimal under laboratory conditions, it may be that in the real world, when the learner is not predisposed to call upon such devices, the lag time may be greater. The length of the lag time would probably depend on the strength of the mnemonic device, the nature of the word and the learner's knowledge of it, the language use situation, and the learner's strategic competence (i.e., knowledge of how to employ strategies such as the keyword mnemonic). In other words, the wait time demanded of the listener may be greater than that which the listener is willing to grant the speaker. If so, perhaps the listener will lose patience and supply a word for the learner—whether the intended word or some other. Upon perceiving that the speaker is a nonnative, some listeners will provide words *each* time the speaker hesitates—sometimes correctly predicting what the speaker wanted to say and sometimes missing the mark.

In addition, the longitudinal studies conducted by cognitive psychologists may include a time span of only a week or so. There is room for research conducted for longer periods of time and also for research that is sensitive to the role that mnemonic devices actually play in the retrieval and use of vocabulary on a daily basis. Such investigations would call for the developing of research techniques capable of tapping this kind of information—such as through verbal report from learners (especially introspective and retrospective self-observation, and think-aloud and talk-aloud self-revelation; see also the minitraining at the end of Chapter 5 and Cohen 1987b).

There are at least two other research issues which could be investigated. The first involves the study of the typical trial-and-error process of self-generated associations, in an effort to learn more concerning efficient ways of generating such associations. The second regards the gathering of information concerning when or whether the keyword is discarded so that the learner does not even remember it.

RESEARCH ON ATTENDING IN THE CLASSROOM

On numerous occasions I have observed language instruction in classrooms and have become quite frustrated when attempting to use such observations as a means for describing the *learning* process. The observation sheet I have been asked to use for observation of language classrooms at the Hebrew University includes an item concerning the level of participation of the learners. Yet, I cannot observe the students' degree of cognitive engagement in the the classroom. Hence, in many respects, the observational approach limits the sample to those students who speak up, and even then the observers frequently have the uncomfortable feeling that they are merely intuiting about how students are learning and not necessarily perceiving their learning patterns accurately. Furthermore, there is little to be learned about the "quiet" students in a typical class session.

Hence, various interventionist approaches were tried out, such as getting the teacher's permission to stop the class in order to ask a particular student a question about why he or she had said something a certain way. Also, when students were paired up in class for the purpose of having dialogs, I would interrupt their interactions to ask questions about their language behavior. In addition, particular students would be questioned at the first break regarding their language intake in that class before the break.

In keeping with these same goals, observers sat next to one student for a whole class period (up to four hours), observing the student's participation and notetaking. Periodically, these observers would ask the students questions about what they had gotten out of specific things that the teacher or fellow students had said, how they had handled new vocabulary words, and why they had written down certain things in their notebooks.

Encouraged by their results, I started videotaping classes and having the learners view the videotape and answer questions as to what they were thinking when one or another classroom event took place. This approach seemed the most successful of all because the learners did not have to depend entirely on their memory to reconstruct the event. Learners reported listening differentially to their fellow students' interlanguage talk according to how much they liked them for whatever reason. For example, students tuned out other students if they felt that the students talked too much or too fast or with an incomprehensible accent.

Yet a drawback of the video research was that there was an inevitable lapse between the taping of the class and the showing of the videotapes to the students, since time was needed for analyzing the tapes to find interesting moments and for scheduling subsequent viewing sessions with the students. It then became clear that the obtaining of really meaningful student data would call for some instant mental replay on the part of the students. Hence, the technique to be described next—that of stopping the class to circulate a questionnaire—emerged.

Whole-Class Self-Observation

The purpose of the research effort was to have all the students in a given classroom inspect their mental states at selected moments during the class sessions. Thus, rather than studying a number of moments for any one student, the focus was on several moments across a number of students. What learners were doing with input that the teacher intended for them to learn was the main focus of the research effort. The question was whether or in what ways this input was being processed as *intake*. The videotape study had already suggested that students filter out the language of their peers to a certain (perhaps great) extent.

Procedures   Foreign and second language classrooms were selected in which the teacher agreed to have the class session interrupted at one or two moments in order for the students to inspect their mental states and then write down what they found (Cohen 1983a). Such self-observational inspection is termed *introspective* if it entails the inspection of specific language behavior while it is still in short-term memory, and *retrospective* if such inspection occurs after the event (usually after 20 seconds or so). See the end of Chapter 5 and Cohen 1987b for more on the terminology for verbal report measures.

The "moment" for stopping the class generally was selected from extended segments of input in the form of teacher talk or student interlanguage talk. For example, a moment might reflect the teacher's elaborated explanation of a grammar point, use of a complex structure, or use of difficult lexical items. It might also consist of a student's report, response, or interaction with other students.

The questionnaire used in the series of studies looked essentially like that reproduced as the exercise requested of the reader in Chapter 3.

1. What were you thinking about right now?
2. What are the thoughts that were "in the back of your mind" while you were listening to the class session just now?

3. If you were tuning out or having difficulty attending, was it because the material was:

too easy_____
too difficult_____
not interesting_____
too condensed_____
other_____?

4. If you *were* thinking about what was being taught, were you:

repeating the material to yourself (orally or in writing)_____
paraphrasing the material in your own words_____
characterizing the material in some way (e.g., labeling it, looking for an example, etc.)_____
relating this material to some other material_____?

The rationale for the last question was to see how actively students were processing the content of the lesson—from simply repeating it (a potentially weak approach to remembering the material) to relating it to other material (a potentially powerful way to remember material, i.e., through associative links).

At the beginning of the class session, the learners were told that they were going to be participating in a study and that the class session would be stopped in order for the learners to fill out a questionnaire anonymously. The learners were told that the purpose of the research was to help improve their learning. The questionnaires were intended to be written in the native language of the learners (wherever possible), and they were to respond in that language. Responses of learners were primarily in English, but some were in Spanish, French, and Russian.

A basic assumption underlying this self-observational approach is that learners can, in fact, be trained to verbalize some of their cognitive processes in language learning. However complex the learners' thoughts may be, it is still considered beneficial to self-observe them introspectively or retrospectively. This approach was employed in seven second language classrooms in Israel—three at the college level (two intermediate Hebrew classes of mostly English speakers and an English class for Arabic speakers), two at the adult school level (an English class for Arabic speakers and a Hebrew class for English-speaking senior citizens), and two at the high school level (a Hebrew class for Farsi and French speakers, and an English class for Hebrew speakers).[3]

[3]The technique was also tried out in first language classrooms and in content subject classrooms.

Findings   On the basis of this relatively small sampling of classrooms, it was possible to get some indication as to patterns of attending and the likelihood as to whether learning was taking place. First, it was found that on the average only about 50 percent of the students were attending to the content of the lesson at the moment that the class was stopped. The senior citizen group was found to have a lower attention rate—25 percent. The average attention level also rose to a relatively high 82 percent, depending on the focus of the lesson.

When students were attending to the instructional content, they may have been making a general observation (e.g., "My English grammar is lacking regarding this grammatical point"—L1 grammar), assessing their general grasp of what was being said (e.g., "I know the grammar points being taught here but not how to use them"), or grappling with a specific problem (e.g., "I am looking for an unknown word in Hebrew that the teacher just used").

When students were tuning out, they may have been evaluating the teacher (e.g., "I was thinking about how good the teacher is"); evaluating another student (e.g., "Why don't people listen the first time?"); or thinking about other academic issues (e.g., "I was thinking about taking exams in Hebrew"), social issues (e.g., "my weekend," "a rugby match," "a friend"), or bodily needs (e.g., "thinking about breakfast," "thinking about a break to go to the bathroom").

When asked about thoughts in the back of their mind, less than a quarter of the students, on the average, reported that they were thinking about the instructional content (e.g., "the difference in meaning between masculine and feminine forms of a word"). Thoughts were spread among the other categories—other academic issues (e.g., "sociology lessons I didn't finish"), social issues ("personal plans for the next few years," "getting money out of the bank," "a girl in my next class"), or bodily needs ("I want to get something to eat").

If students were tuning out, it appeared that all the reasons provided in the questionnaire were equally relevant—that is, the material was considered either too easy, too difficult, not interesting, too condensed (too much), or other (such as "affective reasons"—e.g., a negative reaction to the teacher).

The questions about the way in which the students *were* attending to the instructional context were only posed in the last several studies. The findings suggested that students were mostly just repeating the material to themselves in their minds. Fewer reported that they were characterizing the material in some way (e.g., labeling it or looking for an example). Fewer still reported relating it to other content, and still fewer said that they attempted to paraphrase it. Actually, those reporting a paraphrase were mostly paraphrasing by way of translation—saying the utterances over to themselves in their native language.

What became apparent as students started reporting their thoughts was that they were sometimes attending to more than two thoughts at the same time. This finding is consistent with the capacity model of attention (mentioned in Chapter 3), which suggests that input from more than one source can all be processed simultaneously on a "space-sharing basis," but with each input receiving a differential degree of analysis. In other words, the mind must allocate attention in some order of priority. Hence, some stimuli get complete analysis and others only superficial analysis (Wingfield & Byrnes 1981, Chapter 6).

Implications of Research on Attending

Perhaps the main finding was that students took in less classroom input than might have been predicted. These results would help to explain why what teachers *teach* is not necessarily *learned*. Students do not seem to attend to the instructional content that much. Thus, there appears to be less language *learning* going on in class than one might think. And a reason for this is that language students are not attending in class at a level that will insure that language learning *will* take place—at least, they are not attending to the instructional content at a high level.

A deceptive factor here is that learners may attend at just a high enough level so that they can respond when their name is called or give an answer to a fairly automatic question-answer pattern. At this level of attention, the learner could also perform rather automatic activities that do not require much thought (such as the oral reading of a passage). The teacher may think that the learners are more engaged in the learning task than they are.

A practical step that learners could take to counteract this low-attention phenomenon would be to compensate for fluctuating and relatively low levels of attention by being overly attentive—through techniques such as "being every student in the class," as described in Chapter 3. At moments when attention is predictably low or perceived to be low, the teacher might want to liven up the class through role playing, games, project work, or something of the kind. The teacher could also liven up the class by departing from routine—by going on a field trip with the students or by sending them out into the community to do a survey in the target language.

Further research could involve explicitly training learners in how to use their minds more actively in the second language classroom. For example, the teacher could demonstrate what it means to process a particular grammar explanation receptively as opposed to actively relating it to some other grammar points or to some knowledge that has already been acquired. The students themselves could be trained to be more aware of how their attention wanders—that is, when they start tuning out. It may well be that tuning out begins to happen the more passively the students handle the input.

SPEAKING: THE USE OF SPEECH ACT SETS

In recent years, teachers and curriculum writers have been encouraged to give attention to speech strategies that are expected, and perhaps even essential, in given situations—such as the appropriate strategies for apologizing, complaining, and requesting. The empirical study of *speech acts* (i.e., those routinized utterances that speakers use to perform speech functions like requesting, complaining, and apologizing) has been undertaken to gather information on what appropriate use of linguistic forms in different sociocultural contexts actually comprises. A number of studies have shown that nonnative speakers may fail to communicate effectively in a given situation even though their command of grammar and vocabulary is fine (see Wolfson 1989, Chapter 7).

As the studies begin to multiply, a picture is emerging as to the basic structure of *speech act sets*—that is, the major linguistic and pragmatic strategies which alone or in combination would represent the particular speech act in a given situation. For example, in one situation, "Sorry" may serve quite adequately as a full-fledged apology. In another situation, it may be necessary to say something like "I am really very sorry" in order to obtain the desired effect.

The studies that will be reported on here are intended to serve as illustrative of the kinds of studies that I have been directly involved with, in an effort to determine what speech forms need to be taught to nonnative learners. Again, for purposes of illustration, the discussion will be limited to apologies.

The Apology Speech Act Set

An apology is a speech act which aims to provide support for the hearer who was actually or potentially adversely affected by a violation for which the speaker is at least partially responsible. When apologizing, speakers are willing to humiliate themselves to some extent and to admit to fault and responsibility for the offense. The five strategies which make up the speech act set of apology (Olshtain & Cohen 1983) consist of two which are general and do not depend on contextual constraints and three which are situation-specific. The two general strategies are: *the explicit expression of an apology* which contains the formulaic, routinized apology expressions (e.g., "I'm sorry," "Excuse me," "I regret") and *the expression of responsibility* which reflects the speaker's degree of willingness to admit to fault for the offense. Potentially, the expression of an apology and/or the expression of the speaker's responsibility could constitute an apology act in any situation.

The other three strategies, *an explanation, an offer of repair,* and *a promise of nonreoccurrence,* are situation-specific and semantically reflect the content of the situation. An explanation is an account of the situation which indirectly caused the apologizer to commit the offense (e.g., "The bus was late" as a statement intended to set things right). An offer of repair is a bid by the apologizer to carry out an action or provide payment for some kind of damage which resulted from the offense. In a promise of non-reoccurrence, the apologizer commits himself or herself to not having the offense happen again. The preference for any one of these five strategies or for a combination of them will depend on the specific situation within the given language and cultural group.

In addition to the main strategies which make up the speech act set, there are ways in which the speaker can modify the apology by either intensifying it or by downgrading it. An intensification would make the apology stronger, creating even more support for the hearer and more humiliation for the speaker. The routinized intensification usually consists of internal modification within the apology expression—in the form of a conventional intensifier such as "really," "very," "terribly." External modification can take the form of a comment signaling added concern for the hearer. Such comments intensify the apology since they express stronger interest on the part of the speaker to placate the hearer. External modification which downgrades the apology can take the form of a comment which minimizes either the offense or the harm it may have caused.

Putting all of these components together, we could have the following apology in response to forgetting a meeting with a boss:

> I'm really sorry [*intensified expression of apology*]. I completely forgot about it [*expression of responsibility*]. The alarm on my watch didn't go off as it was supposed to [*explanation*]. Is it possible for me to make another appointment? Can we meet now? [*offer of repair*]. This won't ever happen again [*promise of non-reoccurrence*].

An Initial Study with Intermediate Learners and Natives

Our first apology study (Cohen & Olshtain 1981) involved eight apology situations selected to assess cultural competence. We were looking for language behavior in apologizing that reflected negative transfer from the native language, an avoidance of negative transfer, or lack of grammatical proficiency. Four of the situations were especially set up to elicit different degrees of intensity of regret (e.g., "Sorry" versus "I'm really sorry")—hitting a car, and bumping into a lady, hurting her/just shaking her up/

because she was in the way. The remaining four situations were meant to assess the effect of status of the hearer on the formality of the apology—insulting someone at a meeting, and forgetting a meeting with a boss/a friend/a son.

The situations were randomly ordered and responses elicited without an intended reply from the hearer. The respondents read the situation to themselves, and then the investigator role-played the person who had been offended.

Procedures   The subjects were 44 college students who were on the average 20 years of age. Twelve were native English speakers (E1), who provided data on how English speakers apologize in their native language. The remaining 32 were native Hebrew speakers, 12 of whom provided Hebrew (H1) responses and 20 of whom were enrolled in intermediate-level English classes and provided English as a foreign language (EFL) responses.

Findings   The results revealed situations in which EFL deviations from the cultural patterns of E1 appeared to be a result of negative transfer from H1 apology strategies since the deviant patterns were similar to those present in H1 patterns. For example, EFL speakers did not express an apology as much as E1 speakers for insulting someone at a meeting and for forgetting to take their son shopping. Similarly, EFL speakers did not offer repair as frequently as E1 speakers for forgetting a meeting with their boss or for forgetting to take their son shopping.

There were also situations in which EFL responses were more like E1 than H1 responses. It may have been that in these situations EFL speakers were successful at avoiding negative transfer of sociocultural patterns operating in their native language. For example, EFL speakers expressed an apology frequently for bumping into a lady "because she was in the way," just as the E1 speakers did. This was not the case for H1 speakers. Also, EFL speakers acknowledged responsibility, as did E1 speakers, for forgetting a meeting with the boss and for insulting someone at a meeting.

We found certain situations where EFL responses seemed to indicate a deficiency in linguistic proficiency—situations where E1 and H1 responses were similar and more complete than EFL ones. In other words, there were situations in which EFL respondents may not have been proficient enough in English to include the expected formulaic strategy in their responses readily in the testing situation. For instance, EFL speakers were less likely than E1 or H1 speakers to offer repair for backing into someone's car and for bumping into a lady, hurting her. Likewise, EFL respondents were less likely to acknowledge responsibility in the situation of bumping into a lady, shaking her up a bit.

We also found that EFL responses did not always reflect the appropriate intensity of regret (e.g., "I'm *very* sorry."). For example, in the situations of "forgetting to get together with a friend" and of "bumping into a lady, hurting her," EFL respondents did not intensify their regret as much as E1 respondents. This deviation may well have been the result of native language transfer, since intensity in Hebrew can be signaled by an interjection (like *oi!* ["oh!"]).

A Follow-Up Study with Advanced Learners

A follow-up study was conducted to investigate whether advanced nonnatives would have mastery over the more complex speech act sets such as apologizing and would thus not be in need of remedial instruction (Cohen et al. 1986). The study sought to determine the nature and extent of gaps between native and advanced nonnative apologies. The study asked two questions: (1) What difference do we find between advanced nonnative learners and native speakers in their apology behavior in the five main strategies and as regards modifications of these strategies? and (2) Are there differences in apology behavior resulting from the severity of the offense and/or from the familiarity of the hearer?

The 180 respondents for this study included 96 native speakers of American English, studying at one of six U.S. universities, and 84 advanced learners of English, who were native Hebrew speakers studying at one of five Israeli universities. The respondents responded to eight apology situations, for which the degree of offense (high/low) and the familiarity of the interlocutors (friend/acquaintance/stranger) was varied. Six other speech act situations (compliments, complaints, and regrets) were included so as to avoid a response set. Whereas in the previous study oral responses were tape-recorded and transcribed, in this study respondents were asked to write the responses the way that they would most likely say them.

The basic finding in this study was that nonnatives lacked sensitivity to certain distinctions that natives make, such as between forms for realizing the strategy of expressing an apology such as "Excuse me" and "Sorry." At least one out of every five times a native offered an expression of apology, it was with "Excuse me," while few nonnatives used this form. In addition, nonnatives limited themselves to the use of "Sorry" in contexts where "Excuse me" would also be acceptable and possibly preferable.

While natives and nonnatives did not seem to differ markedly in the use of main strategies for apologizing, striking differences emerged in the various modifications of such apologies, especially in the use of intensifiers such as "very" and "really." Nonnatives intensified their expression of apology significantly more in one situation ("forgetting to help a friend buy a bike") than did the natives. This extra intensity on the part of the nonnatives was not necessarily warranted, given the generally low or moderate severity of the offense in those situations.

Not only did nonnatives tend to intensify more, but also used a wider and more indiscriminate set of forms. Actually, the nonnative pattern was either to overgeneralize one of the forms ("very" and "sorry") or to use a variety of forms ("terribly," "awfully," "truly"). The nonnatives did not use "really" in the way that the natives did. They attributed to the intensifier "very" the same semantic properties as to "really," while the natives tended to make a distinction—"really" reflecting genuine regret (a greater depth of apology and concern) and "very" more a matter of etiquette. For example, in a situation of "scalding a friend with coffee in a cafeteria," the natives tended to use "really sorry" while nonnatives used "very sorry," which sounded less intensified.

With respect to external modification, natives used interjections (e.g., "Oh!") and curses frequently while nonnatives did not. In addition, the natives were more likely to produce comments providing the appropriate social lubricant in difficult situations (such as "Are you O.K.?"). The results of this study raised the issue of whether benefits would accrue from providing overt instruction regarding these fine points of apologizing.

Research on the Teaching of Apologies

Given the growing body of empirical data regarding the apology speech act set, we were interested in knowing whether it was possible to teach the fine points of apologizing so as to close the gap between natives and nonnatives. Hence, we undertook a study which involved the teaching of such forms (Olshtain & Cohen 1990). The two general research questions asked in this study were: (1) Can the fine points of speech act behavior be taught explicitly in the foreign language classroom? What techniques are most suitable for such teaching? and (2) What level of speech act proficiency can be attained? Is a certain level of residual awareness sufficient? The study involved 18 advanced EFL students, 10 studying in private language schools and 8 in a teachers' college, and 11 native speakers of American English. The learners were pretested to determine gaps in their apologizing behavior. They were given the two types of discourse-completion tasks presented above in Chapter 4, they had to write an appropriate utterance and they had to rate the appropriateness of a set of multiple-choice responses. They were then taught a set of three 20-minute lessons aimed at filling in the gaps—information about the strategies within the apology speech act set, and about modifications of apologies through the use of intensification and emotionals. Finally, they were posttested to determine what had been learned.

Our findings showed that after instruction, advanced learners were somewhat more likely to select apology strategies similar to those that native speakers used in that situation. For example, in a situation of "forgetting to buy medicine for a neighbor's sick child," the response of one nonnative before training was a weak expression of responsibility ("Unfortunately not yet . . .") and an offer of repair ("but I'll be happy to do it right now"). After training it was an intensified expression of apology ("I'm deeply sorry") and an offer of repair ("I can do it right now"). Also, after training nonnatives produced shorter utterances, also more in keeping with native behavior.

It is typical of an advanced intermediate-stage of language acquisition that when learners are uncertain how to say something, they overcompensate by using too many words (Blum-Kulka & Olshtain 1986). Prior to instruction, one learner responded to a situation of forgetting to meet a friend with, "Did you wait for me? You must forgive me. I could not come because of problems and I tried to warn you by phone but . . ." After training, the utterance was shorter: "Oh, I'm so sorry. It dropped out of my mind."

Perhaps the area that met with most success was that of the use of intensifiers. Before training, intensifiers were generally absent in situations like forgetting to buy medicine for a neighbor's sick child (only 20 percent use). After training, intensifiers (e.g., "I'm really sorry I forgot . . .") were used in almost all cases (90 percent).

The learners had certain preferences for how they would like to be taught such fine points. They preferred above all else that the teacher give an explanation of these points. They also welcomed information sheets describing the points and saw some value in role play activities to help reinforce the points. They indicated that they got less out of listening to dialogs which incorporated the forms and from pair work.

If the fine points of speech act behavior are to be taught formally in class, another question of interest to us is how this information is processed at the moment when learners are called upon to use it. For example, is it retrieved automatically or do the students call up in their minds the classroom situation in which they learned it? Such information may suggest ways to teach these points most effectively. In this study, when the learners were asked to retrospect briefly as to their source of information for answering the discourse-completion questions, they indicated that they tended to answer by remembering what they had heard in class.

In an apology study conducted in Brazil with 10 intermediate EFL university students, the respondents provided verbal report data just after performing their apology speech acts. They indicated that 40 percent of their speech acts reflected previously learned or internalized structures and that mostly these structures were produced "automatically." What was interesting was how many things they indicated having on their minds while responding. For example, they reported analyzing the situation, which included noting the interlocutor's age and status. They also would quickly think the utterance through in Portuguese and then come back to the English. They would worry about whether they were producing it correctly in terms of the choice of vocabulary and grammar. And finally, there was also some concern for whether they pronounced their English utterance correctly (Motti 1987).

The findings from this last Olshtain and Cohen (1990) study involving direct intervention would suggest that the fine points of speech act behavior such as types of intensification, subtle differences between strategy realizations, and consideration of situational features can be taught. A lingering question is that of how successfully such forms are retrieved in a genuine language-using situation—either in comprehending a speech act used by someone else or in producing one. This question is of interest expressly because of the complex nature of such speech forms.

SUMMING UP

The first section of this chapter not only presented findings showing that associations help in the retention of vocabulary over time, but also made the point that real world conditions may not resemble those attained in a laboratory experiment. The findings with respect to vocabulary learning by association suggest that contextualized learning is more beneficial for the intermediate or advanced learners, and furthermore that the more proficient student may ultimately have an easier time finding associations. It also appeared that the learner's continued use of associations for troublesome words was more beneficial than trying to recognize or produce such words without the extra memory aid.

The chapter also dealt with varied means for learning about attending patterns of learners in a typical foreign language classroom. While videotaping revealed that learners pay differential attention to each other, depending on various sociocultural and linguistic factors, questionnaires distributed after interrupting a class session suggested that learners may tune out as much as 50 percent of what is going on in class. Knowledge of such a reality might provide teachers with an answer to their often-heard query as to why what was taught was not learned.

In addition, the chapter took a look at how nonnatives perform the speech act of apologizing in comparison to natives. The analysis demonstrated the various influences that a learner has when attempting to perform such acts: the possible negative influence of how it is done in the native language (i.e., negative transfer), deficiency in linguistic knowledge, and lack of awareness of seemingly unimportant modifications of such speech acts—such as, intensification ("really" vs. "very"). Actually, advanced learners were seen to select apology strategies similar to those used by natives and even to select similar forms for realizing these strategies for the most part, but to differ in their lack of awareness of modification strategies.

The chapter concluded by showing how the increasing empirical data regarding what natives do in these complex speech situations can actually be fed into minitraining courses (in this case, three 20-minute sessions) to help learners apologize (or realize whatever speech act) in a more nativelike manner.

FURTHER READINGS

Vocabulary Learning

For readers who wish to explore the issue of the learner's mental lexicon, there is a fine book on the acquisition of *native language* vocabulary, edited by McKeown and Curtis, which contains insights on target language vocabulary acquisition as well. The following is a description of one chapter from the book.

Elshout-Mohr, M. and van Daalen-Kapteijns, M. M. 1987. Cognitive processes in learning word meanings. In McKeown, M. G. & Curtis, M. E. (eds.), *The nature of vocabulary acquisition*. Hillsdale, NJ: Lawrence Erlbaum, 53–71. Verbal comprehension is seen as knowledge about word meanings from two sources: the number of word meanings known and the quality of each word meaning. Greater success is expected if the individual has a greater number of knowledge units, if each unit is well structured and can be used as a schema to decontextualize information, and if each unit can be accessed in an efficient way.

There are at least three new books on *target language* vocabulary that include mention of research findings in their coverage of vocabulary learning.

Carter, R. 1987. *Vocabulary: Applied linguistic perspectives*. London: Allen & Unwin. The book explores the notion of core vocabulary and a good portion of Chapter 7 is devoted to research on the learning of vocabulary.
Carter, R. and McCarthy, M. 1988. *Vocabulary and language teaching*. London: Longman. In this volume, the authors provide an update as to what is known about the learning and teaching of target language lexicon, as well as including useful papers from colleagues on new directions in vocabulary research.
Nation, I. S. P. 1990. *Teaching and learning vocabulary*. New York: Newbury House/ Harper & Row. The book considers the goals of vocabulary learning and vocabulary size, the factors involved in learning words, and vocabulary learning associated with the four language skills, and refers frequently to the theoretical and empirical literature.

Most of the research literature on *mnemonics* is on native language vocabulary learning through mnemonics. Target language learning through mnemonics has tended to be relegated to student theses—for example, E. J. Fuentes, An investigation into the use of imagery and generativity in learning a foreign language vocabulary. Unpublished doctoral dissertation, Stanford University, 1976. The leaders in research on the use of mnemonics in language learning have been Michael Pressley and Joel Levin. The following are several of their key review articles.

Levin, J. R., Pressley, M., McCormick, C. B., Miller, G. E., and Shriberg, L. K. 1979. Assessing the classroom potential of the keyword method. *Journal of Educational Psychology, 71* (5), 583–594. This review article found the best results for the keyword method in learning concrete nouns in Spanish among elementary school children. Results at the high school level were less satisfactory. The article contrasts the success of the keyword method in a highly structured laboratorylike setting with its diminished success in the classroom.

Pressley, M., Levin, J. R., and Delaney, H. D. 1982. The mnemonic keyword method. *Review of Educational Research, 52,* 61–91. This article reviews research on the keyword approach to vocabulary learning, comparing it to other means of vocabulary learning. The article examines some of the issues of controversy with respect to use of mnemonics such as whether teachers should supply them.

Pressley, M., Levin, J. R., and McDaniel, M. A. 1987. Remembering versus inferring what a word means: Mnemonic and contextual approaches. In McKeown, M. G. and Curtis, M. E. (eds.), *The nature of vocabulary acquisition.* Hilisdale, NJ: Lawrence Erlbaum, 107–127. The authors distinguish two distinct goals of vocabulary instruction: *remembering* and *inferring.* A review of research in both areas leads the authors to the conclusion that if the purpose is to maximize remembering, then the mnemonic approach is the appropriate strategy. If the objective is to enhance other aspects of vocabulary acquisition and use, then inferring may work—but there is a need for training in how to use internal or external contextual clues systematically and efficiently. The authors are critical of approaches to inferring meanings through contextual clues, suggesting that Sternberg's (1987) system has not been tested rigorously enough at the empirical level, as has the mnemonic method. Also, they feel that the mnemonic approach is facilitative of word comprehension, as is the inferential approach. (This bibliographic item also has relevance to research on reading, discussed in Chapter 8.)

Attending

For a treatment of different models for attention, a book by Wingfield and Byrnes has a useful chapter.

Wingfield, A. and Byrnes, D. L. 1981. *The psychology of human memory.* New York: Academic Press. In Chapter 6, the authors discuss different aspects of attention, such as that of "alertness" which is the relevant one for target language classrooms. Among other things, they discuss "time-sharing" and "capacity" models of attention and bring research evidence to bear in their discussion of each.

In target language research, the focus has been more on the aural comprehension of specific input such as lectures in subject areas than on what is attended to more generally in language classrooms—for example:

Chaudron, C. 1985. A method for examining the input/intake distinction. In S. M. Gass and C. G. Madden (eds.), *Input in second language acquisition*. New York: Newbury House/Harper & Row, 285–300. The author begins by noting that "very little research has explored the connection between input and intake" in target language learning. The researcher was particularly interested in studying the learners' initial perception and segmenting of the input. He reported on the use of a partial dictation recall measure and a listening cloze procedure with EFL students, who viewed two videotaped minilectures on science topics. The tapes were intermittently interrupted to have the learners complete the recall or the cloze task. The respondents also had to indicate whether statements on a summary comprehension quiz were identical to statements made in the lecture. Although the tasks were found to be too easy, the research was seen as a model for the kinds of probes that could be undertaken to determine learners' perceptions of input.

The assumption is often made that what is attended to is what is taught—especially with respect to the more innovative methods such as Suggestopedia, Counseling Learning, and Silent Way. As this chapter has suggested, the reality may be that learners are attending differentially to different input. The problem is that the literature has yet to explore this phenomenon in any depth. One thrust intended to gain insights into the learning process is that of *verbal report* studies. These studies include any efforts to have learners think aloud while they are performing a target language task (e.g., reading) or observe their learning introspectively or retrospectively.

One form of self-observation is that of the diary studies, wherein a learner (or a teacher) records an introspective or retrospective account of his or her own learning or teaching. For readers interested in pursuing this means of obtaining classroom data, here are two references.

Bailey, K. M. and Ochsner, R. 1983. A methodological review of the diary studies: Windmill tilting or social science? In K. M. Bailey, M. H. Long, and S. Peck (eds.), *Second language acquisition studies*. New York: Newbury House/Harper & Row, 188–198. This paper describes available diary studies with a concern for consolidating knowledge about diary studies and thus encouraging the proliferation of such studies. Diary studies are seen as constituting preliminary research for the basis for generating hypotheses.

Bailey, K. M. 1983. Competitiveness and anxiety in adult second language learning: Looking *at* and *through* the diary studies. In H. W. Seliger and M. H. Long (eds.), *Classroom oriented research in second language acquisition*. New York: Newbury House/Harper & Row, 67–103. In this chapter, Bailey demonstrates how diary data can be used to focus on specific aspects of language learning, in this case, on competitiveness and anxiety. She supports the findings from her own diary with those from a series of other (unpublished) studies. She also discusses some contributions the diary study methodology can make to an understanding of second language acquisition.

We note that whereas diaries have not been utilized specifically for the purpose of gathering information on attending strategies, they could be a potential source of data concerning the nature of these strategies.

For researchers interested in exploring alternative means of using verbal reports for obtaining data on attending and on other areas, the Faerch and Kasper volume provides a useful collection of theoretical papers and empirical studies:

Faerch, C. and Kasper, G. 1987. *Introspection in second language research*. Clevedon, England: Multilingual Matters. This volume begins with theoretical descriptions of verbal report measures by Faerch and Kasper, Ericsson and Simon, Grotjahn, and others. It also includes papers which make use of verbal reports in researching lexical search and lexical inferencing, translation, reading, finding compensatory strategies in speaking, and taking word completion tests.

Speech Acts

Perhaps the latest and most up-to-date compendium of the speech act studies is that contained in a new book by Wolfson.

Wolfson, N. 1989. *Perspectives: Sociolinguistics and TESOL*. Chapters 4 through 7 deal most directly with speech act behavior, both in terms of what natives and nonnatives do. The book is also concerned with the methodological issues associated with researching such phenomena.

Another recent book of interest to researchers reports on the findings from a large-scale cross-cultural study of speech acts.

Blum-Kulka, S., House-Edmondson, J., and Kasper, G. (eds.). 1989. *Cross-cultural pragmatics: Requests and apologies*. Norwood, NJ: Ablex. The book describes a large international research program, the Cross-Cultural Speech Act Realization Project (CCSARP). The aim of the project was to describe similarities and differences between L1 and L2 realization patterns of requests and apologies across languages—English (British, American, and Australian), Canadian French, Danish, German, Hebrew, and Russian.

Chapter *8*

Research on Reading
and Writing

In this chapter we will look at some of the research studies that led to the insights converted into points for learners in Chapters 5 and 6 on reading and writing. The chapter also includes a section of "Further Readings" which contains abstracts of other research literature which deals directly or indirectly with strategies in reading and writing.

RESEARCH ON READING

The following is a description of studies that I conducted or supervised, which had as their purpose better understanding of problems encountered in reading texts in a foreign language. The results from these studies were instrumental in formulating the types of insights presented in Chapter 5 above.

Initial Case Studies on Problems in Reading Technical Discourse

The first set of studies on the reading process were an outgrowth of work done with an expert, native-speaking informant concerning a technical text in the field of biology (see Selinker 1979). This work was, in turn, a response to the growing awareness in the late 1970s of the crucial role that different text types of written discourse played in the processing of text (see Selinker & Trimble 1974, for one of the early papers). Out of working with this expert informant in his efforts to interpret the text, it became clear that what was lacking in the study of specialized texts were the interpretations of nonnative students who actually had to read the text as a requirement in their university biology course. In other words, the expert in the field had explained what the text meant to him, rather than having the nonnative students report on what the text had meant to them.[1]

Hence, a series of four studies were conducted to determine the nature of text processing in various areas—general biology, genetics, political science, and history (Cohen et al. 1979). At that time the focus was exclusively on those aspects of text which a group of teacher-researchers predicted to be problematic for readers in three areas: heavy noun phrase subjects or objects,[2] syntactic markers of cohesion,[3] and the role of nontechnical vocabulary in technical texts.[4]

Procedures   The studies were all case studies with limited numbers of informants who were undergraduates at the Hebrew University of Jerusalem—one in the genetics study, two in the biology study, one in the political science study, and eight in the history study. All the informants were native Hebrew speakers except for five English-speaking readers serving as a comparison group in the history study. In the first three studies (genetics, biology, and political science), the student informants were instructed to underline all vocabulary and structures that they found difficult to understand in the text that they were given to read. In the biology and political science studies, the informants underlined the problem areas before the interview sessions. In the political science study, the informant also made note of which words he looked up in the dictionary.

For all four studies, the researchers prepared sets of points to investigate. For the genetics study, the investigator (Glasman) prepared questions based on a series of lexical and grammatical categories that she predicted would be problematic for her informant. Then, she asked probing questions about those lexical and grammatical items that she had identified as problematic but which her informant had not underlined as such. For the biology and political science studies, the researchers (Cohen, Rosenbaum-Cohen, and Ferrara) analyzed the texts in consort with a group of some

---

[1]In a subsequent study by Huckin and Olsen (1984), the actual author of the text was asked to accept or refute the interpretations of his Hebrew University colleague regarding the meaning that he had intended the text to have. He often concurred with his colleague in the interpretation of the major points. Discrepancies tended to deal with questions of lexicon and grammar. The author of the article felt that a closer editing may have eradicated these ambiguous forms from the text.

[2]The term *heavy* with respect to noun phrase subjects or objects was borrowed from Berman (1984) and was intended to suggest that such constructions, although not necessarily appearing lengthy or complex, were nonetheless difficult to process.

[3]This refers to conjunctive words—i.e., words which grammatically signal the interconnection of sentences within a text (e.g., "however," "thus," "also," and "finally") (Halliday and Hasan 1976).

[4]By nontechnical vocabulary in technical texts, we were referring to nontechnical words which may (1) take on a technical meaning in a particular field (Cowan 1974, referred to these as *subtechnical vocabulary*), (2) appear as contextual paraphrases or synonymous phrases for other words or phrases, (3) form part of a specialized nontechnical lexis (e.g., vocabulary items indicating time sequence, measurement, or truth validity).

six or so other EFL teachers and developed a series of questions on the basis of a checklist of features in reading technical English.

The checklist encompassed the following broad categories: graphic organization, rhetorical principles or devices, grammar, and vocabulary. In these first three studies, the researchers' questions focused explicitly on areas predicted to be problematic for the readers—by asking directly whether some word or structure was a problem for them. In the biology and the political science studies, after students had indicated whether a word or structure was problematic, they were also asked whether, in retrospect, this word or structure interfered with comprehension of the sentence, section, or overall passage. In the fourth, the history study, the focus was different; it was not overtly on problematic areas but rather on comprehension. The researchers (Cohen and Fine) asked both *macro-level* comprehension questions, or questions which required some integration or generalization from specific sentences in order to answer, and *micro-level* questions, questions which were focused directly on specific sentences or parts of sentences.

In the genetics and political science studies and in sessions with native English speakers in the history study, the informants were interviewed individually by one or more interviewers. The two subjects in the biology study and the three subjects in the history study were interviewed in a group. Sessions in the biology, political science, and history studies were tape recorded. Although methodological approaches varied, the findings from the different case studies converged.

Findings   Let us look briefly at the major findings, and then consider the implications with respect to the improvement of reading in a foreign language.

Heavy Noun Phrases   As it turned out, heavy noun phrases, in various syntactic functions (e.g., subject of the main clause, subject of a subordinate clause, or object of the preposition), not only caused difficulties for informants across all four studies but were among the few structures that were predictably problematic for students. In the genetics study, for example, all but one of the seven sentences that the informant identified as being problematic had heavy noun phrases in them. An example from the text was presented above in Chapter 5 (p. 83)—that of a 16-word clause functioning as the subject of a subordinate sentence (". . . such treatments as holding cells in buffer after irradiation before placing them on nutrient agar plates . . .").

In the biology study, the text produced troublesome sentences like the following:

> In many unicellular organisms and in some lower plants, nuclei contributing to the zygote are transferred between two cells without the

> formation of obviously specialized gametes by processes such as partial
> and temporary fusion (*conjugation*) of ciliated protozoans. (V. Novikoff
> and E. Holtzman. 1976. *Cells and organelles*. 2nd ed. New York: Holt,
> Rinehart and Winston, 332.)

In this sentence, the relatively short noun phrase subject, "nuclei contributing to the zygote" was troublesome because it was not perceived as one unit.

In the political science study, the informant missed the purpose of the paper because the purpose was stated as the noun phrase object of a preposition.

> The purpose of this paper is to try to redress the resulting imbalance
> by concentrating detailed attention upon the multiple functions, i.e.,
> observable consequences, of voting for individuals and of elections for
> political systems in contemporary societies. (Rose & Mossiwir
> 1967:173–174)

In the history study, we did not ask about structures directly, but rather assessed their difficulty indirectly through comprehension questions. For example, the students were asked to focus on the following paragraph:

> The gap between East and West has also been widened by a growing
> discrepancy in material standards of living. Nowhere is the contrast
> sharper than between Americans and the peoples of Asia. In part be-
> cause of accidents of history and geography, we enjoy a far more fa-
> vorable balance between population and natural resources than do they.
> As a result we live on an economic plane that appears unattainable by
> them under existing conditions. This economic gap perpetuates and
> sometimes heightens the difference between our respective attitudes
> and ways of life. (E. O. Reischauer and J. K. Fairbank. 1960. *East Asia:
> The great tradition*. New York: Houghton Mifflin, 6)

Then the students were asked as a micro question, "Which people have the better balance between population and natural resources?" They answered correctly, "The West." The informants were then asked, "Why?" a question which was meant to probe whether or not they correctly interpreted the adverbial modifier with its noun phrase object "In part because of accidents of history and geography." The natives gave the correct answer right away. One nonnative answered, "Because they understand the existing conditions," and another mentioned "economic plane." So, in this case they appear to have misinterpreted or neglected the embedded noun phrase about historical and geographical accidents.

Syntactic Markers of Cohesion   All four studies revealed that learners were not picking up on the conjunctive words signaling cohesion, not even the more basic ones like "however" and "thus." The informant in the genetics study, for example, noted that she had never known the meaning of "thus," and had simply thought it marked off sentences.

Perhaps the most striking example of difficulty in processing markers of cohesion appeared in the history study, specifically with respect to the sequential correlatives "also" and "finally." The students were asked the macro question, "Why do the authors favor the historical approach?" in reference to the following partially excerpted passage.

> *The Approach to East Asia Through Its History.*   The historical approach seems to us the best for a number of reasons. One is that the peoples of East Asia, more than those of the rest of the world, see themselves in historical perspective. They are strongly aware of their heritage from the past and also conscious of the historical judgment of the future. To approach them through their history is to look at them as they see themselves, which is the first requisite for understanding.
>
> The historical approach is also necessary for a clear understanding of the major aspects of our subject. . . .
>
> A clear understanding of the traditional cultures of those countries, finally is essential to any comprehension of what is happening in East Asia today. . . . (Reischauer & Fairbank, 7–8)

The rationale for the question was to see if students could perceive the cross-paragraph structure, particularly as signaled by these conjunctive elements. We thought that there were three reasons why the authors of the text, Reischauer & Fairbank, favored the historical approach. The natives gave all three reasons, and two of the natives reanalyzed the first reason into three separate reasons, which included "seeing selves in historical perspective," "heritage," and "seeing future judgment in historical terms." The nonnatives did not mention the second and third reasons at all. One spoke of "heritage" and another mentioned "consciousness of historical judgment." Thus, the nonnatives, unlike the natives, did not organize the material that they had read when that organization stretched across different paragraphs, although cross-paragraph markers of cohesion were provided in the text.

Clearly, the task of finding the markers of cohesion is a part of good reading generally, even in the native language. But there is more to the task than basic native reading ability and speed. The nonnatives were not attuned to recognizing the conjunctive words, whereas the natives' responses would suggest that these words played a significant role in their understanding of the passage. Upon closer scrutiny of the text, we note that "also" and "finally" are not conspicuously placed in their respective sentences. In fact, "finally" appears after a long (10-word) noun phrase subject. Such conjunctive words may have particularly little functional value if, in fact, nonnatives read more locally than do natives—in other words, if they have more difficulty linking up parts of sentences, linking sentences with other sentences, and linking paragraphs with other paragraphs.

The Role of Nontechnical Vocabulary in Technical Texts   The series of studies indicated that knowing the technical terms (i.e., terms that have a specialized meaning in a particular field and are used consistently in that field) was not a sufficient condition for successful reading of specialized material. It was, in fact, the nontechnical terms which created more of a problem, as less than a quarter of the problematic words on the average proved to be technical. The informants did not give an accurate translation or target language paraphrase of a surprisingly large number of nontechnical words in context (e.g., "essential," "efficient," "required," "determined," "pattern," "distinctive," "invariable," "assertion," "ambiguities," and "discrepancy"). Specialized nontechnical vocabulary was especially problematic—for example, time lexes such as "succeeding," "preceding," "simultaneously," "consecutively," and "subsequent."

A second area of difficulty was that of nontechnical words taking on a technical meaning in a particular field and the nonnative reader being aware of only one of these meanings (either the technical or the nontechnical one). An example from the genetics text was the term "recognition," which in context appeared to suggest that a particular damage referred to had to be recognized or noticed in some way by the scientist. Checking with a specialist in the field, we learned that the term had a technical meaning in this text; that is, there is some biological system present in the organism that becomes aware that damage has occurred (Selinker 1979).

Still another area of difficulty with respect to vocabulary concerned *contextual paraphrase*, that is, the use of two (or more) words, or phrases, to refer to the same concept. For example, in the genetics study which dealt with the reading of a text on the repair of genetic material in living cells, "repair processes" appeared 10 times in the text, "repair mechanism" four times, "repair mode" three times, and "repair scheme" three times. According to the specialist consultant (a biology professor), "repair processes" and "repair mechanism" were contextual paraphrases in that text, as were "repair mode" and "repair scheme," but the former pair were technically more specific than the latter. Thus, the burden on the nonnative reader was not only to perceive that there were contextually synonymous phrases in the text, but also to determine which were equivalent to which.

Implications for the Foreign Language Learner   The research described above demonstrated among other things that readers from different fields, reading different types of texts and providing information about their reading in somewhat different ways, nonetheless displayed similar types of problems with respect to heavy noun phrases, forms signaling grammatical cohesion, and problematic nontechnical vocabulary. Whereas the study actually began with the question "What is problematic in reading texts from specialized fields in a foreign language?," it ended with the question, "How do learners go about solving problems in reading?" While the former yields findings as to language forms that the reader needs to learn, the latter yields insights into cognitive strategies that need to be learned. Since forms vary in the meaning that is attached to them depending on the text and may even have several acceptable meanings within the same text, readers who have a repertoire of strategies for interpreting such forms are more likely to comprehend the text successfully.

With respect to heavy noun phrases, strategic readers recognize them as such and, in cases where such phrases seem to impair understanding, they assign a meaning that is consistent with the discourse of the particular passage. Although *cohesion* is certainly a lower-level element in obtaining meaning from a text than is *coherence*, correct identification of cohesive markers has been shown here to play an important role in upper-level reading comprehension, a role that the more successful reader usually bears in mind. Finally, better readers may well be cognizant of different categories of nontechnical vocabulary. As to the meanings of the words themselves, these readers are aware that the meanings of such words might vary from text to text and that, for this reason, each text needs to be considered in some ways as a separate entity.

Mentalistic Studies of Reading Comprehension

A series of studies has been conducted since the earlier studies reported above, usually as seminar papers or dissertations. The following is a brief account of some of these.

A Taxonomy for Reading Strategies   As noted in Chapter 5, an in-depth study of high school readers of Hebrew as a native language and English as a foreign language identified 126 strategies and organized them into four types which she referred to then as: technical-aid moves, clarification and simplification moves, coherence-detecting moves, and monitoring moves (Sarig 1985, 1987, 1990). In Chapter 5, they are referred to in more lay terms as support strategies, paraphrase strategies, strategies for establishing coherence in text, and strategies for supervising strategy use, respectively. The real contribution of this research was to lend a categorical perspective to the analysis of a morass of reading strategies. The first three categories were seen to be roughly hierarchical and the fourth a metacategory applying to all the other three. Sarig's study stimulated other studies such as the one to be described next.

The Relationship Between the Number and Variety of Reading Strategies and Success at Foreign Language Reading   An in-depth study of two intermediate-level university EFL readers, a high and a low performer, was conducted (Zupnik 1985), and it was found that Sarig's taxonomy was an effective tool in comparing the types of moves employed by the two readers. In the study, the low performer used more moves and a larger variety of moves than the high performer, but with less successful results, which seemed to refute Olshavsky's (1976/1977) findings that the high performer uses more reading strategies than the low performer.

The explanation appeared when analyzing the types of strategies employed. The low performer was involved mostly in clarification and simplification strategies (e.g., the identification and analysis of specific vocabulary items), while the high performer was focusing more on monitoring strategies (e.g., a critical analysis of the questions asked, self-evaluation of reading success, awareness of lack of comprehension). Also, most of the low reader's strategies had a deterring effect on comprehension whereas almost all of the high performer's strategies were comprehension promoting.

Determining Similarities Between First and Foreign Language Reading   Sarig's case study described above was actually part of a larger study in which 140 Israeli college-bound high school seniors participated. Aside from the taxonomy of reading strategies, another contribution of the study was the finding that readers differ considerably in the way that they tackle a high-level reading task. The subjects were asked to read Hebrew and English texts which had been equated for difficulty by means of (1) a scale of pragmatic, textual, and linguistic variables assessed by expert readers, (2) a discourse cloze,[5] and (3) a comparative rhetorical analysis between the texts. The respondents were trained in how to provide verbal report data: they received a sheet with examples of mentalistic data, were given a demonstration of think-aloud and introspective techniques by the researcher, and then practiced verbalizing actively with the researcher supervising and giving support (Sarig 1985).

Sarig's research provided various insights regarding similarities between first and foreign language reading. With respect to combinations of strategies, moves in the two languages correlated highly for each of the 10 readers. Eight of the 10 readers transferred their first language reading style to reading in the foreign language. Of the two who did not, one was an intermediate reader and the other a poor reader in the foreign language. Sarig interpreted these findings as indicating that ability to transfer reading skills from first to foreign language is not dependent on foreign language

[5]A test wherein only those words are deleted which mark, in one way or another, relationships between propositions (Levenston, Nir, & Blum-Kulka 1984:207).

proficiency, but rather is an individual cognitive trait. Likewise, she found that successful transfer of strategies to the foreign language did not necessarily promote comprehension. Both low- and high-performing readers were characterized by transfer of moves that promoted and deterred comprehension, and in almost all cases the readers differed from one another with regard to the extent of transfer and the degree to which it promoted comprehension.

Sarig also found that differences across individuals characterized both first and foreign language reading. There were found to be four dimensions along which individuals differed in their strategy behavior: (1) the actual combination of strategies utilized, (2) the subtask that contributed most to success in reading, (3) the frequency of use of each strategy, and (4) the extent of transfer and whether it had positive or negative effects.

There was only one noticeable area where a given reader's strategies were found to differ across languages. With respect to clarification and simplification moves, especially the moves involving the decoding of propositions (or information units), there was a low correlation between comprehension-promoting moves in first and foreign language. The explanation that the researcher gave was that clarification and simplification strategies were more dependent on language proficiency than were the other sets of reading strategies in her taxonomy. Hence, it was easier to identify propositions or basic ideas in a first language than in a foreign language, which accounted for the nonsignificant correlation.

Whereas a *short-circuit hypothesis* has been posited stipulating that readers will not transfer their reading skills to the second language if their language proficiency in that language has not reached a certain threshold level (Clarke 1979), Sarig's findings suggested to her that a *compensation hypothesis* might more accurately reflect the situation as revealed through her research, namely, that when readers lack adequate second language proficiency, they will rely on first language strategies *more* than they do in their first language. This reliance is intended to compensate in part for lack of foreign language proficiency. This hypothesis is in line with Stanovich's (1980) *interactive compensatory model of reading* and with the empirical findings of Perkins (1983) and Haynes (1983).

Strategies for Comprehending Target Language Vocabulary

Two studies on target language vocabulary were conducted under my supervision in Brazil, both concerned with the strategies that learners use in understanding foreign language vocabulary. The first study, a replication of Bensoussan and Laufer (1984), dealt with the extent to which context aids in determining meanings of words and the nature of lexical inference strategies (Teixeira 1987). Five advanced EFL students at the B.A. level served as respondents for the study. The subjects were given a list of 40 EFL words without context and were requested to provide a translation into Portuguese. The words selected were considered to have meanings that could be guessed from context.

A week later the subjects received the words in the context of the text from which they were extracted. After reading the text, the subjects had individual interview sessions in which they were asked three general reading comprehension questions, and then were given the list of 40 English words for which they were once again asked to supply Portuguese translations. As the subjects assigned meanings to the words, they were asked to verbalize the lexical inference strategies they used, including indicating which context assisted them, if any. If they left items blank, they were to indicate what stopped them from assigning meanings. Whereas some of these reports were of a think-aloud nature (i.e., immediate, unanalyzed verbal reports of thought processes), most of them reflected retrospective self-observation (delayed inspection of thought processes).

The quantitative results for the five subjects showed that with only 17 percent of the words the use of context facilitated guessing of meaning. The most popular lexical inference strategy was found to be that of using words most immediately adjacent to the unknown word. If that did not work, then subjects reread the entire phrase containing the word. Often this strategy was not successful, but the respondents continued to use it, rather than looking for clues to meaning in other sentences. Another popular strategy was to analyze the word to see if it was a cognate with Portuguese or if it had recognizable segments. In various instances the respondent understood the word but was unable to find an equivalent in Portuguese. The protocol data also showed that in some cases, subjects were wary of assuming that English words were cognates with Portuguese when, in fact, they actually were. For example, "intangible" is equivalent to *intangível* in Portuguese, yet subjects did not see the link or accept them as true cognates.

The strategies that were actually shown to produce the best results were top-down inferences based on knowledge of the topic of the text and inferences based on intersentential context. The subjects' conclusion that the context did not help them much was based on a distorted view of what *using the context* meant. Their use of context was limited only to the context immediately adjacent to the word and/or to the somewhat broader intrasentential context.

In the second study, the aim was to determine the words that students would identify as cognates in an EFL text and to investigate how learners used these cognates in reading the text (Rodríguez 1986). Seventeen Brazilian graduate students participated in the study. The students were requested to underline and translate into Portuguese all the words that were similar to Portuguese in an English passage of 460 words, of which 95 were actually cognates. When the students' comprehension of the text as a whole was correlated with ability to identify cognates, there was found to be a significant correlation between the ability to recognize cognates in context and the ability to comprehend the text. Four of the students provided verbal reports as well. The verbal protocols showed that the students did look for cognates and other unknown words in order to understand the text. Most cognates were identified in the initial quick reading of the text.

The Implications of the Mentalistic Studies   The findings from this series of studies would offer various pointers for improving foreign language reading. Sarig's (1987) taxonomy can help a learner to see that there are different levels of strategies—from the lower-level support strategies such as underlining and marginal notetaking to the higher-level strategies for determining the overall meaning of the text. On a practical level, the average reader may simply need to learn a few of these strategies. This calls for a diagnosis of each reader's individual reading profile, which can then serve as a basis for deciding which strategies to teach or unteach.

Zupnik's study would suggest that the use of a few well-placed strategies may be more effective than the use of a large variety. It would appear that the conscious use of higher-level strategies in conjunction with lower-level ones—under the supervision of metacognitive strategies—is likely to produce the best results in reading.

We learned in Sarig's work that it is natural to fall back on native language reading strategies for reading in a foreign language. This practice can help us up to a certain point. Once we go beyond our level of linguistic knowledge, it becomes difficult or impossible to comprehend a text even if reading strategies are used effectively—unless we are called upon to perform low-level recoding or decoding (see Chapter 5).

Teixeira's study pointed out the limited use that learners make of context in guessing unknown words. Her work would suggest that a reader who looks beyond the immediate sentence for clues to the meaning of an unknown word may do better than the reader who only looks for more local clues. Finally, Rodríguez' study would suggest that the reader who looks for cognates as a way to facilitate reading in a foreign language may be more likely to understand the vocabulary of a text than someone who does not. Obviously it would make a difference if the two languages have numerous cognates, like English and Portuguese, as opposed to few, like English and Hebrew.

RESEARCH ON WRITING.

Research on the Feedback Process

Survey Research on Student Processing of Feedback   While teachers may spend hours marking student papers, the question has been raised as to whether such corrections make a difference (Marzano & Arthur 1977, Semke 1984). It has been suggested that when students get their written work returned to them embellished by teacher corrections, they simply groan, put it away, and hope that somehow they will get fewer red marks next time (Raimes 1983). It has been noted that teachers tend to concern themselves more often with accuracy in form—that is, with surface-level features of writing—than with meaning. Furthermore, their feedback has been found to reflect misreadings of the text which have led to misguided feedback, as well as corrections and recommendations that are unclear or imprecise (Zamel 1985). Given this state of affairs, the question arises as to the extent to which learners pay attention to teacher feedback and what they do with it.

A survey was undertaken to obtain verbal report data from students of first and second languages regarding the way that they relate to teacher comments on the papers they write (Cohen 1987a). The study sought to determine whether there was justification in providing students access to a repertoire of processing strategies for dealing with feedback. The query that motivated the study was whether without such a repertoire, most students would simply ignore teacher feedback.

The students were 217 American university students. All were studying in courses in which the writing of papers and the receiving of teacher feedback was an integral part. The courses that they participated in included native English rhetoric, ESL, French, German, and Hebrew as a foreign language. A questionnaire was designed that would be brief (one page) yet informative regarding the form and substance of teacher feedback and the ways in which learners dealt with this feedback. It asked the respondents to think of the last paper that their teacher had returned to them (usually one or two days prior to receiving the questionnaire). The survey questionnaire was not administered at the same time that the students were given their papers back so as to avoid the possibility that it would influence their handling of teacher's comments.

The findings revealed that, whereas most students read over all or most of a paper returned to them and attended to all or most of the corrections, still one-fifth of the students surveyed reported doing so only sparingly or not at all. The self-rated poorer learners were also less likely to read through the paper and attend to the corrections. For the students who were attending to comments, these teacher comments were being transmitted primarily in the format of single words or short phrases, dealing primarily with mechanics and grammar, both in the elementary and in the more advanced courses. When students indicated that they did not understand teacher comments, these comments tended, in fact, to be in the most frequently used form, namely, in single words or short phrases such as "confusing" or "not clear."

Not only did students report paying considerable attention to teacher comments concerning mechanics and grammar, but they also reported paying much attention to comments regarding vocabulary, organization, and content—areas where teacher comments were reportedly lacking. Those rating themselves as better learners paid more attention to comments on vocabulary, grammar, and mechanics than did poorer learners. With regard to the strategies that students used for processing the feedback, the most popular by far seemed to be that of simply making a mental note of the teacher's comment. The rewriting of papers was reportedly limited and more prevalent among students who rated themselves as poor writers—apparently because these students had more surface errors that their teachers required them to fix up.

The results of this survey suggested that the activity of teacher feedback as currently constituted and realized might have more limited impact on the learners than the teachers would desire. It appeared that often there was somewhat of a mismatch between the type of information sought by the learners (i.e., feedback on content, organization, and vocabulary) and that provided by their teachers (i.e., feedback on grammar and mechanics).[6] The results prompted more in-depth studies of the feedback process, and so a series of such studies was undertaken.

Case Study Research on the Feedback Process   Three small-scale studies aimed at investigating in greater detail the relationship between what teachers provide as feedback on compositions and what students think about and do with the feedback were conducted in Brazil (Cohen and Cavalcanti 1987a, 1987b, in press). One study dealt with feedback on Portuguese L1 compositions and the other two studies with feedback on EFL compositions. The Portuguese L1 study and one of the EFL studies were carried out at the university level. The other EFL study was conducted at an adult language institute. The studies called for the three teachers to provide verbal report protocol data, while making written comments on the compositions of three students (a high, intermediate, and low performer, respectively) selected from each teacher's classroom, and then to fill out a questionnaire. The students selected also provided verbal report protocols concerning their reactions to the feedback and filled out a questionnaire about their handling of the feedback, as did the other students in their respective classes.

The findings included a description of what the teachers felt they gave as feedback, what the students perceived them as giving, the feedback that was actually given, what students understood of that feedback, their in-

---

[6]A recent survey of 158 high intermediate ESL students in New York City yielded somewhat different results—that learners preferred feedback regarding grammar and vocabulary to the correction of ordering of ideas and connectors. Learners also expressed a preference for teacher correction directed at the whole class as opposed to peer correction while working in pairs of students or groups of four (Ultsch, Tragant, & Orkin 1989).

tended strategies for dealing with it, and their preferences for feedback. While the fit between teachers' and students' perceptions and the actual feedback situation was generally good, there were certain mismatches between what the students wanted and what they received. Generally speaking, the students wanted more feedback on content and organization than their teachers provided. Furthermore, the students' repertoire of strategies for handling feedback was found to be limited. For the most part, students simply made a mental note of teachers' comments rather than recording the feedback systematically. If they felt they did not understand a comment, they indicated that they would be more likely to ask the teacher than to consult a grammar book, a dictionary, a peer, or a previous composition. These findings are consistent with those from the earlier survey research mentioned above (e.g., Cohen 1987a).

The Implications of the Research on Teacher Feedback   The findings from the studies described above would suggest the advisability of training students at all proficiency levels in the use of alternative strategies to the ones that they are currently using. One such strategy for those who were not using it would be the judicious use of revision, incorporating the teacher's comments. Both the teachers in the survey research from New York State (Cohen 1987a) and in the EFL case studies from Brazil (Cohen & Cavalcanti 1987a, 1987b, in press) indicated that as a rule their students did not revise their compositions except, perhaps, for writing in a correction on the original essay above the teacher's comment. In the New York study, apparently only the poorer students revised in what amounted to rewriting the paper so as to clean up a number of surface errors. In effect, then, there seems to be a tendency for the rewriting of papers to be conducted —if at all—at the level of surface edits for grammar and mechanics, and not at that of revision for content, organization, and vocabulary.

The feedback situation as reflected by this line of research is probably not atypical of situations in many classrooms where writing is taught around the world. In other words, there are benefits to be accrued from the typical approaches to feedback, yet there appear to be missing ingredients. One such ingredient is a clear agreement between teacher and student as to what will be commented on and how such comments might be categorized. Another such ingredient would be the discussion of possible repertoires of strategies students could use in order to derive maximum benefit from the feedback provided by the teacher. Clear teacher-student agreements as to feedback procedures and student training in repertoires of strategies for handling feedback could lead to more productive and enjoyable composition writing in the classroom.

Research on Reformulation

The research conducted on the technique of reformulation was prompted by an earlier case study with three students selected from an advanced ESL class which demonstrated that teacher and peer feedback is, at best, partial and unsystematic (Cohen & Robbins 1976). The results revealed a striking lack of consistency in feedback to students on written work over a 10-week university-level ESL course that I taught. When 15 samples of English writing from each of three Chinese speakers in the class were scrutinized, with a focus on the students' grammatical usage, it became clear that the corrections had been unsystematic—sometimes catching conspicuous errors, sometimes not. There was also inconsistency in the diagnosis of what the source of the problem was. And this was all with respect to a relatively simple area to give feedback on, namely, grammar. It could be assumed that systematic and consistent feedback on vocabulary, organization, and content is even more taxing of the teacher's skills.

The inconsistent and limited nature of teacher feedback in its traditional form, then, led me to seek more comprehensive forms of feedback. Levenston's reformulation technique appeared to provide an important complement to the typical form of error analysis that characterizes the feedback that learners usually receive with respect to their written work (Levenston 1978).

Levenston took an essay written in English by an eleventh-grade Israeli student and demonstrated how, even after surface errors were eliminated, the essay was still in need of correction of the kind often provided by teachers of native language composition—correction regarding problems such as lexical inadequacy, syntactic blending (two separate ideas in one syntactic construction), conceptual confusion, rhetorical deviance (after Kaplan 1966), and ambiguity. Levenston proposed that we distinguish a first stage aimed at removing "goofs," which he termed *reconstruction* (after Corder 1974) from a further stage of *reformulation* aimed at improving the style and clarity of thought. But he stopped short of proposing that such a technique be utilized in the second language classroom. He asked, ". . . what second-language teacher has time for such detailed treatment, much of which should be handled in the first-language classroom?" (Levenston 1978:11).

Initial Studies   Intrigued by the technique, I responded to Levenston's challenge and applied his idea to the second language classroom. While on sabbatical leave at the University of California, Los Angeles, in Fall 1980, I had foreign students in the advanced ESL writing class (English 106J) that I taught compare the revised version of an essay that each one wrote with a reformulated version. The students then had to produce a list of differences. Their response to the technique was quite positive. (For more details on what the reformulation technique entails, see Chapter 6.)

The preliminary research effort consisted of close-order comparisons of the revised student essay and the reformulation. For example, the following are the opening lines of a revised essay from a student in that course.

> If the time ever comes when a woman is elected to the presidency of the United States, how well will she perform? Will she be able to rule better than our male presidents have? Will she be able to handle the problems of running a country? In this essay, I'm going to answer these questions by analyzing the women who have ruled in other countries.
>
> One woman is Cleopatra. She became ruler of Egypt at the age of eighteen. Even at that young age she had a strong thrust for power . . .

With regard to the revisions suggested to the student, I had made no changes in the opening paragraph. In the second paragraph I had suggested changing the first sentence from "One woman is Cleopatra" to "One such woman leader is Cleopatra," and wrote the word "cohesion" in the margin. I had also changed "thrust" to "lust" in the second sentence of that paragraph, while the student probably meant "thirst."

The student then had the essay reformulated by a friend. The reformulation of this excerpt was as follows:

> How well will a woman perform if she is ever elected president of the United States? Will she execute the duties of her office better than males? Will she be able to handle our country's problems? In this essay I will explore these questions by analyzing women rulers of other countries.
>
> One such woman is Cleopatra. At the tender age of eighteen she ascended Egypt's highest office. Even at such an early age she had a strong compulsion for power. . . .

I then compared the slightly revised version to the reformulated one. In terms of selection of vocabulary, the native writer replaced or modified a number of the lexical phrases just in these few lines. For example, "able to rule" was replaced by "execute the duties of her office," "answer these questions" by "explore these questions," "become ruler of Egypt" by "ascended Egypt's highest office," "the age of eighteen" by "the tender age of eighteen," "young age" by "early age," and "lust for power" by "compulsion for power."

The native writer also replaced the informal "I'm going to (answer)" with "I will (explore)." In addition, the native supplied several questionable forms such as, "males" (line 2) instead of "men" or "a man," in contrast to "woman"; and "office" instead of perhaps "throne." Critics of reformulation voice a concern that on occasion the reformulation might be less appropriate than the original. These last two lexical choices were perhaps examples of such inappropriate changes.[7]

In comparing the syntax of the two versions, it was seen that the native chose not to begin the essay with the "if" clause, but rather to reverse the order. In the second sentence of the second paragraph, the native fronted the adverbial clause. Otherwise the nonnative's syntactic patterns were preserved. The native also introduced a grammatical error in using "ascended" (line 6) instead of "ascended to." With respect to cohesion, the native switched the pronominal referent "our" from reference to "our male presidents" to "our country's problems." Finally, with respect to discourse functions, the native chose to focus immediately on the rhetorical questions introduced by "how," rather than leading with the "if" clause.

Careful scrutiny of the revised and reformulated papers assigned in the course indicated that the reformulation exercise added a dimension in feedback that had been lacking up to that point. As a follow-up to this study, a UCLA native English-speaking graduate student did a study on reformulation. She reformulated a friendly letter written by a Chinese ESL student, a letter which basically looked quite acceptable. Yet a systematic comparison of the revised version and the reformulation revealed that this nonnative was incorrectly transferring the discourse functions (e.g., opening, closing, apology, and invitation) from business English to her friendly letter. Such functions were consistent with her work experience with business English, but incompatible with the nature of the friendly letter that she was writing (Dally 1981).

Thus, it was found that reformulation could point up major deviations from nativelike writing in the writing of nonnative students—deviations which if overlooked, could well lead to significant fossilization.[8] The intriguing potential of this reformulation technique encouraged me to try it out on myself.

Case Study with Author As Subject   In this study I made myself a subject in the research on reformulation to get a participant observer's view of how it works and of its possible benefits. The study investigated the extent to which (1) the best edit of a nonnative paper would still sound awkward, (2) reformulation would provide breakthroughs in second language writ-

----

[7]My experience, however, is that the native choices are usually better, even far better, than those of the nonnative and that in questionable cases, there is an opportunity for discussion about style—that there often is not a right and a wrong word for a given context, but rather options, with some possibly better than others. The traditional form of feedback deals primarily in "right" and "wrong."

[8]A process in which incorrect linguistic features become a permanent part of the way a person speaks or writes a target language (Selinker 1972).

ing, and (3) different reformulators of the same essay would agree on what to change and how (Cohen 1983c).

I wrote an essay of about 600 words in Hebrew as a second language on the topic, "What is Psycholinguistics?" A native speaker trained in translation then corrected the essay thoroughly. She suggested 90 changes in the areas of vocabulary, syntax, cohesion, rhetorical functions, and paragraphing (one change every seven words on the average). Three of my colleagues in applied linguistics were then asked to reformulate this reconstructed version of the essay.[9] Each made on the average 50 changes.

In response to the first issue, it was found that all three reformulators of the essay dealt considerably more with syntactic changes, matters of cohesion, and rhetorical functions than did the person doing the thorough edit. She had focused considerably more on vocabulary than they (86 percent of the changes versus 47 percent of changes by the reformulators). Regarding the second issue, I did experience a number of significant breakthroughs in my learning of written Hebrew. With respect to vocabulary, it was found that I tended to use the same vocabulary in writing that I used in speaking. Register difficulties were particularly noticeable in my use of conjunctions and adverbs. In other words, I learned that while I had a working knowledge of technical terms in writing, I did not have a similar working knowledge of function words in writing—largely because they differed from ones used in speech. For example, in Hebrew speech, "also" is expressed by *gam*, whereas the results for the reformulation research would suggest that the preferred expression in academic writing is *k'mo-xen*.

With regard to syntax, several rules that I had heard in passing in one class or another were underscored by the fact that the reformulators heeded them. For example, there is a rule in Hebrew which calls for inverting the order of the subject noun phrase and verb phrase following an adverbial phrase with sentences in the past tense. I used the NP + VP order (e.g., "the researchers investigated . . .") which is generally acceptable except after an adverbial phrase (correct: *Ad lifney eser shanim, xakru haxokrim . . .* 'Until ten years ago, investigated the researchers . . .'). This violation in written syntax passed the thorough correction or reconstruction of the essay, but not the reformulation.

With respect to cohesion, the reformulators made over three times as many changes proportionate to total changes as did the person doing the reconstruction. Furthermore, they provided me with a breakthrough: seeing that Hebrew does not tolerate as much use of pronominal reference as does English. In Hebrew, lexical substitution would be more appropriate. Thus, after writing "the second language learners," the next mention in Hebrew might be "the language learners," and then "the learners," and

---

[9]The colleagues were Rafael Nir, Shoshana Blum-Kulka, and Elite Olshtain.

perhaps then "they," while in English the writer might jump immediately to "they" in the second mention. I had read about this stylistic difference in the literature (e.g., Levenston 1976, Berman 1980) but had not applied it in my own writing.

As for the issue of similarity in reformulation by the three reformulators, it was found that they usually did change the same words, phrases, and sentences. They had a similar number of changes within each category. Although these reformulators differed somewhat in vocabulary, in syntactic structures, and sometimes in their interpretation of the text—usually where the text was ambiguous—these results would suggest that the use of one competent reformulator is adequate. This study demonstrated to me that reformulation has the potential of pointing up important matters of style, vocabulary, and syntax, that often lie outside the realm of traditional feedback. The results prompted additional research.

Small-Scale Study of EFL and H2 Reformulations   In an effort to further pursue the reformulation procedure, a small-scale study was undertaken at the Hebrew University of Jerusalem (Cohen 1983b). The major issues concerned (1) differences in changes made in correcting essays and in reformulating them, and (2) ways in which students might benefit from reformulation.

Seven English as a foreign language (EFL) learners in their second year of a B.A. in English language and literature and six Hebrew as a second language (H2) learners studying in advanced-level Hebrew courses participated in the study. The students were asked to write a short, informal composition in which they presented their suggestions for improving student life at the new Hebrew University campus on Mount Scopus. The teachers corrected these essays and returned them to the students who then produced reconstructed versions and submitted them to native-speaking research assistants serving as reformulators. The research assistants then conducted interviews with the students, having the learners compare the reconstructed and the reformulated versions. The students were first asked to indicate differences they noticed between the two versions. Then the assistants called attention to a series of points and asked the students to react.

It was found that both with the EFL and H2 essays, the reformulations produced many more changes than were found in the version corrected by the teacher (two times more in the EFL essays and five times more in the H2 essays). The nature of changes was similar in most categories except that of cohesion, where there were more changes in the reformulated versions in both languages. Consistent with this finding, the instances of real student insights about writing in the second language were mostly with respect to matters of cohesion. For example, an H2 writer gained an insight about how she was not linking sentences with conjunctions as the native Hebrew speaker did. In addition, several EFL writers gained the insight that, whereas they used lexical repetition to refer to something already mentioned in the composition, the native English speaker switched to pronominal reference.

When asked to evaluate the procedure, the students' reactions were generally favorable. Most "liked it," thought it was "a good idea," and found it "valuable." One even regretted not having used a system like this from the start of her studies. The students found the feedback in the reformulation to be deeper than that in typical corrective feedback—actually illustrating to the student an appropriate way to write what they wanted to express. A student made the point that often from the limited teacher's corrections, learners would get the false impression that most of what they had written was fine when it was not. Students pointed out that whereas the teacher's correction may help with the technical problems in language that the student already knows well enough to use, it may not really improve the student's style. In other words, it was felt that when the teacher corrects essays, the student's own limited expressions remain, whereas the reformulation is written on a different level altogether, with the richness, variety, and subtleties of the language.

Comparative Study of Reformulation Versus Correction   As a follow-up to the two studies already described, a larger-scale comparative study to investigate the benefits of reformulation was subsequently conducted (Cohen 1983c).

In this study, 53 advanced H2 learners wrote three compositions during a two-month intensive summer course at the Hebrew University of Jerusalem. A reformulation group obtained teacher correction of their essays, had native acquaintances reformulate their essays, and then compared the reconstructed and the reformulated versions individually under the direction of a research assistant. A correction group also gave their essays to the teacher for correction and then met with research assistants to discuss the teacher's corrections. Each of the three research assistants was assigned to an equal number of reformulation and correction group students and continued to meet individually with these students for 30 minutes to an hour over the two-month period, each time that the students received one of their three compositions back—reformulated or corrected, respectively.

Eighteen native-speaking Hebrew teachers served as judges in the rating of the three reconstructed and the three reformulated essays of eight students randomly selected from the reformulation group, and the three corrected essays from the eight students randomly selected from the correction group. These 72 essays were then arranged into six sets of 12 so that neither two essays from the same student nor the reconstructed and the reformulated version of an essay appeared in the same set. The judges rated each essay according to four scales—vocabulary, syntax, cohesion, and total. The students were also asked to rate on a five-point scale the extent to which their Hebrew studies improved their ability to write in Hebrew, the usefulness of the meetings with the research assistants, and the helpfulness of the reformulation technique.

It was found that although there were no significant differences in gains from the first to the second, nor from the second to the third, essays on any of the scales, the mean gain score from the first to the third composition was significantly higher ($p < 0.05$) for the correction group than for the reformulation group on the syntax, cohesion, and total scales. What produced significant differences in this comparison was the fact that the means for the reformulation group dropped on the third essay to levels even below those on the first essay, while the means for the correction group increased slightly beyond those on the second essay, suggesting that the reformulation group was no longer taking the task seriously the third time around.

This study also sought to see if the judges would rate the reformulated versions higher than the reconstructed versions. This proved to be the case for the vocabulary and syntax scales on the second composition and for the vocabulary scale on the third.

With respect to the popularity of the two techniques in the eyes of the student consumers, the correction group students rated the type of feedback that they received significantly higher than the reformulation group rated theirs in several areas. Specifically, the correction technique was rated as contributing more to "general writing ability" and to the "ability to write cohesively" than was the reformulation technique. The correction group students were also significantly more positive about the extent to which the assistants helped them.

The reformulation group students had more mixed reactions. Of the 20 who participated in the study, 12 were basically positive in their views. They noted that the technique gave them an opportunity to see exactly what their writing problems were and then to work on them. Half of these students indicated that they would continue to use the technique beyond the summer language course. For one student, learning about connectives and about the importance of cohesion in writing were major breakthroughs. Corroborating his self-report, the research assistant working with this student noted an improvement in these areas from the first to the second composition, and his teacher noted an improvement as well. Another student was aware that the technique helped him learn expressions in Hebrew as well as learning something more about Hebrew sentence structure.

A main reason for the reformulation group students' poor performance on the third essay was their fatigue at having to devote so much time to the project. Students repeatedly objected to the time needed not only to submit and get back three essays, but also to find a reformulator and then get back the reformulated version. In reality, the reformulation group had more to do than the correction group. It was never envisioned that reformulation would serve as "the answer" to feedback at the advanced levels on second language compositions. It was simply envisioned as supplementing other approaches. It was seen largely as a tool for diagnosing areas for development. Hence, one or two such sessions were considered to be adequate for such diagnosis. This study showed that students were no longer enthusiastic about the method when they were asked to engage themselves in more than two such essay reformulations in an eight-week period.

The Implications of the Reformulation Research   Perhaps a major implication emerging from the research on reformulation is that the technique may be beneficial for some students some of the time. Care needs to be taken not to overuse the technique. When used in moderation, the technique has the potential of being a powerful tool for improving target language writing style—particularly at the intermediate and advanced levels. An important effect of the technique is that it inadvertently emphasizes the fact that there is more than one correct way to write things in a target language, and that these various correct ways may be noticeably different from any of the nonnative versions.

SUMMING UP

This chapter has reviewed some of the principle research studies that colleagues, students, and I have undertaken regarding issues addressed in the earlier chapters on reading and on writing. The research on reading made extensive use of verbal report techniques in an effort to understand the reading process better. The case studies on technical discourse demonstrated how students from a variety of different technical fields may share similar problems in reading technical texts—problems such as contending with heavy noun phrases, correctly interpreting markers of cohesion, and perceiving accurately the role of nontechnical vocabulary in technical texts. The latter studies described in the chapter illustrate the importance of developing a broadly based taxonomy of reading strategies—one that accurately depicts the number and variety of reading strategies involved in the reading of text. It was seen that in many ways foreign language reading is like native language reading. The section ended by discussing research on the interpretation of foreign language vocabulary, with the focus on the extent to which context aids in the interpretation process.

The section on writing looked at research on two kinds of feedback— the first being the more traditional teacher feedback and the second being an innovative approach to feedback, namely, "reformulation." Shortcomings in teacher feedback procedures and in those used by students to deal with this feedback were highlighted both in preliminary survey work and then in follow-up case study work.

Research on reformulation—that is, a technique whereby a nonnative essay is rewitten by a native, preserving the ideas of the author—was then presented. The types of studies that were described ranged from classroom research with the teacher as observer/researcher to the investigation of my own second language essay writing to small- and larger-scale studies of university students engaged in analyzing reformulations of their essays. Given the problems inherent in the ways that feedback is currently provided, reformulation, as an innovative alternate, is seen to be a potentially beneficial means of providing feedback as to the finer aspects of writing proficiency in a target language. It was also noted that the technique should not be overworked because learners can experience fatigue in carrying it out more than twice in a semester course.

FURTHER READINGS

Reading Strategies

Since numerous topics were covered with respect to reading, this section will be selective, calling attention only to a few of the many references available dealing with reading strategies.

These first references are to research studies that have demonstrated the advantages of training readers in the use of reading strategies.

Baumann, J. F. 1984. The effectiveness of a direct instruction paradigm for teaching main idea comprehension. *Reading Research Quarterly 20* (1), 93–115. In this study involving 66 sixth graders, a strategy group got intensive direct main idea instruction, a basal group got an intensive set of lessons on main idea comprehension from a basal reader series, and a control group did unrelated vocabulary exercises. Measures of ability to recognize and produce explicit and implicit main ideas at the paragraph and short-passage levels showed the strategy group to be performing significantly better than the other groups. The conclusion reached was that direct training in reading strategies was preferable to the other means.

Brown, A. L., Palincsar, A. S., and Armbruster, B. B. 1984. Instructing comprehension-fostering activities in interactive learning situations. In H. Mandl et al. (eds.), *Learning and comprehension of texts*. Hillsdale, NJ: Lawrence Erlbaum, 255–286. The paper reports on a series of three studies demonstrating that cognitive skills in reading can be taught to poor seventh-grade readers and that such training is durable and generalizable. The authors note that good readers are generally given more class time for comprehension fostering tasks than poor readers—tasks such as clarifying the purpose for reading, activating relevant background knowledge, allocating attention so that the focus is on major content not trivia, critical evaluation of content for internal consistency and compatibility with prior knowledge, monitoring ongoing activities, drawing and testing inferences, predicting, and drawing conclusions. The areas selected for training of readers were summarizing (self-review), questioning, clarifying, and predicting.

Hosenfeld, C. 1984. Case studies of ninth grade readers. In J. C. Alderson and A. H. Urquhart (eds.), *Reading in a foreign language*. London: Longman, 231–244. The author describes two case studies in which she had a ninth-grade learner of French and a ninth-grade learner of Spanish read a text in their respective target languages, producing a verbal report protocol as they read. On the basis of the protocol, Hosenfeld identified areas in which the students could benefit from the use or better use of reading strategies. She found that once the students were alerted to these strategies and had had practice in using them, their reading abilities dramatically improved.

Hamp-Lyons, L. 1985. Two approaches to teaching reading: A classroom-based study. *Reading in a Foreign Language*, 3 (1), 363–373. Twenty-four ESL students were split into "text-strategic" and traditional approaches to reading. In the text-strategic approach, focus was on meaning, schemata, discourse, and silent reading. This treatment did better.

Barnett, M. A. 1988. Teaching through context: How real and perceived strategy use affects L2 comprehension. *Modern Language Journal*, 72 (2), 150–162. The author studied 272 fourth-semester French FL college students. Nine sections were taught traditionally and four with experimental and innovative reading materials, emphasizing effective reading strategies. The main strategy that was taught was considering the context and noting the interrelationship of words, actions, and ideas—a "text-level" as opposed to a "word-level" strategy. It was found that those who considered and remembered context as they read understood more than those who did not. As readers used more strategies, their perception that they did so was found to increase. The results showed that teaching students to apply strategies did not significantly improve their reading comprehension and did not make them more aware of using suggested strategies. The researcher could not explain this finding other than to suggest that perhaps the effects of the training would show up slowly.

The next references are to descriptions of case studies in which reading processes are described:

Haas, C. and Flower, L. 1988. Rhetorical reading strategies and the construction of meaning. *College Composition and Communication*, 39 (2), 167–183. This case study involved 10 readers (four graduate students, six undergraduates—half average and half above-average readers) trying to understand a complex college-level text, using think-aloud protocols. The study investigated differences between experienced readers and freshman readers with regard to rhetorical reading—that is, going a step beyond the text to account for the author's purpose, context, and effect on the audience. The experienced readers were found to have more rhetorical strategies (13 percent versus one percent) in their verbal protocol. They not only just created a gist and paraphrased the content, but also inferred the author's purpose.

Wolff, D. 1987. Some assumptions about second language text comprehension. *Studies in Second Language Acquisition, 9* (3), 307–326. Eight stories were read by native English speakers and videotaped. Between 40 to 50 interviews were held with German L1 informants (12 to 18 years old) who provided recall data on each story (350 informants in all). Then the respondents were asked to give retrospective verbal reports to provide information on the cognitive strategies used. The researcher found that top-down processing played a more important role in L2 comprehension than in L1 comprehension. The general conclusion was that L2 learners process texts in the same way as in their L1 and make up for deficiencies in their language knowledge by relying more heavily on top-down processing, by referring more efficiently to their world knowledge.

The following articles focus on the area of self-supervision or meta-cognition in reading:

Garner, R. 1987. *Metacognition and reading comprehension.* Norwood, NJ: Ablex. The book summarizes research on metacognition. Among many other things, the book deals with methodological concerns—such as metacognitive interviews, think-aloud data, and training students to use strategies.

Jolley, J. S. 1985. Metacognition and reading: Theoretical background and implementation strategies for classroom teachers. ERIC ED 259 301. The monograph defines *metacognition* and *comprehension monitoring*. It also reviews the literature on strong and weak readers. An emphasis is placed on self-control training —such as, shifting responsibility to the reader. Strategies for prereading, reading, and postreading are discussed, including the notion of a learning log for the reader to jot down confusing points, questions about information, and important insights during the reading.

The remaining two references are to a research article with a general coverage of the reading strategy literature and an article on reading vocabulary.

Swaffar, J. K. 1988. Readers, texts, and second languages: The interactive processes. *Modern Language Journal, 72* (2), 123–149. The article provides an extensive review of the literature on interactive processes in reading. The author starts by noting the new conceptual model of the comprehension process. She considers textual meaning and reader processing (problems in assessing interactive variables), schematizing and learning (including processing styles revealed through oral interviews), language competency and interactive processes (with an emphasis on vocabulary, and strategy training). The article also provides implications for the classroom based on the review of the literature: (1) Readers need to choose their own vocabulary to learn and then need strategies for monitoring their learning and use, (2) readers need to be taught certain syntactic forms such as modifiers and logical connectors, (3) there needs to be more exploring of how readers arrive at decisions as to the meaning of a text, (4) more attention needs to be given to the influence of edited or doctored texts on readers, and (5) more emphasis should be placed on the use of computer technology.

Nation, P. and Coady, J. 1988. Vocabulary and reading. In R. Carter and M. McCarthy (eds.) *Vocabulary and language teaching*. London: Longman, 97–110. The authors focus on contextualized vocabulary and guessing in reading. The chapter deals with the issue of the unknown-word ratio—the percent of words that readers need not know and still comprehend the text (15 percent in L1, 5 to 7 percent in L2). They report that the effects of preteaching reading vocabulary are mixed. They indicate that the L1 research is not clear on how much learning of words takes place through reading, but that if there is an advantage, it goes to the good reader. They note that learning from context is incremental (Nagy et al. 1985). They also elaborate on Clarke and Nation (1980) with respect to guessing from context: First, find the part of speech of the unknown word, then look at the immediate context and simplify if necessary, next look at the wider context, then guess the meaning, and finally check if the guess is correct. Looking for clues in the structure of the word is no longer included in the list. The authors also cite research regarding instances when the context does not aid in guessing meaning.

Writing Strategies

As in the case of references on reading strategies, it is necessary to be selective in this section because of the numerous references available. The following are just a sampling of some of the research or reviews of research that the researcher may wish to consult. The first three deal with L1 composing, with the first two focusing on the the writer and the third on the feedback interaction between teacher and writer.

Bereiter, C. and Scardamalia, M. 1987. *The psychology of written composition*. Hillsdale, NJ: Lawrence Erlbaum. This book introduces two models for the composing process—*knowledge telling* and *knowledge transforming*. The first model is considered to represent how most people write. The second, more complex, model is depicted as usually producing better results and involves the use of reflective processes to formulate and solve problems in composition. Actually, the second has a knowledge telling component but it also allows for two-way interaction between continuously developing knowledge and continuously developing text. Immature writers are seen to use their knowledge in ways that leave it little better integrated than it was before they committed it to text—hence, "inert knowledge" or "knowledge telling." The point is made that many class exercises encourage knowledge telling. Chapter 11 reports on an experiment involving revision in which the revisions of 10 to 14-year-olds were found to reflect additions rather than changes of text already produced.

Pringle, I. and Freedman, A. 1985. *A comparative study of writing ability in two modes at the grade 5, 8, and 12 levels.* Publication Centre, 880 Bay St., Toronto, Ontario M7A 1N8: Ontario Ministry of Education. The monograph reports on a study in which students in grades 5, 8, and 12 in two Ontario school districts took a writing task—half writing an argumentative task and half a narrative task. Ten percent were randomly selected for analysis of story structure, argumentation, affective development, syntactic complexity, and mechanical and conventional errors. Although syntactic ability was found to be high, and mechanics and use of conventions were fine, even at the twelfth-grade level, the students did not display an ability to write argumentative discourse satisfactorily. Furthermore, most students were found to have little or no awareness of how to revise. Even tidying up mechanics was not done through effective strategies. Revision consisted mostly of substituting, with some adding and deleting, but little reordering. The investigators found few revisions at all and usually at the micro-level (words, phrases, sentences) rather than at the macro-level (ideas, sections, whole draft). The analysis was conducted by means of listening to a tape recording of the first draft while viewing the second. It was concluded that for many writers, preparing the final draft means only making it visually presentable.

Ziv, N. D. 1984. The effect of teacher comments on the writing of four college freshmen. In R. Beach and L. S. Bridwell (eds.) *New directions in composition research.* New York: Guilford, 362–380. The chapter offers an excellent review of literature on teacher feedback and then describes a case study of four college students involved in writing in three draft stages. They wrote their papers and then read them aloud in groups of four or five. The writers then prepared second drafts. These were given to the teacher. Learners then read their corrected papers aloud and commented on the teacher's comments. Next, the learners were to express a reaction which was tape recorded. The learners were given an example by the teacher of how to do this. The students received detailed teacher comments on structural and lexical issues, at both the micro- and macro-levels. The study looked at student perceptions of these comments and student action taken. It was found that these writers—all inexperienced revisers—responded most favorably to explicit cues at the macro- and micro-levels. Implicit cues were not helpful at the sentential level because learners did not recognize what the problems were and/or did not have strategies needed to revise them. "Can you rephrase this?" or "Rewrite this sentence" did not work. On the lexical level, "wrong word" had poor results. Corrections were not helpful because learners copied them without understanding. It was found to be more beneficial for the teacher to assume the role of interested adult rather than that of evaluator and judge.

The next three references deal with studies comparing L1 and L2 writers, with the first concerning the issue of general writing style.

Arndt, V. 1987. First and foreign language composing: A protocol-based study. In T. Bloor and J. Norrish (eds.), *Written language.* London: Centre for Information on Language Teaching and Research (CILT), 114–129. The article reports on a comparative, protocol-based study of Chinese L1 and EFL writing processes of six postgraduate EFL students writing academic discourse at Nankai University in Tianjin, China. Students composed aloud into tape recorders in booths in a language lab. She found that the writers differed in their approaches to writing, but used similar approaches in L1 and FL writing. The researcher found the students to display six distinct styles: (1) *the outliner*—who needed an entire session to orient himself to the topic, producing only outlines, no text; (2) *the lister*—who started writing without an orientation period, filling the paper with fragments of ideas, large quantities of text without concern for how they fit together; (3) *the reviser*—writing effortlessly and spontaneously, aware of the total text and monitoring progress; (4) *the struggler*—who found writing painful and struggled to have her words match her intended meaning; (5) *the thinker*—who was concerned with getting to the logical heart of ideas, making rational sense, without planning or outlining but with considerable time thinking about what she would write; (6) *the planner*—who could only write after tracing out elaborate superstructural frameworks (introduction, main points, examples, conclusion) as taught, but whose actual writing did not fit his frameworks. Three problems were found to be common to all writers: lack of global planning for coherent text, concern only for the meaning at the local level; inadequate evaluation, criticism of the generated text; and lack of serious commitment to the writing task because it was considered to be just an exercise.

Cumming, A. 1988. Writing expertise and second language proficiency. Vancouver: Department of Language Education, University of British Columbia. The study marked the rigorous assessment of L1 writing (holistic ratings of French L1 composition, self-ratings of writing, self-report of professional experience in writing), yielding three categories: professionally experienced, average, and basic. The participants were 23 undergraduates at Ontario University, native French-speaking ESL students in an English-French bilingual program. They received three writing tasks: an informal letter, an argument, and a summary. Think-aloud protocols were collected for each of the writing tasks. The researcher identified different types of decision statements: knowledge telling, problem identification/resolution/ evaluation. Professionally experienced writers devoted much attention to evaluating their expression at the word and phrase levels together and were quick to make decisions about gist and organization. Inexperienced writers focused on a single phrase, sentence, or thought level. It was found that preplanning or on-line planning was not necessarily a function of expertise in L1 writing, because there were cases where experienced and inexperienced ESL writers were both preplanners. The main finding was that writing ability and L2 proficiency are two largely independent phenomena.

Raimes, A. 1987. Language proficiency, writing ability, and composing strategies: A study of ESL college student writing. *Language Learning*, 37 (3) 439–468. The article reports on a study of four ESL writers in remedial courses and four in college-level writing courses. They were given two writing tasks for think-aloud composing. The results were related to course placement, holistic evaluation of students' writing, and scores in language proficiency. While the L2 writers were found to use many strategies in common with L1 writers, L2 writers were less concerned about making errors—hence, they displayed fewer efforts to edit. In addition, nonremedial writers spent more time planning, rehearsing, rescanning, revising, and editing than did remedial writers.

This last reference deals with L2 composing exclusively, and provides a listing of what were found to be the characteristic strategies of good target language writers.

Zamel, V. 1983. The composing processes of advanced ESL students: Six case studies. *TESOL Quarterly*, 17 (2), 165–187. Six writers (Chinese, Spanish, Portuguese, Hebrew, Persian), two good and four poor, had their behavior and what they wrote observed while composing ESL texts. The writers were interviewed after writing. A series of conclusions were reached with regard to good writers: (1) They were not sidetracked by a gap in their knowledge as they wrote—they would write the word and circle it, leave it blank, or write an L1 word; (2) they made meaning-level changes for the most part; (3) they related to composing as a process of discovering and exploring ideas and constructing the best framework for these ideas—not always based on a sense of direction or clear plan; (4) they distanced themselves from the text, taking into account the reader's point of view; (5) they did not let language-related difficulties interrupt the writing process; and (6) they did not view writing as a sequential completion of separate tasks (e.g., generating a thesis sentence, topic sentences, and so forth).

Chapter 9

Conclusions

This book has been intended as an exercise in consciousness-raising, for both learners and teachers. The challenge is to become conscious of those usually automatic learning patterns so that you, the learner, can have some choice or control over them. This book has given numerous suggestions for what learners themselves can do to become more aware of how they learn, and subsequently to exercise more conscious control over the learning process. Needless to say, there are many other suggestions that could be added. While there is no one single formula for success, this book has suggested options that seem to have a payoff for language learners with different learning styles and at different levels of proficiency.

Assuming learners take over some or many of the functions that were expected of teachers formerly, how does this affect the teacher's role? In fact, having a degree of learner autonomy introduced into the learning process frees the teacher to be more creative and innovative in the teaching process. Much of the energy that the teacher usually expends "directing traffic" can now be channeled into assisting students at crucial moments. Lessons may well go quicker because the learners are better able to cope with them and are more aware of the action to take if they are not able to cope (e.g., conferencing with the teacher after class, or making comments in their dialog journal).

Another important role in the learning process is that of researcher. There is a continual need to have researchers explore more fully what the learning process entails. For too many years pronouncements about how people learn language and what they actually learn were based largely or exclusively on intuition. Intuitions are not necessarily invalid. Often they are most insightful, but they may not provide a complete picture and may even be unfounded. In recent years, we are finally beginning to see a growing number of *empirical* studies regarding aspects of second or foreign language acquisition that had previously been left to intuition. Such studies have brought with them some surprises with regard to what learners actually do as opposed to what they were thought to be doing in order to learn and use a target language.

By way of conclusion, let us go back over some of the principal points raised within the five chapters dealing with the language learning skills.

VOCABULARY

This book has demonstrated the potential benefits of having learners focus on how they go about learning vocabulary. Once you are aware of what you do as a learner, you may have a better idea of what is working and what is not. The next step would be to try out other approaches that may be more effective. There are times when you beat your head against a wall, in a manner of speaking. In other words, you engage in learning techniques that are unlikely to produce positive results in your case—just a sore head (literally and figuratively). For example, a certain vocabulary learning technique—such as repeating a word to yourself by rote 10 times—may not be helpful to you, but you do it because this is the way your friend or classmate or sibling does it and it works for them. It is important to identify strategies or habits that do not benefit you. If the words are simply not accessible the next day or ever, then something is wrong with the approach in your case.

The truth is that learners have different learning styles and that they need to discover what works best for them. Experimenting to find out what works best can be a "liberating" experience for you. For example, the most effective way for you to learn certain concrete nouns so that you do not forget them at a later time may be to learn them through actual or mental pictures. For other such nouns, you may do better using structural association or mnemonic keywords. In any event, conscious choice is the key factor here. The lack of *dependence* on the teacher in some ways may actually make you better able to benefit from your teacher's guidance and suggestions. You can select from among those hints, aids, and clues that the teacher supplies, those that are likely to have an impact on your own learning.

Not only is it suggested that you choose the strategies for vocabulary learning that are most likely to work for you, but also that *you* choose the words that you wish to learn. As pointed out by Swaffer (1988:137), if learners themselves decide which words are important to commit to memory, the words will have greater salience for the learners and the rate of retention will be higher. As a rationale for having students identify the words they need to know, she notes that students differ in terms of the words that they need to learn.

The book has put considerable emphasis on learning words through association, especially through mnemonic devices, because research results have shown that learners do not use such aids systematically. You would have to see whether this applies to you. If you think that you would benefit from more systematic choices regarding how you will learn given words and what type of association you might use, then let this book serve as an invitation to you to be more systematic. If in the exercise with Aymara vocabulary (the exercise leading off Chapter 2), you noticed that a particular form of association worked for you, be willing to use it in other vocabulary learning situations.

The final comment here is simply not to be discouraged if words seem to slip away. Forgetting vocabulary is as natural as learning it. Sometimes reviewing vocabulary helps keep it available. As we saw, there is much to learn in mastering vocabulary words in a language, and mastery takes time. Even "minimal familiarity" calls for some or possibly great effort. For these reasons, any and all strategies that are consciously applied to the learning process can help to make the task easier. Remember that making the task easier does not necessarily mean *simplifying* it because the process may actually introduce extra, sometimes complex elements—such as when a mnemonic keyword is introduced in order to learn a word. This means one extra, perhaps complex piece of data to process. Yet the point is that the learning becomes easier all the same.

ATTENDING

In some ways, the skill of listening in a target language is the most frustrating because in authentic interactions it seems that there is so little we can do—that things are out of our hands. With speaking, we can decide when and how to speak, and with reading and writing, we usually have time to sort things out (as far as our competence will allow us). With respect to listening, we actually may know all or most of the words being used but find that the very speed of delivery undermines our best efforts to understand. Or perhaps the pronunciation or stress given words is unexpected. If we have the luxury to ask for the message to be repeated, so much the better. If we do not, then we may have a problem, depending on the patience and kindness of the speaker(s).

It is expressly because of difficulties that may arise in comprehending oral language that attending strategies have an important role to play. Motivated learners might try to improve their speed listening by exposing themselves more to natives speaking the language naturally or to more advanced learners in conversation. The advantages of taping a portion of an interaction cannot be overstressed. The repeated playing back of such snippets of conversation, sections of a lecture, or whatever, can help you to break the sound barrier, so to speak.

This book has been written to train learners to benefit more from their target language studies regardless of the quality of the teaching. This tack was taken since there are numerous instances when you have little control over who teaches you and how. In the case of the 12 languages I have studied over the years, I have had some stimulating teachers and some less so. The challenge is to learn the maximum amount under each of these circumstances without having the teacher do anything different.

SPEAKING

The book has endeavored to underscore the complexities of speaking in a target language. It is for this reason that the wise language learner looks for communication strategies to ease the burden—such things as getting around not knowing a word by using a general word, an approximation, or a description (paraphrase or circumlocution). For some learners, learning how to speak a language—particularly in the early stages—becomes an exercise in avoiding errors. And ironically the more "agitated" attention given to producing error-free or error-reduced utterances, the more errors may result. In other words, a preoccupation with form may get in the way of producing correct forms "naturally."

There need to be moments of letting go—of simply speaking from the knowledge base that you have acquired. Certainly this does not rule out the benefits of self-monitoring. It may pay for you to check through your utterances after you have said them to make sure that they came out correctly, and if they have not, to then make the necessary corrections, if possible. It is also important to receive outside feedback, but as was pointed out, there is a proper time and place for feedback on speaking. In other words, corrections are important and make a real contribution, but only when you are ready for them and can benefit from them. Otherwise, they may simply have a discouraging effect on your self-concept as a target language learner.

Whereas we are now beginning to see what utterances are acceptable as instances of speech act behavior—as in apologizing, complaining, requesting, and complimenting, we still know little about what you, the learner, needs to go through in order to produce such speech acts, especially in the case of the more complex ones like apologies. For this reason, it is easy enough to give you advice like, "Be more aware of how natives perform these speech acts and perhaps even ask natives for acceptable utterances in given situations." However, we do not yet have a set of empirically tested methods to suggest for selecting the elements to include in, say, apologies in each given situation, beyond the general guidelines given in Chapter 4.

In other words, you are encouraged (1) to pay attention to the nature of the situation and the familiarity that you have with the other interlocutors, (2) to see which of the strategies for the given speech act seem appropriate for use (in the case of apology: expression of apology, acknowledgement of responsibility, explanation, offer of repair, promise of nonreoccurrence), and (3) to select the actual speech forms (e.g., "Sorry," "Excuse me," "very," and "really") with care. Eventually, it may be possible to describe the ways that more successful target language speakers process these types of information in order to produce their speech act utterances.

READING

In order to improve your target language reading, you need to read a lot. Many target language learners shy away from reading, because it seems to be so difficult to do. However, the alert learner can make the task easier. Reading material that is uninteresting to you or too laden with unknown words will only produce frustration and lack of desire to continue reading. Hence, it is important to find material that you want to read—that is relevant to your purposes for reading—and that is not too difficult. This may call for utilizing material that is simplified, as well as authentic texts that have been specially glossed to facilitate reading by nonnatives with limited vocabulary.

One of the main messages with regard to reading is that it is not what you think it is. There is little or nothing that is actually "passive" with respect to reading for comprehension. Successful reading comprehension calls for an active approach to the text, involving the use of various skills. We have also seen that the implementation of these skills (e.g., skimming, summarizing, and guessing word meanings from context) can be enhanced through the use of strategies. Thus, once you have material that you want to read, the challenge is to apply strategies that will support successful reading. This involves a conscious effort. Remember that even readers trained in speed reading need to make a conscious effort to practice the techniques that they learned in order to have them accessible to them (Just & Carpenter 1984).

WRITING

Just as we may be hard put to write a single draft of a business letter or professional paper in our native language such that it comes out the way it should, so in a target language we are likely to need to write several drafts before our text is up to standard. The process approach to writing is based on the assumption that you will not get it right the first time. The important thing is being aware of the options that you have for reworking your writing—whether through checking with peers, conferencing with your teacher, or turning to an outside reformulator—if the purpose for writing warrants it. As you take responsibility for your own learning, you begin to ask yourself, "Who should I turn to now in order to get the best feedback regarding the piece that I just wrote?"

In addition, you would want to be conscious of the strategies you use for dealing with the feedback that you receive. In other words, what do you do if you do not understand the feedback fully or at all? What means are at your disposal for maximizing the benefits of the feedback? The dialog journal, in some ways, provides a novel means for receiving ongoing interactive feedback sessions with your teacher without the need to schedule regular conferences, as well as allowing you an opportunity to practice writing communicatively. You may wish to incorporate such an approach into your learning—whether with a tutor or teacher. A teacher, for instance, may be willing to respond to queries you have written into a journal regardless of whether the rest of the class is also writing dialog journals.

One way of making the job of writing in a target language easier is to identify those forms of writing that you are most called upon to indulge in and to concentrate your efforts on learning them. If, for example, you need to compose business letters, then the reformulation technique may serve as a shortcut method to obtain a working knowledge of a business letter. By writing your own version and then having it reformulated by a native, you would have the benefit of being able to see the gaps between what you know how to do in writing and what you still need to learn. In essence, you are getting an instant diagnosis for the specific purpose at hand.

In many ways, the reformulation technique allows you to incorporate several different purposes for writing into your routine. After you have received the reformulation and gone over the differences, you could write your own version of the reformulated text, in large part *imitating* what was written. You may wish to have the act of reformulation serve to *train* you in the use of linguistic forms by copying out several of the sentences into a separate notebook in which you keep examples of the way that natives employ certain grammatical structures in connected text.

Diligent learners may actually generate various other lists of insights gained from reformulation beyond that of grammatical structures. For instance, such lists could also contain (1) discourse connectors (e.g., "moreover," "albeit," or whatever) for which the reformulation exercise provided meanings or new meanings, or (2) technical terms, or nontechnical terms used technically, for which the meaning became clear or clearer through the exercise. The advantage of having these insights categorized is that it facilitates retrieval at the moment that you are engaged in writing and want to jog your memory as to some of the more effective means for making your points.

FINAL THOUGHTS

Will the techniques suggested in this book enter into your personal collection of tools for perfecting language skills? Might these ideas simply be one more set of interesting ideas that are soon forgotten? The intention of the book has been to provide new directions for learners to be active participants in the process of learning the new language—beyond the forms of participation normally conceived of as pertaining to the learner. Rather than providing a cookbook of dozens of techniques for the learner, the emphasis here has been more to expose you, the learner, to ways of being an effective language learner. It will be up to you to expand upon these ways and to become truly responsible for your own learning.

This book is intended to perform the role of language learning coach—to help assure that you, the learner, will come away from a target language learning experience with greater success than you would have otherwise. The time you have spent going through this book and working through the various suggested exercises should enhance the time you spend in both formal and informal language learning. For the teacher, the book has been intended to provide you with a number of suggestions for how to train your students to be more effective learners. For the researcher, it is hoped that the discussion of research in target language learning may have motivated you to commence or continue empirical investigation in the field so that we may have increasingly greater insights into means for improving language learning.

References

Alamari, Manal. 1982. Type and immediate effect of error correction for Hebrew second-language learners. Jerusalem: School of Education, Hebrew University. (In Hebrew)

Allen, E. D. & Valette, R. M. 1977. *Classroom techniques: Foreign languages and English as a second language.* 2nd ed. New York: Harcourt Brace Jovanovich.

Allwright, R. L. 1975. Problems in the study of the language teacher's treatment of learner error. In M. K. Burt & H. C. Dulay (eds.), *New directions in second language learning, teaching and bilingual education.* Washington, DC: Teachers of English to Speakers of Other Languages (TESOL), 96–109.

Allwright, R. L. 1980. Turns, topics, and tasks: Patterns of participation in language learning and teaching. In D. Larsen-Freeman (ed.), *Discourse analysis in second language research.* New York: Newbury House/Harper & Row, 165–187.

Anderson, P. L. 1981. The use of editing to teach composition to adults. Honolulu: Department of English as a Second Language, University of Hawaii.

Anderson, R. C. and Pearson, P. D. 1984. A schema-theoretic view of basic processes in reading comprehension. In P. D. Pearson (ed.), *Handbook of reading research.* New York: Longman, 255–291.

Arndt, V. 1987. First and foreign language composing: A protocol-based study. In T. Bloor & J. Norrish (eds.), *Written language.* British Studies in Applied Linguistics 2. London: Centre for Information on Language Teaching and Research (CILT), 114–129.

Asher, J. J. 1977. *Learning another language through actions.* Los Gatos, CA: Sky Oaks.

Atkinson, R. C. 1975. Mnemotechnics in second language learning. *American Psychologist, 30,* 821–828.

Bailey, K. M. 1980. An introspective analysis of an individual's language learning experience. In R. C. Scarcella & S. D. Krashen (eds.), *Research in second language acquisition.* New York: Newbury House/Harper & Row, 58–65.

Baker, L. & Brown, A. L. 1984a. Cognitive monitoring in reading. In J. Flood (ed.), *Understanding reading comprehension.* Newark, DE: International Reading Association, 21–44.

Baker, L. & Brown, A. L. 1984b. Metacognitive skills and reading. In P. D. Pearson (ed.), *Handbook of reading research.* New York: Longman, 353–394.

Bamberg, B. 1984. Assessing coherence: A reanalysis of essays written for the national assessment of educational progress, 1969–1979. *Research in the Teaching of English, 18* (3), 305–319.

Barnard, H. 1971. *Advanced English vocabulary: Workbook one.* New York: Newbury House/Harper & Row.

Barnett, J. E., Di Vesta, F. J., & Rogozinski, J. T. 1981. What is learned in note taking? *Journal of Educational Psychology, 73* (2), 181–192.

Beaugrande, R. de. 1984. Reading skills for foreign languages: A processing approach. In A. K. Pugh & J. M. Ulijn (eds), *Reading for professional purposes.* London: Heinemann, 4–26.

Bejerano, Y. 1987. A Cooperative small-group methodology in the language classroom. *TESOL Quarterly, 21* (3), 483–504.

Bellezza, F. S. 1981. Mnemonic devices: Classification, characteristics, and criteria. *Review of Educational Research, 51,* 247–275.

Bensoussan, M. & Laufer, B. 1984. Lexical guessing in context in EFL reading comprehension. *Journal of Research in Reading, 7* (1), 15–32.

Berman, R. A. 1980. Postposing, lexical repetition and the like—a study in contrastive stylistics. *Balshanut Shimushit* (Applied Linguistics), *2,* iii–xxvi.

Berman, R. A. 1984. Syntactic components of the foreign language reading process. In J. C. Alderson & A. H. Urquhart (eds.), *Reading in a foreign language.* London: Longman, 139–159.

Blum, S. & Levenston, E. A. 1978. Universals of lexical simplification. *Language Learning, 28* (2), 399–415.

Blum-Kulka, S. & Olshtain, E. 1986. Too many words: Length of utterance and pragmatic failure. *Studies in Second Language Acquisition, 8* (2), 165–179.

Bodman, J. W. & Lanzano, M. K. 1984. *Milk and honey: An ESL series for adults.* Book 4. New York: Harcourt Brace Jovanovich.

Brewster, E. T. & Brewster, E. S. 1976. *Language acquisition made practical: Field methods for language learners.* Pasadena, CA: Lingua House (Order from Academic Publications, Summer Institute of Linguistics, Dallas, TX).

Bridwell-Bowles, L., Johnson, P., & Brehe, S. 1986. Composing and computers: Case studies of experienced writers. In A. Matsuhashi (ed.), *Writing in real time: Modelling product processes.* London: Ablex, 81–107.

Brière, E. J. 1966. Quantity before quality in second language composition. *Language Learning, 16,* 141–151.

Bright, J. A. & McGregor, G. P. 1970. *Teaching English as a second language.* London: Longman.

Brown, A. L., Campione, J. C., & Day, J. D. 1981. Learning to learn: On training students to learn from text. *Educational Researcher, 10,* 14–21.

Brown, A. L. & Day, J. D. 1983. Macrorules for summarizing texts: The development of expertise. *Journal of Verbal Learning and Verbal Behavior, 22,* 1–14.

Brown, H. D. 1987. *Principles of language learning and teaching.* 2nd. ed. Englewood Cliffs, NJ: Prentice-Hall.

Busch, D. 1982. Introversion-extraversion and the EFL proficiency of Japanese students. *Language Learning, 32,* 109–132.

Calkins, L. M. 1986. *The art of teaching writing.* Portsmouth, NH: Heinemann.

Canale, M. 1982. Evaluating the coherence of students writing in L1 and L2. Toronto: Centre for Franco-Ontarian Studies, Ontario Institute for Studies in Education.

Canale, M. & Swain, M. 1980. Theoretical bases of communicative approaches to second language teaching and testing. *Applied Linguistics, 1,* 1–47.

Candlin, C. N. & Saedi, K. L. 1981. Processes in discourse. Unpublished manuscript, Department of Linguistics and Modern English Language, University of Lancaster, England.

Carrell, P. L. 1988. Some causes of text-boundedness and schema interference in ESL reading. In P. L. Carrell, J. Devine, & D. Eskey (eds.), *Interactive approaches to second language reading*. Cambridge: Cambridge University Press, 101–113.

Carrell, P. L. & Eisterhold, J. C. 1983. Schema theory and ESL reading pedagogy. *TESOL Quarterly, 17* (4), 553–573.

Carrier, C. A. & Titus, A. 1981. Effects of notetaking pretraining and test mode expectations on learning from lectures. *American Educational Research Journal, 18* (4), 385–397.

Carter, R. 1987. *Vocabulary: Applied linguistic perspectives*. London: Allen & Unwin.

Carter, R. 1988. Vocabulary, cloze and discourse: An applied linguistic view. In R. Carter & M. McCarthy, *Vocabulary and language teaching*. London: Longman, 161–180.

Casey, F. 1985. *How to study: A practical guide*. Basingstoke, England: Macmillan.

Chomsky, N. 1965. *Aspects of the theory of syntax*. Cambridge, MA: MIT Press.

Chaudron, C. 1983. Evaluating writing: Effects of feedback on revision. Los Angeles: ESL Section, English Department, University of California at Los Angeles.

Chaudron, C. 1984. The effects of feedback on students' composition revisions. *RELC Journal, 15*, 1–14.

Chaudron, C. 1988. *Second language classrooms: Research on teaching and learning*. Cambridge: Cambridge University Press.

Chibnall, B. 1987. *Teaching for effective study*. London: Croom Helm.

Clarke, D. F. & Nation, I. S. P. 1980. Guessing the meanings of words from context: Strategy and techniques. *System, 8* (3), 211–220.

Clarke, M. A. 1979. Reading in Spanish and English: Evidence from adult ESL students. *Language Learning, 29* (1), 121–150.

Cohen, A. D. 1983a. Introspecting about second language learning. *Studia Anglica Posnaniensia, 15*, 139–146.

Cohen, A. D. 1983b. Reformulating second-language compositions: A potential source of input for the learner. ERIC ED 228 866.

Cohen, A. D. 1983c. Writing like a native: The process of reformulation. ERIC ED 224 338.

Cohen, A. D. 1984. On taking language tests: What the students report. *Language Testing*, (1), 70–81.

Cohen, A. D. 1987a. Student processing of feedback on their compositions. In A. L. Wenden and J. Rubin (eds.), *Learner strategies in language learning*. Englewood Cliffs, NJ: Prentice-Hall, 57–69.

Cohen, A. D. 1987b. Studying language learning strategies: How we get the information. In A. L. Wenden and J. Rubin (eds.), *Learner strategies in language learning*. Englewood Cliffs, NJ: Prentice-Hall, 31–40.

Cohen, A. D. 1987c. The use of verbal and imagery mnemonics in second-language vocabulary learning. *Studies in Second Language Acquisition, 9* (1), 43–62.

Cohen, A. D. 1989. Attrition in the productive lexicon of two Portuguese third-language speakers. *Studies in Second Language Acquisition, 11* (2), 135–149.

Cohen, A. D. In press. English testing in Brazil: Problems in using summary tasks. In C. Hill & K. Parry (eds.), *The test at the gate: Ethnographic perspectives on the assessment of English literacy*. Cambridge: Cambridge University Press.

Cohen, A. D. & Aphek, E. 1979. Easifying second language learning. A research report under the auspices of Brandeis University and submitted to the Jacob Hiatt Institute, Jerusalem. ERIC ED 163 753.

Cohen, A. D. & Aphek, E. 1980. Retention of second-language vocabulary over time: Investigating the role of mnemonic associations. *System*, *8* (3), 221–235.

Cohen, A. D. & Aphek, E. 1981. Easifying second language learning. *Studies in Second Language Acquisition*, *3* (2), 221–236.

Cohen, A. D. & Cavalcanti, M. C. 1987a. Giving and getting feedback on compositions: A comparison of teacher and student verbal report. *Evaluation and Research in Education*, *1* (2), 63–73.

Cohen, A. D. & Cavalcanti, M. C. 1987b. Viewing feedback on compositions from the teacher's and the student's perspective. *The ESPecialist*, *16*, 13–28. (PUC-SP/CEPRIL, R. Monte Alegre, 984, 05014—São Paulo, SP, Brazil)

Cohen, A. D. & Cavalcanti, M. C. In press. Feedback on compositions: Teacher and student verbal reports. In B. Kroll (ed.), *Second language writing: Research insights for the classroom*. Cambridge: Cambridge University Press.

Cohen, A. D., Glasman, H., Rosenbaum-Cohen, P. R., Ferrara, J., & Fine, J. 1979. Reading English for specialized purposes: Discourse analysis and the use of student informants. *TESOL Quarterly*, *13* (4), 551–564. Reprinted in P. L. Carrell, J. Devine, and D. Eskey (eds.), *Interactive approaches to second language reading*. Cambridge: Cambridge University Press, 1988, 152–167.

Cohen, A. D. & Olshtain, E. 1981. Developing a measure of sociocultural competence: The case of apology. *Language Learning*, *31* (1), 113–134.

Cohen, A. D., Olshtain, E., & Rosenstein, D. S. 1986. Advanced EFL apologies: What remains to be learned. *International Journal of the Sociology of Language*, *62* (6), 51–74.

Cohen, A. D. & Robbins, M. 1976. Toward assessing interlanguage performance: The relationship between selected errors, learners' characteristics, and the learners' explanations. *Language Learning*, *26* (1), 45–66.

Collins, A., Brown, J. S., & Newman, S. E. In press. Cognitive apprenticeship: Teaching the craft of reading, writing, and mathematics. In L. B. Resnick (ed.), *Cognition and instruction: Issues and agendas*. Hillsdale, NJ: Lawrence Erlbaum.

Connor, U. 1984. A study of cohesion and coherence in ESL students' writing. *Papers in Linguistics: International Journal of Human Communications*, *17* (3), 301–316.

Corder, S. P. 1974. Error analysis. In J. P. B. Allen & S. P. Corder (eds.), *Techniques in applied linguistics*. The Edinburgh Course in Applied Linguistics, vol. 3, 122–154.

Coulmas, F. (ed.) 1981. *Conversational routine*. The Hague: Mouton.

Cowan, J. R. 1974. Lexical and syntactic research for the design of EFL reading materials. *TESOL Quarterly*, *8* (4), 389–399.

Cowan, J. R. 1976. Reading, perceptual strategies and contrastive analysis. *Language Learning*, *26* (1), 95–109.

Craik, F. I. M. 1977. Depth of processing in recall and recognition. In S. Dornic (ed.), *Attention and performance VI*. Hillsdale, NJ: Lawrence Erlbaum, 679–697.

Craik, F. I. M. & Lockhart, R. S. 1972. Levels of processing: A framework for memory research. *Journal of Verbal Learning and Verbal Behavior*, *11*, 671–684.

Cramer, N. A. 1985. *The writing process: Twenty projects for group work*. New York: Newbury House/Harper & Row.

Cumming, A. 1985. Responding to the writing of ESL students. In M. Maguire & A. Pare (eds.), *Patterns of development*. Ottawa: Canadian Council of Teachers of English, 58–75.

Cumming, A. 1986. Intentional learning as a principle for ESL writing instruction: A case study. *TESL Canada Journal*, Special Issue 1, 69–83.

Cumming, A. 1989a. Second language learning through second language writing: Thinking episodes. Vancouver: Department of Language Education, University of British Columbia.

Cumming, A. 1989b. Writing expertise and second language proficiency. *Language Learning, 39* (1), 81–141.

Dally, P. 1981. Contrastive analysis of Chinese letter writing in English as a second language: With special attention to discourse function. Term paper. Los Angeles: English as a Second Language Section, English Department, University of California at Los Angeles.

Dam, L. & Gabrielson, G. 1988. Developing learner autonomy in a school context: A six-year experiment beginning in the learners' first year of English. In H. Holec (ed.), *Autonomy and self-directed learning*. Strasbourg, France: Council for Cultural Co-operation, Council of Europe, 19–30.

Deese, J. & Deese, E. K. 1979. *How to study*. New York: McGraw-Hill.

Dickinson, L. 1987. *Self-instruction in language learning*. Cambridge: Cambridge University Press.

DiPardo, A. & Freedman, S. W. 1988. Peer response groups in the writing classroom: Theoretic foundations and new directions. *Review of Educational Research, 58* (2), 119–149.

Dubin, F., Eskey, E., & Grabe, W. 1986. *Teaching second language reading for academic purposes*. Reading, MA: Addison-Wesley.

Dubin, F. & Olshtain, E. 1981. *Reading by all means*. Reading, MA: Addison-Wesley.

Dunkel, P. 1988. The content of L1 and L2 students' lecture notes and its relation to test performance. *TESOL Quarterly, 22* (2), 259–281.

Ellis, G. & Sinclair, B. 1989. *Learning to learn English: A course in learner training.* (Teacher's Book, Learner's Book, Cassette) Cambridge: Cambridge University Press.

Ellis, R. 1985. *Understanding second language acquisition*. Oxford: Oxford University Press.

Eskey, D. E. 1986. Theoretical foundations. In F. Dubin, D. E. Eskey, & W. Grabe (eds.), *Teaching second language reading for academic purposes*. Reading, MA: Addison-Wesley, 3–23.

Faerch, C., & Kasper, G. 1983. Plans and strategies in foreign language communication. In C. Faerch & G. Kasper (eds.), *Strategies in interlanguage communication*, London: Longman, 20–60.

Ferris, D., Ferris, R., Hared, M., Kowal, K., Lapp, R., & Patthey, G. G. 1989. The influence of conferencing on student writing and revision. Los Angeles: Program in Applied Linguistics, University of Southern California.

Flower, L. 1979. Writer-based prose: A cognitive basis for problems in writing. *College English, 41,* 19–36.

Flower, L. & Hayes, J. R. 1984. Images, plans, and prose: The representation of meaning in writing. *Written Communication, 1* (1), 120–160.

Freedman, A. & Clarke, L. 1988. *The effect of computer technology on composing processes and written products of grade eight and grade twelve students.* Ottawa, Toronto: Queen's Printer.

Freedman, R. 1985. *1,000 identicals and near-identicals, Hebrew-English.* Molokai, HI 96742: Words, Ltd. (Similar lists available for French, Spanish, German, Italian, and Russian with English.)

Freedman, S. W. 1987. *Response to student writing*. Urbana, IL: National Council of Teachers of English.

Gaskill, W. H. 1983. Problems and revisions in the composing processes of a Taiwanese ESL student. Los Angeles: Program in Applied Linguistics, University of California at Los Angeles.

George, H. V. 1972. *Common errors in language learning*. New York: Newbury House/ Harper & Row.

Gilette, B. 1987. Two successful language learners: An introspective approach. In C. Faerch & G. Kasper (eds.), *Introspection in second language research*. Clevedon, UK: Multilingual Matters, 268–279.

Gimenez, T. N. 1984. Legibilidade de textos academicos em ingles da área de servício social. M.A. thesis, Graduate Program in Applied Linguistics, Pontifícia Universidade Católica de São Paulo.

Goodman, K. S. 1967. Reading: A psycholinguistic guessing game. *Journal of the Reading Specialist*, 6, 126–135.

Grala, M., Oxford, R., & Schleppegrell, M. 1987. *Improving your language learning: Strategies for Peace Corps volunteers*. Washington, DC: Center for Applied Linguistics.

Graves, D. H. 1983. *Writing: Teachers and children at work*. Portsmouth, NH: Heinemann.

Gregg, K. R. 1984. Krashen's monitor and Occam's razor. *Applied Linguistics*, 5 (2), 79–100.

Grellet, F. 1981. *Developing reading skills: A practical guide to reading comprehension exercises*. Cambridge: Cambridge University Press.

Gremmo, M. 1988. Autonomie dans l'apprentissage: L'évaluation par les apprenants d'un système auto-dirigé. In H. Holec (ed.), *Autonomy and self-directed learning*. Strasbourg, France: Council for Cultural Co-operation, Council of Europe, 107–120.

Grice, H. P. 1975. Logic and conversation. In P. Cole & J. Morgan (eds.), *Syntax and semantics 3: Speech acts*. New York: Academic Press, 41–58.

Haas, C. 1988. How the writing medium shapes the writing process: Effects of word processing on planning. Pittsburgh, PA: English Department, Carnegie Mellon University.

Hague, S. A. 1987. Vocabulary instruction: What L2 can learn from L1. *Foreign Language Annals*, 20 (3), 217–225.

Halliday, M. A. K. & Hasan, R. 1976. *Cohesion in English*. London: Longman.

Hammer, P. No date. English-French cognate unit. Edmonton, Alberta: University of Alberta.

Hammer, P. 1979. The interrelationship of languages. Edmonton, Alberta: University of Alberta.

Hanawalt, P. C. 1972. Repair of genetic material in living cells. *Endeavor*, 31, 83–87.

Harris, M. 1987. *Teaching one-to-one: The writing conference*. Urbana, IL: National Council of Teachers of English.

Hatch, E., Shapira, R., & Gough, J. 1978. Foreigner talk discourse. *ITL Review of Applied Linguistics*, 39/40, 39–60.

Hayes, E. B. 1988. Encoding strategies used by native and nonnative readers of Chinese Mandarin. *Modern Language Journal*, 72 (2), 188–195.

Hayes, M. F. & Daiker, D. A. 1984. Using protocol analysis in evaluating responses to student writing. *Freshman English News*, 13 (2), 1–5.

Haynes, M. 1983. Patterns and perils of guessing in second language reading. In J. Handscombe, R. A. Orem, & B. P. Taylor (eds.), *On TESOL '83*. Washington, DC: TESOL, 163–176.

Haynes, M. 1987. A closer look at learning vocabulary from reading. East Lansing, MI: 1626C Spartan Village.

Helmore, H. 1985a. *A report on a self-directed learning course. Part 1*. Waterloo, NSW 2017, Australia: Institute of Technical and Adult Teacher Education, Sydney College of Advanced Education, P.O. Box 375.

Helmore, H. 1985b. *A report on a self-directed learning course. Part 2*. Waterloo, NSW 2017, Australia: Institute of Technical and Adult Teacher Education, Sydney College of Advanced Education, P.O. Box 375.

Helmore, H. 1987. *Self-directed learning: A handbook for teachers: 1. Helping individual learners*. Waterloo, NSW, Australia: Learning Assistance Centre, Sydney College of Advanced Education.

Hidi, S. & Anderson, V. 1986. Producing written summaries: Task demands, cognitive operations, and implications for instruction. *Review of Educational Research, 56* (4), 473–493.

Higa, M. 1963. Interference effects of interlist word relationships in verbal learning. *Journal of Verbal Learning and Verbal Behavior, 2*, 170–175.

Higbee, K. L. 1979. Recent research on visual mnemonics: Historical roots and educational fruits. *Review of Educational Research, 49*, 611–629.

Holec, H. 1986. La recherche en didactique du F.L.E. futuribles. *Études de Linguistique Appliquée, 64*, 55–63.

Holec, H. (ed.). 1988. *Autonomy and self-directed learning: Present field of application*. Project No. 12: Learning and Teaching Modern Languages for Communication. Strasbourg, France: Council for Cultural Co-operation, Council of Europe.

Holley, F. M. & King, J. K. 1971. Imitation and correction in foreign language learning. *Modern Language Journal, 55* (8), 494–498.

Holmes, J. 1986. Sharks, quarks and cognates: An elusive fundamental particle in reading comprehension. *The ESPecialist, 15*, Centro de Pesquisas, Recursos e Informação em Leitura, Pontifícia Universidade Católica de São Paulo.

Hosenfeld, C. 1976. Learning about learning: Discovering our students' strategies. *Foreign Language Annals, 9* (2), 117–129.

Hosenfeld, C. 1977. A preliminary investigation of the reading strategies of successful and unsuccessful second language learners. *System, 5* (2), 110–123.

Hosenfeld, C. 1979. Cindy: A learner in today's foreign language classroom. In W. C. Born (ed.), *The learner in today's environment*. Montpelier, VT: Capital City Press, 53–75.

Hosenfeld, C. 1984. Case studies of ninth grade readers. In J. C. Alderson & A. H. Urquhart (eds.), *Reading in a foreign language*. London: Longman, 231–249.

Hosenfeld, C., Arnold, V., Kirchofer, J., Laciura, J., & Wilson, L. 1981. Second language reading: A curricular sequence for teaching reading strategies. *Foreign Language Annals, 14*, 415–422.

Huang, X. & van Naerssen, M. 1987. Learning strategies for oral communication. *Applied Linguistics, 8* (3), 287–307.

Huckin, T. & Olsen, L. 1984. On the use of informants in LSP discourse analysis. In A. K. Pugh & J. M. Ulijn (eds.), *Reading for professional purposes*. London: Heinemann, 120–129.

Huttunen, I. 1988. Towards learner autonomy in a school context. In H. Holec (ed.), *Autonomy and self-directed learning*. Strasbourg, France: Council for Cultural Co-operation, Council of Europe, 31–40.

Jahn, J. No date. The study of vocabulary. In *Effective strategies for second language learning*. Unpublished manuscript, Montreal, Canada.

Jolley, J. S. 1985. Metacognition and reading: Theoretical background and implementation strategies for classroom teachers. ERIC ED 259 301.

Jones, S. 1983. Attention to rhetorical information while composing in a second language. In C. Campbell, V. Flashner, T. Hudson, & J. Lubin (eds.), *Proceedings of the 4th Los Angeles Second Language Research Forum*. Vol. 2. Los Angeles: University of California at Los Angeles, 130–143.

Jones, C. S. & Tetroe, J. 1987. Composing in a second language. In A. Matsuhashi (ed.), *Writing in real time: Modeling the production processes*. Norwood, NJ: Ablex, 34–57.

Just, M. A. & Carpenter, P. A. 1984. Reading skills and skilled reading in the comprehension of text. In H. Mandl, N. L. Stein, & T. Trabasso (eds.), *Learning and comprehension of text*. Hillsdale, NJ: Lawrence Erlbaum, 307–329.

Just, M. A., Carpenter, R. A., & Masson, M. E. J. 1982. *What eye fixations tell us about speed reading and skimming* (Technical Report). Pittsburgh: Carnegie-Mellon University.

Just, M. A. & Carpenter, P. A. 1987. *The psychology of reading and language comprehension*. Boston: Allyn and Bacon.

Kahneman, D. 1973. *Attention and effort*. Englewood Cliffs, NJ: Prentice-Hall.

Kaplan, R. B. 1966. Cultural thought patterns in intercultural education. *Language Learning*, 16, 1–20.

Kaplan, R. B. 1983. Contrastive rhetorics: Some implications for the writing process. In A. Freedman, I. Pringle, & J. Yalden (eds.), *Learning to write: First language/second language*. London: Longman, 139–161.

Kaplan, R. B. 1987. Cultural thought patterns revisited. In U. Connor & R. B. Kaplan (eds.), *Writing across languages*. Reading, MA: Addison-Wesley, 9–21.

Keller, E. & Warner, S. T. 1976. *Gambits 1: Conversational tools*. Ottawa: Canadian Government Publishing Centre.

Keller, H. H. 1978. *New perspectives on teaching vocabulary*. Language in Education: Theory and Practice 8. Arlington, VA: Center for Applied Linguistics.

Kellog, R. T. 1980. Is conscious attention necessary for long-term storage? *Journal of Experimental Psychology*, 6 (4), 379–390.

Kennedy, D. B., Kenyon, D. M., & Matthiesen, S. J. 1989. *Newbury House TOEFL preparation kit*. New York: Newbury House/Harper & Row.

Kezwer, P. 1987. The extroverted vs. the introverted personality and second language learning. *TESL Canada Journal*, 5 (1), 45–58.

Kintsch, W. & van Dijk, T. A. 1978. Toward a model of text comprehension and production. *Psychological Review*, 85 (5), 363–394.

Kramsch, C. J. 1979. Word watching: Learning vocabulary becomes a hobby. *Foreign Language Annals*, 12 (2), 153–158.

Kramsch, C. J. 1981a. *Discourse analysis and second language teaching*. Washington, DC: Center for Applied Linguistics.

Kramsch, C. J. 1981b. Teaching discussion skills: A pragmatic approach. *Foreign Language Annals*, 14 (2), 93–104.

Krashen, S. 1982. *Principles and practice in second language acquisition*. Oxford: Pergamon.

Krashen, S. 1985a. *The input hypothesis: Issues and implications.* London: Longman.

Krashen, S. 1985b. The power of reading. In S. Krashen, *Inquiries and insights.* Hayward, CA: Alemany Press, 89–113.

Kreeft, J., Shuy, R. W., with Staton, J., Reed, L., & Morroy, R. 1984. *Dialogue writing: Analysis of student-teacher interactive writing in the learning of English as a second language.* Washington, DC: Center for Applied Linguistics.

Larsen-Freeman, D. 1986. *Techniques and principles in language teaching.* New York: Oxford.

Laufer, B. & Sim, D. D. 1983. To what extent is L2 reading comprehension a function of L2 competence rather than of reading strategies? Haifa, Israel: Department of English, Haifa University.

Leu, D. J., Jr. 1982. Oral reading error analysis: A critical review of research and application. *Reading Research Quarterly, 17* (3), 420–437.

Levenston, E. A. 1976. Towards a comparative stylistics of English and Hebrew. *English Teachers' Journal (Israel), 15,* 16–22.

Levenston, E. A. 1978. Error analysis of free compositions: The theory and the practice. *Indian Journal of Applied Linguistics, 4* (1), 1–11.

Levenston, E. A. 1979. Second language lexical acquisition: Issues and problems. *Interlanguage Studies Bulletin, 4,* 147–160.

Levenston, E. A., Nir, R., & Blum-Kulka, S. 1984. Discourse analysis and the testing of reading comprehension by cloze techniques. In A. K. Pugh & J. M. Ulijn (eds.), *Reading for Professional Purposes.* London: Heinemann, 202–212.

Levin, J. R. 1981. The mnemonic '80s: Keywords in the classroom. *Educational Psychology, 16,* 65–82.

Levine, A. & Reves, T. 1985. What can the foreign language teacher teach the mother tongue reader? *Reading in a Foreign Language, 3* (1), 329–339.

Long, M. H. 1981. Input, interaction, and second language acquisition. In H. Winitz (ed.), *Native-language and foreign language acquisition.* New York: New York Academy of Sciences, 259–278.

Martin, A. V., McChesney, B., Whalley, E., & Devlin, E. 1977. *Guide to language and study skills for college students of English as a second language.* Englewood Cliffs, N.J.: Prentice-Hall.

Marzano, R. J. & Arthur, S. 1977. Teacher comments on student essays: It doesn't matter what you say. University of Colorado at Denver. ERIC ED 147 864.

McLaughlin, B. 1978. The monitor model: Some methodological considerations. *Language Learning, 28* (2), 309–332.

Meara, P. 1980. Vocabulary acquisition: A neglected aspect of language learning. *Language Teaching and Linguistics: Abstracts, 13* (4), 221–247.

Meara, P. 1982. Word associations in a foreign language: A report on the Birkbeck vocabulary project. *Nottingham Linguistic Circular, 11* (2), 29–37.

Moore, L. K. 1986. Teaching students how to evaluate writing. *TESOL Newsletter, 20* (5), 23–24.

Motti, S. T. 1987. Competência communicativa em língua estrangeira: O uso de pedido de disculpas. Seminar paper. São Paulo, Brazil: Program in Applied Linguistics, Pontifícia Universidade Católica de São Paulo.

Muller, M., Schneider, G., & Wertenschlag, L. 1988. Apprentissage autodirigé en tandem à l'université. In H. Holec (ed.), *Autonomy and self-directed learning.* Strasbourg, France: Council for Cultural Co-operation, Council of Europe, 65–76.

Nagy, W. E., Herman, P. A., & Anderson, R. C. 1985. Learning words from context. *Reading Research Quarterly, 20* (2), 233–253.

Naiman, N., Frolich, M., Stern, H. H., & Todesco, A. 1975. *The good language learner.* Toronto: Modern Language Center, Ontario Institute for Studies in Education.

Nash, R. 1976. Phantom cognates and other curiosities in Puerto Rican Englañol. *La Mundo Lingvo-Problema, 5*, 157–167.

Nation, I. S. P. 1990. *Teaching and learning vocabulary.* New York: Newbury House/ Harper & Row.

Nation, P. & Coady, J. 1988. Vocabulary and reading. In R. Carter & M. McCarthy (eds.) *Vocabulary and language learning.* London: Longman, 91–110.

Neubach, A. & Cohen, A. D. 1988. Processing strategies and problems encountered in the use of dictionaries. *Dictionaries, 10*, 1–19.

Nichols, R. G. 1986. Word processing and basic writers. *Journal of Basic Writing, 5* (2), 81–97.

Nuttall, C. 1982. *Teaching reading skills in a foreign language.* London: Heinemann Educational Books.

Oller, J. W., Jr. & Tullius, J. R. 1973. Reading skills of non-native speakers of English. *IRAL, 11* (1), 69–80.

Olshavsky, J. E. 1976/77. Reading as problem solving: An investigation of strategies. *Reading Research Quarterly, 12* (4), 654–674.

Olshtain, E. & Cohen, A. D. 1983. Apology: A speech act set. In N. Wolfson and E. Judd (eds.), *Sociolinguistics and language acquisition.* New York: Newbury House/Harper & Row, 18–35.

Olshtain, E. & Cohen, A. D. 1990. The learning of complex speech act behavior. The *TESL Canada Journal, 7* (2).

Omaggio, A. C. 1986. *Teaching language in context.* Boston: Heinle & Heinle.

O'Malley, J. M. & Chamot, A. J. 1990. *Learning strategies in second language acquisition.* Cambridge: Cambridge University Press.

Ott, C. E., Blake, R. S., & Butler, D. C. 1976. Implications of mental elaboration for the acquisition of foreign language vocabulary. *IRAL, 14* (1), 37–48.

Oxford, R. L. 1985. A new taxonomy of second language learning strategies. Washington, DC: Center for Applied Linguistics.

Oxford, R. L. 1988. Problems and solutions in foreign/second language vocabulary learning: The potential role of semantic mapping. University Park, PA: Intensive English Communication Program, Pennsylvania State University.

Oxford, R. L. 1990. *Language learning strategies: What every teacher should know.* New York: Newbury House/Harper & Row.

Oxford, R., Cohen, A. D., Crookall, D., Lavine, R., & Sutter, W. In press. Learning strategy training: Cross-cultural comparisons and a model. University Park, PA: Intensive English Communication Program, Pennsylvania State University.

Oxford, R. & Ehrman, M. 1989. Psychological type and adult language learning strategies: A pilot study. *Journal of Psychological Type, 16*, 22–32.

Perkins, R. 1983. Semantic constructivity in ESL reading comprehension. *TESOL Quarterly, 17* (1), 19–27.

Perl, S. 1980. Understanding composing. *College Composition and Communication, 31* (4), 363–369.

Porat, M. 1988. Dialogue journals—A new and practical way of combining the teaching of writing and reading with getting to know your students. *English Teachers' Journal (Israel)*, 36, 84–86.

Poulisse, N. 1989. The use of compensatory strategies by Dutch learners of English. Doctoral dissertation, Department of Applied Linguistics, University of Nijmegen, the Netherlands.

Poulisse, N., Bongaerts, T., & Kellerman, E. 1984. On the use of compensatory strategies in second language performance. *Interlanguage Studies Bulletin—Utrecht*, 8, 70–105.

Prokop, M. No date. A student's guide to effective foreign language study. New York: ACTFL Materials Center, 2 Park Avenue, NY 10016.

Pugh, A. R. 1978. *Silent reading*. London: Heinemann.

Raimes, A. 1983. *Techniques in teaching writing*. New York: Oxford University Press.

Raimes, A. 1987a. *Exploring through writing: A process approach to ESL Composition*. New York: St. Martin's Press.

Raimes, A. 1987b. Why write? From purpose to pedagogy. *English Teaching Forum*, 25, 36–41, 55.

Raimes, A. 1987. Language proficiency, writing ability, and composing strategies: A study of ESL college student writing. *Language Learning*, 37 (3), 439–468.

Raugh, M. R. & Atkinson, R. C. 1975. A mnemonic method for learning a second-language vocabulary. *Journal of Educational Psychology*, 67, 1–16.

Reid, J. M. 1987. The learning style preferences of ESL students. *TESOL Quarterly*, 21 (1), 87–111.

Reinert, H. 1976. One picture is worth a thousand words? Not necessarily! *Modern Language Journal*, 60, 160–168.

Richards, J. C. 1973. A noncontrastive approach to error analysis. In J. W. Oller, Jr. & J. C. Richards (eds.), *Focus on the learner*. New York: Newbury House/ Harper & Row, 96–113.

Richards, J. C. 1976. The role of vocabulary teaching. *TESOL Quarterly*, 10 (1), 77–89.

Richards, J. C. & Rodgers, T. S. 1986. *Approaches and methods in language teaching*. Cambridge: Cambridge University Press.

Rickard, R. B. 1980. First language perceptual strategies and reading in a second language. *TESL Studies*, 3, 183–198.

Rinvolucri, M. 1983. Writing to your students. *ELT Journal*, 37, 16–21.

Rivers, W. M. 1979. Learning a sixth language: An adult learner's daily diary. *Canadian Modern Language Review*, 36, 67–82.

Rivers, W. M. 1981a. Apples of gold in pictures of silver: Where have all the words gone? *Studia Linguistica*, 35 (1–2), 114–129.

Rivers, W. M. 1981b. *Teaching foreign-langue skills*. 2nd ed. Chicago: University of Chicago Press.

Robinson, F. P. 1970. *Effective study*. New York: Harper & Row.

Rodríguez, L. 1986. Words identified as cognates in an EFL text. Seminar paper. São Paulo, Brazil: Graduate Program in Applied Linguistics, Pontifícia Universidade Católica de São Paulo.

Rose, A. 1982. Spoken versus written criticisms of student writing: Some advantages of the conference method. *College Composition and Communication*, 33 (3), 326–330.

Rose, R. & Missiwir, R. 1967. Voting and election: A functional analysis. *Political Studies*, 15, 173–201.

Rosenstein, D. S. 1932. The efficacy of correcting recurrent oral errors among E.F.L. students. Beersheva, Israel: Department of English as a Foreign Language, Ben-Gurion University.

Rossier, R. E. 1975. Extroversion-introversion as a significant variable in the learning of English as a second language. Unpublished doctoral dissertation, University of Southern California.

Rubin, J. 1975. What the "good language learner" can teach us. *TESOL Quarterly*, 9 (1), 41–51.

Rubin, J. 1981. The study of cognitive processes in second language learning. *Applied Linguistics*, 2 (2), 117–131.

Rubin, J. 1987. Videodisc teaches language learning skills. *Foreign Language Annals*, 20 (3), 275.

Rubin, J. & Thompson, I. 1982. *How to be a more successful language learner*. Boston, MA: Heinle & Heinle.

Russell, B. 1950. An outline of intellectual rubbish. *Unpopular essays*. London: Allen & Unwin, 95–145.

Sanaoui, R. 1984. The use of reformulation in teaching writing to French second language students. *Carleton Papers in Applied Language Studies*, 1, 139–146.

Sarig, G. 1985. Comprehension of academic texts in the mother tongue and in a foreign language. Unpublished doctoral dissertation, School of Education, Hebrew University of Jerusalem. (In Hebrew)

Sarig, G. 1987. High-level reading in the first and in the foreign language: Some comparative process data. In J. Devine, P. L. Carrell, & D. E. Eskey (eds.), *Research in reading in English as a second language*. Washington, DC: Teachers of English to Speakers of Other Languages (TESOL), 105–120.

Sarig, G. 1988. Composing a study-summary: A reading-writing encounter. Ramat Aviv, Israel: Open University.

Sarig, G. 1990. Comprehension-promoting strategies: The sum of the parts and the whole. *Communication and Cognition*, 23 (1).

Scardamalia, M. & Bereiter, C. 1986. Research on written composition. In M. Wittrock (ed.), *Handbook of research on teaching*. 3rd ed. New York: Macmillan, 778–803.

Schachter, J. 1983. A new account of language transfer. In S. Gass & L. Selinker (eds.), *Language transfer in language learning*. New York: Newbury House/Harper & Row, 98–111.

Schachter, J. 1984. A universal input condition. In W. E. Rutherford (ed.), *Language universals and second language acquisition*. Philadelphia: John Benjamins, 167–183.

Schlue, K. 1977. An inside view of interlanguage. In C. A. Henning (ed.), *Proceedings of the Los Angeles Second Language Research Forum*. Los Angeles: ESL Section, Department of English, University of California, 342–348.

Schmidt, R. W. 1984. The strengths and limitations of acquisition: A case study of an untutored language learner. *Language Learning and Communication*, 3 (1), 1–16.

Schulz, R. A. 1986. From achievement to proficiency through classroom instruction: Some caveats. *Modern Language Journal*, 70 (4), 373–379.

Scott, M. 1986. The understanding to direct: Conscientização and reading. Working Paper No. 18 CEPRIL-PUC/SP, R. Monte Alegre, 984, 05014—São Paulo, SP, Brazil.

Seliger, H. W. 1980. Utterance planning and correction behavior: Its function in the grammar construction process for second language learners. In H. W. Dechert & M. Raupach (eds.), *Temporal variables of speech*. The Hague: Mouton, 87–89.

Seliger, H. W. 1983. Learner interaction in the classroom and its effect on language acquisition. In H. W. Seliger & M. H. Long (eds.), *Classroom oriented research in second language acquisition*. Rowley, MA: Newbury House, 246–267.

Selinker, L. 1972. Interlanguage. *IRAL, 10*, 201–231.

Selinker, L & Trimble, L. 1974. Formal written communication and ESL. *Journal of Technical Writing and Communication, 4* (2), 81–90.

Selinker, L. 1979. On the use of informants in discourse analysis and "language for specialized purposes." *IRAL, 17* (3), 189–215.

Semke, H. D. 1984. Effects of the red pen. *Foreign Language Annals, 17* (3), 195–202.

Shaw, P. A. 1982. Fluency and the ESL writing skill. M.A. Thesis, Department of Linguistics, University of Southern California.

Skehan, P. 1989. *Individual differences in second-language learning*. London: Edward Arnold.

Smith, F. 1982. *Writing and the writer*. London: Heinemann.

Sommers, N. 1982. Responding to student writing. *College Composition and Communication, 33*, 148–156.

Sperling, M. 1988. I want to talk to each of you: Writing conference discourse and individualizing the process of learning to write. Berkeley, CA: School of Education, University of California, Berkeley.

Sperling, M. & Freedman, S.W. 1987. A good girl writes like a good girl: Written response to student writing. *Written Communication, 4* (4), 343–369.

Stanovich, K. E. 1980. Toward an interactive-compensator model of individual differences in the development of reading fluency. *Reading Research Quarterly, 16*, 32–71.

Staton, J., Peyton, J. K., & Gutstein, S. (eds.). 1986. Focus on the teacher: Benefits, strategies, time. *Dialogue, 3* (4). (Center for Applied Linguistics, Washington, DC).

Stern, H. H. 1975. What can we learn from the good language learner? *The Canadian Modern Language Review, 31* (3), 304–317.

Sternberg, R. J. 1987. Most vocabulary is learned from context. In M. G. McKeown & M. E. Curtis (eds.), *The nature of vocabulary acquisition*. Hillsdale, NJ: Lawrence Erlbaum, 89–105.

Stevick, E. W. 1982. *Teaching and learning languages*. Cambridge: Cambridge University Press.

Stevick, E.W. 1984. Curriculum development at the Foreign Service Institute. In T. V. Higgs (ed.), *Teaching for proficiency, the organizing principle*. Lincolnwood, IL: National Textbook, 85–112.

Stewner-Manzanares, G., Chamot, A. V., O'Malley, J. M., Kupper, L., & Russo, R. P. 1983. *A teacher's guide for using learning strategies in acquiring ESL*. Rosslyn, VA: InterAmerica Research Associates.

Swaffer, J. K. 1988. Readers, texts, and second languages: The interactive processes. *Modern Language Journal, 72* (2), 123–149.

Tarone, E., Cohen, A. D., and Dumas, G. 1976. A closer look at some interlanguage terminology: A framework for communication strategies. *Working Papers on*

Bilingualism, 9, 76–90, ERIC ED 125 313. Reprinted in C. Faerch and G. Kasper (eds.), *Strategies in interlanguage communication.* London: Longman, 1983, 4–14.

Teixeira, A. L. 1987. Considerações sobre estrategias de inferência lexical em contexto na leitura de segunda língua. Seminar Paper, Graduate Program in Applied Linguistics, Pontifícia Universidade Católica de São Paulo.

Tullius, J. 1971. Analysis of reading skills of non-native speakers of English. M.A. Thesis. Los Angeles: ESL Section, Department of English, University of California at Los Angeles.

Ulijn, J. M. 1981. Conceptual and syntactic strategies in reading a foreign language. In E. Hopkins & R. Grotjahn, *Studies in language teaching and language acquisition.* Bochum: Brockmeyer, 129–166.

Ultsch, S., Tragant, E., & Orkin, N. 1989. Students' preferences for written error correction in grammar: An exploration paper. Paper presented at the 23rd TESOL Convention, San Antonio, TX, 7–11 March 1989. (Available through Elsa Tragant, 1230 Amsterdam Ave #302, New York, NY 10027.)

Weaver, C. 1980. *Psycholinguistics and reading: From process to practice.* Cambridge, MA: Winthrop.

Wenden, A. 1987. A curricular framework for promoting learner autonomy. Jamaica, NY: York College, CUNY.

Wenden, A. & Rubin, J. 1987. (eds.) *Learner strategies in language learning.* Englewood Cliffs, NJ: Prentice-Hall.

Williams, E. 1984. *Reading in the language classroom.* London: Macmillan.

Willing, K. 1985. *Learning styles in adult migrant education.* Sydney, NSW 2000, Australia: Adult Migrant Education Service (AMES), 167 Kent Street.

Willing, K. 1989. *Teaching how to learn: Learning strategies in ESL.* (Teachers' Guide, Activity worksheets.) Sydney, Australia: National Centre for English Language Teaching and Research, Macquarie University.

Wingfield, A. & Byrnes, D. L. 1981. *The psychology of human memory.* New York: Academic Press.

Witbeck, M. C. 1976. Peer correction procedures for intermediate and advanced ESL composition lessons. *TESOL Quarterly, 10* (3), 321–326.

Wolfson, N. 1989. *Perspectives: Sociolinguistics and TESOL.* New York: Newbury House/Harper & Row.

Wolfson, N. & Manes, J. 1980. The compliment as a social strategy. *Papers in Linguistics, 13* (3), 391–410.

Yorkey, R. C. 1970. *Study skills for students of English as a second language.* New York: McGraw-Hill. (2nd ed., 1982)

Zamel, V. 1983. The composing processes of advanced ESL students: Six case studies. *TESOL Quarterly, 17* (2), 165–187.

Zamel, V. 1985. Responding to student writing. *TESOL Quarterly, 19* (1), 79–101.

Zhang, S. & Jacobs, G. 1989. The effectiveness of peer feedback in the ESL writing class. Honolulu, HI: Department of Educational Psychology, College of Education, University of Hawaii at Manoa.

Zupnik, Y. 1985. A comparison of cognitive processes in foreign language and first-language responses. Seminar Paper, School of Education, Hebrew University of Jerusalem.

Index

Abraham, 13
Alamari, 61
Alderson, 182
Allen, 5
Allwright, 55, 60
Anderson, 85, 89, 117
Aphek, 25, 29, 128, 133–134, 138
aptitude, 19
Armbruster, 181
Arndt, 106, 185
Arnold, 5, 73
Arthur, 110, 170
Asher, 55
associations. *See* vocabulary learning,
    mnemonic associations
Atkinson, 27, 30, 133
attending
  capacity models, 42–43, 147, 157
  differential listening, 143
  input vs. intake, 144
  self-observation of mental states, 144
  self-test of, 41
  silent performance, 49
  teaching vs. learning, 147
  tuning out, 146

Bailey, 48, 157–158
Baker, 85
Bamberg, 121
Barnard, 37
Barnett, 130, 182
Baumann, 181
Beach, 185
Beaugrande, 75
Bejerano, 50
Bellezza, 25
Bensoussan, 167
Bereiter, 107, 109, 184
Berman, 160, 177
Blake, 133

Bloor, 185
Blum, 57
Blum-Kulka, 44, 65, 153, 158, 166, 176
Bodman, 70
body language, 47
Bongaerts, 56
Brehe, 127
Brewster, E. S., 7
Brewster, E. T., 7
Bridwell, 185
Bridwell-Bowles, 127
Brière, 118
Bright, 38
Brown, 17, 55, 85, 89, 181
Busch, 55
Butler, 133
Byrnes, 43, 147, 156

Calkins, 109, 110
Campione, 89
Canale, 54, 121
Candlin, 75
Carpenter, 77, 81, 193
Carrell, 85
Carrier, 129, 130
Carter, 22, 57, 155, 184
Casey, 6, 129
Cavalcanti, 171
Chamot, 9, 13
Chaudron, 60, 112, 157
Chibnall, 6, 129
Chomsky, 63
Clark, 87
Clarke, 32–33, 107, 167, 184
classroom research
  classroom observation, 6
  use of video replay, 143
Coady, 33–34, 184
cognates, 33, 88

Cohen, 3, 4, 13, 25, 29, 42, 56, 65, 67, 69, 83, 87, 90, 94, 100, 110, 128, 134, 138, 142, 144, 148–149, 151–152, 154, 160–161, 170–173, 176–177
coherence. *See* reading, coherence
cohesion. *See* reading, cohesion
Collins, 17
commentator talk, 44
communication strategies, 53, 57–59
  confirmation checks, 64
  correctors, 55
  planners, 55
compensatory strategies, 56, 158
comprehensible input. *See* input
conferencing. *See* writing, feedback
Connor, 107
Consciousness-raising, 189
contextual paraphrase. *See* reading problems
conversational discourse, synthesizing strategies, 14, 20
Corder, 173
core rules, 63
core vocabulary. *See* vocabulary learning; vocabulary use
  core words, 57
core word. *See* vocabulary use, core word
Coulmas, 58
Cowan, 82, 160
Craik, 22, 40
Cramer, 112
Crookall, 4
Cumming, 19, 107, 112, 186
Curtis, 155–156

Daiker, 116
Dally, 175
Dam, 11
Day, 89
decoding. *See* reading, decoding
Deese, E. K., 6, 129
Delaney, 156
Devlin, 6, 32
dialog journals. *See* writing, dialog journals
diary studies. *See* self-observation, diary studies
Dickinson, 11
dictionaries
  bilingual, 87
  monolingual, 33, 87
Dijk, 89
DiPardo, 50

discourse cloze, 166
discourse knowledge, 54
discourse planning strategies, 58
discussion group, 50
Dubin, 73
Dunkel, 130

Ehrman, 55
Eisterhold, 85
Ellis, 8, 63
Elshout-Mohr, 155
Ericsson, 158
error correction, 59. *See also* writing, feedback
  delayed teacher response, 62
  oral errors, 53
  public error, 61
  secret error, 61
  self-correction, 62
  self-monitoring, 192
  self-repair, 55
errors, cross-associational, 36
Eskey, 73, 75

Faerch, 158
Fairbank, 162–163
Ferrara, 3, 83, 160
Ferris, 109
Fine, 3, 83, 161
flash cards. *See* vocabulary learning, flash cards
Flower, 106, 109, 182
foreigner talk, 44
Freedman, 33, 50, 107, 109–110, 184
Frolich, 6
Fuentes, 156
function words, 35

Gabrielsen, 11
gambits, 58
Garner, 183
Gaskill, 107
Gass, 157
George, 36
Gilette, 129
Gimenez, 90
Glasman, 3, 83, 160
good learners, 47
Goodman, 75, 76
Gough, 44
Grabe, 73
Grala, 8

Graves, 109
Gregg, 48
Grellet, 73
Gremmo, 12
Grice, 54
Grotjahn, 158
Gutstein, 113

Haas, 106, 182
Hague, 36
Halliday, 160
Hammer, 33, 35
Hamp-Lyons, 182
Hanawalt, 83
Harris, 109
Hasan, 160
Hatch, 44
Hayes, 78, 79, 106, 116
Haynes, 88, 167
Helmore, 10–11
Hidi, 89
Higa, 36
Higbee, 25
high input generators, 59
Holec, 11, 13, 37
Holley, 62
Holmes, 90
Holtzman, 162
homework, 12
Horowitz, 13
Hosenfeld, 5, 48, 73, 85, 182
House-Edmondson, 158
Huang, 18
Huckin, 159
Huttunen, 12

illocutionary meaning, 64
imagery link. See vocabulary learning,
    imagery link
input, 44–46, 51
input vs. intake, 157
intake, 42, 46, 51
interlanguage talk, 45

Jacobs, 112
Jahn, 29, 33
Johnson, 127
Jolley, 90, 183
Jones, 107
Just, 77, 81, 193

Kahneman, 42
Kaplan, 120, 173
Kasper, 158
Keller, 33, 59
Kellerman, 56
Kennedy, 100
Kenyon, 100
keyword, 27, 47
Kezwer, 55
King, 62
Kintsch, 89
Kirchofer, 5, 73
Kowel, 109
Kramsch, 35, 57
Krashen, 25, 44–45, 48, 60, 89
Kreeft, 113–114
Kupper, 9

Laciura, 5, 73
language acquisition device, 63
language drills, mechanical, 43
Lanzano, 70
Lapp, 109
Larsen-Freeman, 4
Laufer, 86, 167
Lavine, 4
learner contracts, 11
learner training, 5, 13
learning
    automatic, 25, 48, 189
    autonomous, 11–12
    conscious, 25
    controlled processing, 48
    self-directed, 10
learning strategies, 5, 13–14, 58–59
learning styles, 10, 18, 190
Leu, 81
Levenston, 21, 57, 118, 166, 173, 177
Levin, 27, 156
Levine, 74
linguistic knowledge, 53
linguistic universals, 63
listening comprehension
    identification of elements, 46
    selection of elements, 46
    world knowledge, 47
Lockhart, 22, 40
Long, 50, 157–158
low input generators, 59

McCarthy, 155, 184
McChesney, 6, 32

McCormick, 156
McDaniel, 156
McGregor, 38
McKeown, 155–156
McLaughlin, 48
Madden, 157
Mandl, 181
Manes, 64
Martin, 6, 32
Marzano, 110, 170
Masson, 81
Matthiesen, 100
Meara, 21, 29, 37, 78
memorization techniques, 18, 36
memory, 42
    short-term, 35
    traces, 40
    visual imagery, 29
mental lexicon, 37, 39, 155
Miller, 156
miscue analysis. *See* reading
mnemonic associations. *See* vocabulary
        learning, mnemonic associations
monitoring. *See* self-assessment
Moore, 112
Mossiwir, 162
Motti, 154
Muller, 12

Nagy, 184
Naiman, 6
Nash, 88
Nation, 22, 32–34, 36–37, 155, 184
native speaker talk, 44
negative input, 64
negative transfer, 45, 63
Neubach, 87
Newman, 17
Nichols, 106
Nir, 166, 176
Norrish, 185
notetaking, 6, 39, 128–129, 143, 194
Novikoff, 162
Nuttall, 73

Ochsner, 157
Oller, 77
Olsen, 159
Olshavsky, 166
Olshtain, 65, 67, 69, 73, 148–149, 151–154,
        176
Omaggio, 5

O'Malley, 9, 13
Orkin, 171
Ott, 133
overgeneralization, 45, 63
Oxford, 1, 4, 8, 13–14, 35–36, 55

Palincsar, 181
Patthey, 109
Pearson, 85
Peck, 157
peer tutoring, 11, 50
Perkins, 167
Perl, 107
Peyton, 113
Porat, 113
positive transfer, 63
Poulisse, 56
Pressley, 156
Pringle, 184
Prokop, 37
propositional meaning, 64
Pugh, 80

quasi-experimental designs, 3

Raimes, 103, 105, 107, 111, 170, 186
reading
    authentic vs. simplified texts, 193
    bottom-up, 86
    coherence, 79
    cohesion, 79, 94, 160, 163, 165
    contextual paraphrase, 90, 164
    decoding, 78
    heavy noun phrases, 82, 94
    identification skills, 75
    ideographic writing systems, 78
    inferences, 81
    interactive compensatory model, 167
    interactive model, 75
    interactive processes in, 183
    interpretive skills, 75
    orthographic features, 78
    prediction, 75
    psycholinguistic guessing game, 75
    recoding, 77
    regressions, 76
    saccades, 77
    speed reading, 81
    SQ3R technique, 90
    syntax, importance of, 83
    top-down, 85, 183

types, 80–82
word substitution, 87
reading problems, 161–165
  nontechnical words, 94
  technical words, 94
reading research
  cognates, 168
  compensation hypothesis, 167
  contextual guessing, 167–168
  L1 and L2 reading, 74, 82, 166
  lexical inference strategies, 167–168
  metacognition, 183
  short-circuit hypothesis, 167
  unknown-word ratio, 184
  verbal report, 166, 169, 182
reading skills, 83
reading strategies, 74, 83
  clarification of purpose, 85
  coherence, strategies for establishing, 165
  comprehension monitoring in, 183
  contextual guessing, 83, 87
  global, 83
  metacognitive strategies, 91, 165, 183
  monitoring, 91, 166
  paraphrase, 92, 165
  prediction, 90
  reading for meaning, 85
  reading in broad phrases, 88
  scanning, 81
  search for text organization, 85
  self-supervision, 93
  skimming, 5, 84
  summarizing, 89
  support strategies, 92, 165
  training in, 181–182
  use of dictionary, 87
recoding. See reading, recoding
Reid, 18
Reinert, 29
Reischauer, 162–163
research
  classroom, 16
  observational, 7
Reves, 74
Richards, 4, 38, 63
Rickard, 82
Rinvolucri, 112
Rivers, 5–6, 40, 47
Robbins, 173
Robinson, 90
Rodgers, 4
Rodriguez, 168

Rogozinski, 130
Rose, 109, 162
Rosenbaum-Cohen, 3, 83, 160
Rosenstein, 61, 67, 151
Rossier, 55
rote learning, 190
rote memory, 25, 29
Rubin 4, 7–8, 13
Russell, 96–97
Russo, 9

Saedi, 75
Sanaoui, 122
Sarig, 74, 84, 89, 92–93, 95, 165–167, 169
Scardamalia, 107, 109, 184
Schachter, 64
schemata
  content, 47, 85
  language, 85
  textual, 85
Schleppegrell, 8
Schlue, 62
Schmidt, 6
Schneider, 12
Schulz, 4
Scott, 73, 76
self-access resources, 11
self-assessment, 10, 15, 111
self-awareness, 15
self-instruction, 11
self-observation, diary studies, 48, 157–158
Seliger, 55, 59, 158
Selinker, 45, 63, 159, 164, 175
Semke, 110, 170
Shapira, 44
Shaw, 118
Shriberg, 156
Shuy, 113–114
Sim, 86
Simon, 158
Sinclair, 8
Skehan, 19
skimming. See reading strategies, skimming
small-group interactions, 49
Smith, 107
Sommers, 107, 110
speaking. See communication strategies
speaking success, extroversion, 55
speech acts, 18, 64, 148, 158, 192
  apology speech act, 18, 66
    choice of speech act strategy, 151
      downgraders, 149

five strategies, 148
intensifiers, 69, 71, 149, 151
interjections, 152
lack of linguistic proficiency, 150
negative transfer, 151
research on teaching apologies, 152
verbal report on apologizing, 153
cross-cultural comparisons, 158
familiarity of interlocutors, 70
improving competence, 70
rules of appropriateness, 65
rule violation, 66
severity of offense, 70
status of interlocutors, 70
Sperling, 109–110
Stanovich, 86, 167
Staton, 113
Stern, 4, 6–7
Sternberg, 156
Stevick, 21, 35, 47
Stewner-Manzanares, 9–10
strategies, 13, 47, 54
cognitive, 9
information-processing, 10
metacognitive, 9
study skills, 6, 32
successful speakers, 53, 55–56
summaries
private (writer-based), 89
public (reader-based), 89
reconceptualization, 89
Sutter, 4
Swaffer, 183, 190
Swain, 54

tandem learning, 12
target language, 2
teacher talk, 44
teacher training, 5
Teixeira, 167
Tetroe, 107
Thompson, 7, 13
Titus, 129–130
Todesco, 6
Tragant, 171
translation, 7, 36, 39
literal, 56
translation equivalent, 29
Trimble, 159
Tullius, 77

Ulijn, 77, 82
Ultsch, 171
Urquhart, 182

Valette, 5
van Daalen-Kapteijns, M. M., 155
Vann, 13
van Naerssen, 18
verbal report, 16, 157–158. *See also* writing
research
self-observation, 96
introspective, 144
retrospective, 144, 168, 183
self-revelation, 96
Vesta, 130
videodisc, 8
vocabulary learning
context, 22, 32, 137, 141, 156, 184
core vocabulary, 57, 155
denotations, 38
depth of processing, 22, 40, 43
flash cards, 35, 40, 129
frequency of contact, 139
imagery link, 9, 27
keyword mnemonic, 156
lists, 21
mental lexicon, 34
mnemonic associations, 22, 24–26, 40, 42,
133, 135, 138, 141
mnemonic devices, 16, 34, 156, 190
recall strategies, 14, 20
residual learning, 138
semantic mapping, 36
topic group, 26
translation in, 39
word equivalents, 39
vocabulary use
approximation, 57
core word, 57
general word, 57
word coinage, 57

Warner, 59
Weaver, 78
Wenden, 13, 19
Wertenschlag, 12
Whalley, 6, 32
whole-class method, 50
Williams, 73
Willing, 10
Wilson, 5, 73
Wingfield, 43, 147, 156

Witbeck, 117
Wolff, 183
Wolfson, 64, 148, 158
word analysis. *See* vocabulary learning, context
writers, types of, 106
writing
  dialog journals, 112–113, 193
  edits, 105–106
  feedback, 15, 103
    conferencing, 109–110
    lack of clarity, 111
    misguided feedback, 170
    oral vs. written, 109–110
    peer feedback, 105, 111
    presentation of typical errors, 117
    typical situation, 116
  grammar and mechanics, 106
  modeling, 15, 20
  monitoring of, 106
  multiple drafts, 105
  one-draft submissions, 105
  process approach, 105, 184
  product approach, 105
  purposes for, 103–104
  rapid and free writing, 118
  reformulation, 103, 115, 118–119, 173, 194
    cohesion, 121, 176

    discourse function, 121
    nonnative reformulators, 120
    reconstruction, 119, 122, 173
    student evaluation, 178
    stylistic changes, 116
  review, 106
  revision, 106, 118
  rhetorical function, 103
  self-assessment, 105
  strategies of effective writers, 107–109, 187
  types, 104
writing assessment, 107
writing research
  feedback on grammar and mechanics, 171
  reformulation, 173–180
  revision strategies, 185
  student use of feedback, 172
  student writing styles, 186
  teacher feedback, 170, 173, 185
  verbal report, 107, 171, 186

Yorkey, 6, 32

Zamel, 107, 170, 187
Zhang, 112
Ziv, 185
Zupnik, 166, 169